McKenrick

Corporate Security Administration and Management

Corporate Security Administration and Management

J. Kirk Barefoot, CPP
and
David A. Maxwell, J.D., CPP
University of New Haven

Butterworths
Boston London Durban Singapore Sydney Toronto Wellington

All references in this book to personnel of male gender are used for convenience only and shall be regarded as including both males and females.

Library of Congress Cataloging-in-Publication Data

Barefoot, J. Kirk.
Corporate security administration and management.

Includes index.
1. Industry—Security measures—Management.
I. Maxwell, David A., 1930– . II. Title.
HV8290.B37 1987 658.4'7 86–14693
ISBN 0–409–95106–4

Butterworth Publishers
80 Montvale Avenue
Stoneham, MA 02180

10 9 8 7 6 5 4 3 2 1

Printed in the United States of America

To Janice

J.K.B.

To Liz, Danny, and Dave, Jr.

D.A.M.

Contents

Foreword

The basic rights to one's own life and property, and the obligation to respect the lives and property of others are as old as civilization itself. On the other hand, our lives and property are constantly at risk from the actions of external elements. It is no wonder, then, that any competent manager instinctively senses the moral obligation to preserve assets entrusted to him or her, or, at least, to minimize the loss from the uncontrollable elements. This helps to explain why society is severe in punishing any lapse by a manager in fulfilling these responsibilities.

As organizations have grown in size, the preservation of human and property values has occupied the attention of owners, whether the owner be a single proprietor working in the corner grocery store or owners represented by the board of directors of a multinational corporation. This concern may be expressed by very detailed policies on theft, by simple locks and alarms, by very complex calculations as to the worth of a piece of property, or by insurance to replace any loss of value whether by nature or through human weakness.

Principles and concerns are idealistic and, unfortunately, most people tend to vary from the ideal now and then. Many find no problem in walking home with a company pencil or carrying a towel or an ashtray from a hotel. Others have habits that range from psychotic to criminal. We do not know all the reasons that drive people to covet the property of others and know less about why this turns into stealing, lying, and cheating.

The social sciences and religion have given us some hints. Economists tell us that when identical items appear in great numbers each has less value than a single item standing alone. So why get excited about one shirt on a table filled with shirts? Church leaders say that in a society of plenty the maldistribution of goods is a strong temptation to steal by the "have nots." Sociologists tell us that the media project a living standard beyond the reach of most of their readers, listeners, and viewers. With a bit of clever bookkeeping or a little money "on the side," why not claim my entitlement in this land of plenty?

We need not agree with the reasoning involved, but it brings us to the point of this book. The security function is no longer the province of a lonely night watchman checking for fires and an occasional theft, or the auditor making sure the books of account are correct. It is not hiring a retired F.B.I. agent or policeman to apprehend those who would steal. Nor is it a clever array of insurance coverages for the risks we know. Security has become a major function headed by a professional who knows the economics, the sociology, and the ethics, and who is dedicated to crime prevention rather than just crime detection.

Looking across the functional spectrum of the modern corporation, managing the security function involves an understanding of the people involved in accounting, computer operation, insurance, purchasing, personnel, maintenance, and all the other major activities of any given business. Above all, it means being a manager.

While this book is encyclopedic, practically a handbook for the security professional, the authors have kept a management perspective throughout. It covers planning and budgeting, controlling, organizing, and staffing in a way that will appeal to those already involved in the security function. Of great interest, however, should be the constant emphasis not only on the coordinating function but also on cooperating. This is an area of management that is too often neglected.

No professional manager can fully understand the details involved in the jobs reporting to him or her. This is especially true of the security manager. The authors have deftly outlined how the professional approaches questions associated with such well-developed disciplines as finance, insurance, and law as well as helping vendors, customers, and top management.

There is no absence of nitty-gritty. Here you will find recommendations on formal preparation to be a security manager, outlines to follow to assure loss prevention, how to set up a plan for dealing with a strike, how to formulate a budget, and how to conduct an appraisal. The reader is going to find this book an artful blend of all the science and art that any well-managed company would want in its security function.

There are three kinds of people who should read this book: those who are or wish to be security professionals, those who want to become managers of a modern security function, and top managers who wish to renew their resolve to preserve the assets of their companies. I predict that history will note this as a seminal book in the field.

James L. Hayes
Chairman, Human Resource Industries, Inc.;
Former President and Chairman,
American Management Association

Preface

Our society is in a state of change . . . change through globalization of an ever-shrinking world . . . change in the corporate world through mergers, acquisitions, and divestitures . . . change from an industrial society to an information society . . . and, over the past few years, a change in the very meaning of the term *private security industry*. The private security manager of today works in the corporate suite and has responsibilities that range from implementing multifaceted loss prevention techniques using sophisticated equipment to devising a profit center out of the security function. The thrust of this book is to provide up-to-date, practical, and usable information on how to handle and carry out the vital corporate security function during this period of change. It is an attempt to fill the void left by virtually all schools of business administration—the financial contribution that a good security program can have on the profit and loss statement of many corporations. To do this, the book serves as a blueprint for the security administrator and top management who wish to structure the security department accordingly.

Chapter 1, The Nature of Modern-Day Corporate Security Administration, discusses some of the diverse challenges facing the contemporary corporate security director. It also points out, with statistics, the numerous advantages of having a formal education in the security management discipline. Other important matters discussed include interaction by the security manager with various corporate departments.

Chapter 2, Organizing the Corporate Security Department, treats the proper structuring of the security department within the corporation. This chapter also explains the concept of centralization versus decentralization of the security department.

Chapter 3, Strategic and Operational Management, deals with the mandate and functions of a corporate security department, as well as how to justify its existence. An extensive discussion of the responsibilities-indicators-goals (RIG) approach and the management by objectives (MBO) theory is included.

Chapter 4, Management Techniques, touches on various theories of management, some managerial tools, management styles of several corporate security managers, and guidelines for managerial success. Management is a vast subject. Hundreds of books have been written about it, many of which can be found in your local library, and it is a subject taught in numerous colleges and universities throughout the world. The purpose of this chapter is to acquaint the reader with some of the more well-known aspects of this topic from which one can direct further inquiry.

Chapter 5, Staffing, gives the reader some insights into the recruitment process, from sourcing up through interviewing. From there, the reader is given material that will prove helpful in training a new staff. Follow-up in the form of work force appraisals is dealt with.

Chapter 6, Finance, provides suggestions on budgetmaking and monitoring a current budget. The reader also is presented with material designed to help him or her understand inventory variances and their detrimental effect on the profit and loss statement of the company.

Chapter 7, Loss Prevention, deals extensively with approaches to loss prevention and the reasons why prevention is the only logical approach to a corporation's security problems.

Chapter 8, Investigations Management, discusses the need for expertise in investigations in any corporation regardless of preventive efforts. It charts the correct course of action whether the case be white- or blue-collar crime.

Chapter 9, Risk Management: A Total Integration, serves as a blueprint for integrating the security function in the total risk management concept. A risk management matrix, showing all the interrelationships, also is presented. This chapter places the insurance function in proper perspective and strips away some of the mystique that continually cloaks the insurance industry.

Chapter 10, Legal Considerations, deals with the primary objective of any security director: the prevention of loss to the corporation. The monetary legal judgments in our increasingly litigious society are greater than ever before, and the corporate security manager should be aware of potential areas where security mistakes could create massive financial losses. By understanding the problems in these areas, the manager can concentrate on reducing potential losses.

Chapter 11, Protecting Corporate Information, stresses the fact that information is the strategic corporate resource of today and more sophisticated efforts are necessary to protect it from loss through industrial espionage or other means. Outlined in this chapter are management cycles pertaining to the protection of this vital and critical resource and various legal ways of protecting it. Implementation of suggested guidelines may help the corporation prevail in litigation pertaining to the loss of certain types of information.

Chapter 12, Managing the Security Function of a Labor-Organized Company, is a must for companies that are unionized or about to become so. It becomes clear that dealing with organized labor unions may well be a major part of the security director's job. This chapter also gives insight into the inner workings of unions.

Chapter 13, Control of Contract Security Services, points up the need for adequate control over outside security vendors. In many cases, this is a major part of a security director's job. Suggestions are made as to how agreements with outside vendors can be tightened up in favor of the director.

Chapter 14, Security and Outside Relations, deals with the outgrowth of mutual types of assistance between security departments and the possibility of offering successful corporate security capabilities to others for profit, or at least to help defray the costs of one's own security budget. The reader should keep in mind trends enumerated in the Hallcrest Report and other information relative to the privatization of local, state, and federal governments.

While no one can say with certainty what the future will bring, Chapter 15, Security in the Future, cites research that can help the corporate security executive determine trends. Growth in the private security area is not limited to personnel; it includes rapid advances in areas such as electronics, robotics, personal identification, computerization, and even new types of substance abuse. The modern corporate security director should keep abreast of the exciting new developments in the field of loss prevention.

Acknowledgments

Special thanks go to Mr. Richard D. Paterson, director of security of McKesson Corporation and president of the Professional Certification Board of the American Society for Industrial Security (ASIS). Mr. Paterson is one of the best-versed practitioners in applying modern management techniques to the corporate security function. He is the author of Chapter 3, contributed heavily to Chapter 2, assisted with the outline of the book, and made other contributions throughout.

Thanks go to Lieutenant Gayle V. Blomberg, USAF, an ASIS chapter scholarship winner and magna cum laude security management graduate of the University of New Haven, for her time, support, help, and administrative assistance.

Special kudos to Jane V. Brown, not only for her superb technical skills in editing, correcting, and typing but even more for giving incalculable amounts of time, encouragement, support, and critically incisive and constructive analyses and evaluations of portions of the book.

And thanks go to Greg Franklin, Editor, Butterworths, for his patient support, suggestions, and recommendations.

Last but not least is a special appreciation to Patricia McQuaid, who, in addition to a masterful job of editing, assisted in blending the authors' two distinct writing styles.

Chapter 1

The Nature of Modern-Day Corporate Security Administration

Corporations fall into a variety of settings and industries, such as manufacturers, utilities, computer centers, retail outlets, health care providers, transportation and cargo companies, and educational institutions. Each industry has its own problems peculiar to that particular field and not necessarily common to other industries. Yet the general threads of security concepts and principles remain the same for all loss prevention problems. Today's corporate world is becoming more diverse through the thousands of mergers, takeovers, and buy-outs in the past few years. The diverse areas that may need to be protected can be demonstrated by the 1986 acquisition of the Radio Corporation of America (RCA) by the General Electric (GE) Corporation. This conglomerate will now handle items such as refrigerators, locomotives, dishwashers, nuclear reactors, insurance, data processing, consumer credit, aircraft engines, guidance systems, broadcasting, entertainment, and consumer electronics.

The new corporate security manager must be aware of the future growth of these corporations, many of which are now headed toward the electronics and financial services fields. As corporations grow, so will the job of the corporate security manager, requiring him to be on the alert for new concepts, processes, and devices to prevent loss of assets.

Unlike older professions, the security field is just now formalizing education standards and requirements. Twenty years ago, top security positions were filled from outside the field by retirees from various agencies such as the FBI, the Secret Service, the state police, and municipal police departments.

Many of these people were college graduates, but some were not. Few possessed degrees in applicable fields such as police science, criminal justice, or industrial security. Even candidates with degrees seldom had course background in the many disciplines that make the security professional successful today. Courses in accounting, budgeting, computer science, logic, and business administration were unheard of for a security person.

Only with the acceptance of the fact that the modern security practitioner must be able to think, talk, and perform as a businessperson to be successful has the value of a college degree been recognized.

In the future, the function of the security manager will include managing, staffing, budgeting, administering, supervising, investigating, inspecting, and evaluating. Subsequent chapters will discuss staffing, business management, and investigations management. The security manager must be able to set short- and long-term goals, make timetables to accomplish these goals, and be able to prioritize them.

In addition, the corporate security manager must be able to interact with local, state, and federal law enforcement and administrative agencies, as well as with organizations such as hospitals, disaster relief agencies, and community groups. He must be able to handle a diverse, unusual, and complex array of known and unforeseen problems. The challenge is extremely broad and exciting, as the field of corporate security is on the threshold of explosive growth and change.

Good managerial skills will be essential for a security professional to be able to get others to carry out the necessary policies and procedures, and the manager must be able to do this with tact and diplomacy.

BENEFITS FOR THE DEGREED PERSON

A person with a college degree has a better chance of obtaining a favored loss prevention position.[1] Of course, the degree of education required will be commensurate to and measured by the degree of security responsibility.[2] In one survey of eighty-eight security professionals concerning whether they would be interested in hiring a college graduate with a bachelor of science degree in security, sixty (68 percent) responded affirmatively. Twenty-six of the respondents said that they would hire college graduates at the supervisory level, and forty-three stated that they would hire such persons as management trainees.[3] Some

---

[1]Philip P. Purpura, *Security and Loss Prevention* (Stoneham, MA: Butterworths, 1984), p. 471 (hereafter cited as *Loss Prevention*).

[2]Eugene D. Finneran, *Security Supervision: A Handbook for Supervisors and Managers* (Stoneham, MA: Butterworths, 1981), p. 22.

[3]Robert R. J. Gallati, *Introduction to Private Security* (Englewood Cliffs, NJ: Prentice-Hall, Inc., 1983), p. 174.

Table 1–1 Survey of the Education Level of Security Directors

Education Level	*Percent*
Some High School	1
High School	4
Some College	29
Associate's Degree	13
Bachelor's Degree	26
Postgraduate Study	14
Master's Degree	10
Ph.D.	3

Reprinted with the permission of *Security World.*

felt that an important qualification for the position of security director "would ideally be a four-year degree in industrial security."[4]

Studies have shown that the more formal the education of the security practitioner, the higher his or her salary and benefits will be. Additionally, in the past few years the number of security directors with more formal education has increased.

Industry responses in 1983 reported that the percentage of security directors who have a bachelor's degree jumped from 21 percent to 26 percent between 1980 and 1983.[5] For this group, the median education level climbed from an associate's degree to a bachelor's degree. Also, the most noticeable change in education occurred at the low end, where the percentage with only a high school education dropped from 15 percent to 5 percent, and those with some college instruction rose from 23 percent to 29 percent. It was interesting to note in this study that the younger security directors had achieved higher education levels. The results of a 1983 poll are shown in Table 1–1.

This study also found a direct correlation between education and salary, as those with advanced study or degrees were earning a larger salary (Table 1–2).

In addition, the study noted that the highest paid received the largest package of fringe benefits, as indicated by Table 1–3.

Moreover, this study reflected a direct progression on the bonus chart, taking into consideration education and salary levels in the sense that the higher the salary and the higher the education level, the more cash was received (Table 1–4).

A survey conducted by Abbott, Langer & Associates in October 1983 of all members of the American Society for Industrial Security

---

[4]David L. Berger, *Industrial Security* (Stoneham, MA: Butterworths, 1979), p. 37.

[5]Thomas J. Serb, "Security Director Profile," *Security World,* August 1983, p. 57.

Table 1–2 Correlation between Education and Salary

	No College	*Associate's Degree*	*Bachelor's Degree*	*Advanced Degree*
Under $20,000	13%	10%	11%	9%
$20,000–$24,999	40%	29%	15%	12%
$25,000–$29,999	14%	25%	20%	16%
$30,000–$34,999	13%	17%	20%	21%
$35,000–$39,999	13%	11%	12%	14%
$40,000–$44,999	0%	4%	7%	9%
$45,000–$49,999	7%	2%	5%	8%
$50,000 or more	0%	2%	10%	11%
Average ($000)	$27.6	$28.6	$32.8	$34.7

Reprinted with the permission of *Security World*.

Table 1–3 Correlation between Education and Fringe Benefits

	No College	*Associate's Degree*	*Bachelor's Degree*	*Advanced Degree*
Insurance				
Health	87%	93%	91%	94%
Life	87%	92%	91%	90%
Dental	53%	69%	64%	76%
Other	33%	29%	20%	36%
Monetary				
Profit Sharing	33%	24%	28%	25%
Bonus	27%	26%	30%	21%
Overtime Pay	7%	9%	6%	2%
Future Income				
Pension Fund	67%	59%	60%	74%
Stock or Options	20%	28%	20%	32%
Other				
Membership Dues	47%	61%	63%	63%
Tuition	7%	48%	36%	60%
Car	7%	20%	19%	27%
Average	40%	46%	44%	50%

Reprinted with the permission of *Security World*.

(ASIS) in the United States revealed that the "level of education is also an important determinant of salary for security managers."[6] This study clearly indicated that respondents who had a bachelor's or graduate degree made much more money than those who did not, with the median

---

[6]Steven Langer, Ph.D. "Who Makes What and Why: Highlights of the 1983 Salary Survey," *Security Management*, July 1984, p. 46.

Table 1–4 Correlation between Education and Bonuses

	No College	*Associate's Degree*	*Bachelor's Degree*	*Advanced Degree*
Total Percent Receiving a Bonus	53%	49%	42%	50%
$1–$999	25%	27%	14%	21%
$1,000–$1,999	0%	21%	26%	5%
$2,000–$2,999	25%	11%	11%	14%
$3,000–$3,999	13%	11%	12%	7%
$4,000–$5,999	25%	12%	12%	14%
$6,000–$7,999	0%	8%	11%	7%
$8,000–$9,999	0%	4%	3%	0%
$10,000 or more	12%	6%	11%	32%
Average ($000)	$3.8	$3.3	$3.9	$5.4

Reprinted with the permission of *Security World.*

salary range of a bachelor's degree holder at $40,000 and that of the graduate degree holder at approximately $45,000.

A 1984 study noted that the trend for higher education among security professionals was continuing.[7] While 48 percent indicated that they had college degrees in 1980 and 53 percent did the same in 1983, 58 percent of the 1984 respondents acknowledged this education level. The 1984 study included an additional 21 percent who had matriculated in studies more advanced than a bachelor's degree. Eighteen percent of the respondents indicated that they had a master's degree. This study also indicated that the education median for security directors and managers in 1980 was an associate's degree, while the median in 1984 was a bachelor's degree. In addition, the study revealed that the salary difference between those with an associate's degree and those with only some education was negligible. "However, Bachelor-degreed respondents fared better than those with Associate's Degrees, some $4,000 on the average."[8] Holders of advanced degrees or some postgraduate study earned $4,000 more than those with bachelor's degrees.

A recent special report in trends in security[9] indicated that security education will advance in the coming years, both at the academic and practical levels. This report also indicated that the security practitioner will tend to become more business-oriented and that the educational environment will put pressure on the security industry in terms of the increased expectations it generates in the graduates of its security pro-

[7]Kerrigan Lydon, "Security Staff Salaries," *Security World,* June 1984, p. 29.

[8]Ibid., p. 30.

[9]Wayne Siatt and Sally Matteson, "Special Report: Trends in Security," *Security World,* January 1982, p. 21 (hereafter cited as *Trends in Security*).

grams. In regard to the academic environment, the report also noted that the new breed of business-oriented security professionals might come into conflict with an older generation of security professionals who see security and business management as two separate functions.

Selling a corporate security program to management, to employees, and to visitors is extremely important. The corporate security director must be informative and articulate in his written and spoken communications. Promoting one's program, establishing confidence in the program, and furthering one's thoughts and ideas can be better accomplished if that person is formally educated, as he is accustomed to doing research and expressing himself. Having professional credibility makes the corporate security director's job of selling security much easier, and part of this credibility is having business acumen. Business acumen can be achieved through a number of educational processes, which include formal training such as college courses.[10] The corporate security director becomes the overall educator of the employees and executives of the corporation. A formal educational background will help the director accomplish his task.

SECURITY WITHIN THE CORPORATE FRAMEWORK

Just as the security manager must have the ability to motivate employees, he also must have the skills to educate top executives. With their help, support, input, and communication, the manager's job will be infinitely easier and successful. To do this, however, the security department must be structured in an appropriate slot in the total corporate picture. Although the manager may not report directly to the chief executive officer (CEO), the security director certainly must have access to the CEO. In times of crisis, it is not feasible to relay assessments of particular situations through a layer of superiors in an attempt to convey a clear picture to the CEO. Furthermore, the security director must have the ability to probe into all facets of the corporation concerning compliance with corporate policies. By the very nature of his job, he becomes the watchdog and protector of the corporation from wrongdoing inside and outside the organization. If the corporate security director is not in a position to enable him to communicate freely with top corporate executives, the director should make every attempt to change the situation. If this is not possible, then change can come

---

[10]Clifford C. Evans, "Fitting Security Into the Management Structure," *Security Management,* November 1982, p. 15.

about only when a new director is brought in and makes this a condition of the job. Without proper placement of the security department, recruitment of top professionals in the security industry will be impossible. Once a corporation has made the decision to seek out a top professional, then the time for change and improvement of the corporate security stature is at hand.

Security must have communications that cross organizational lines. It must have the authority to monitor department functions that affect the security of the company and to make evaluations of security hazards and risks to the corporation. For these reasons alone, support of top management is essential.

The role of the corporate security manager depends on the desires, needs, and aims of the corporation. The manager must operate within corporate policy, the principal aim of which is to make a profit. The responsibilities of the director or manager of corporate security may vary widely and should be spelled out in written form, which will be the corporate security policy known to all. The authority of the security manager should, of course, be commensurate with his assigned responsibilities within the scope of the security policy.

The corporate security manager should think in terms of preventing, controlling, reducing, or eliminating loss from problems such as criminal activities, fires, accidents, natural hazards, and labor problems. (Chapter 7, Loss Prevention, will go into further detail.) Not only must the manager be able to communicate up the corporate ladder, he also must be able to communicate to employees down the ladder and to the public, which includes customers, vendors, contractors, and, in some instances, the media. Chapters 13 and 14 will discuss security and outside relations, along with control of outside vendors.

Note that a security manager cannot do it all and that everyone in the corporation is responsible for the protection of corporate assets. The manager should keep in mind that with corporate expansion and the shrinkage of global time and distance, communication may be necessary with other countries and cultures, especially as some third-world countries are now becoming industrial nations.

The corporate security department should be set up, if at all possible, as a profit center, or at least looked upon as such. This is easier to do in some companies than in others, but even in those corporations not involved in the manufacture or handling of consumer products, certain policies can make the department appear to be operating as a profit center. We will deal with this more in Chapter 6.

To realize the full potential of a modern-day corporate security department, we must understand that the department interacts with various other corporate departments. To give the reader an idea of the broad range of interaction, a number of areas of joint interest follow.

Finance and Accounting

Probably the most common area for interaction between corporate security and finance/accounting is inventory shortages. Typically, accounting and financial people attempt to analyze inventory shortages with a view toward finding an accounting explanation. When they are unable to do this, they assume some type of internal or external crime and turn to the corporate security department. The security department must have sufficient intelligence on various inventories either to accept the possibility of criminal wrongdoing and take action or to reject this contention and refer the matter back to the financial people. Simply by knowing the company and being on top of distribution and inventory, the security director often is able to rule out the possibility of widespread theft as an explanation for inventory shortages. These same lines of intelligence also will enable the director to accept the possibility of criminal activity.

Internal Audit

Here the interaction takes place on any type of financial wrongdoing such as embezzlements and the like. Experience has proven that in investigating cases of this type, a team approach is best, whereby an internal auditor can work hand in hand with the security investigator who is examining the case. In many embezzlements it is necessary for the security investigator to obtain admissions from the embezzler so that the internal auditor can corroborate these in the financial records. It is the authors' experience that in many embezzlements, although the internal audit group might be convinced that an embezzlement has taken place, the group is unable to pinpoint the method used and track the various numbers until the perpetrator makes a full admission.

One of the best things the security director can do in interaction with the internal audit group is educate auditors to think more like investigators when conducting an audit. Instead of looking indefinitely for a financial solution to a problem, they should keep an open mind that perhaps the human element caused the problem deliberately.

Sales Department

Customer relations is a common area for interaction under the heading of the sales department. Customer relations can be adversely affected by untimely and inordinate transportation losses of goods being shipped to customers. In this regard, although transportation losses by common carriers generally are reimbursed once proven, the damage to customer goodwill still takes place. Much of this can be eliminated or kept to a minimum if the security department periodically evaluates the security of the various common carrier transporation companies. By constantly monitoring transportation losses, the security department can more readily evaluate weak transportation companies that have no security and encourage transportation by companies that are more enlightened in this regard.

Another area of assistance to be rendered to a sales department would be the diversion of goods. Many companies have designated only approved outlets for distribution of their manufactured products. When the company's products begin showing up in unauthorized outlets, obviously some form of diversion has taken place. The security department usually can be of excellent assistance in determining the point of diversion, thus enabling the sales department to police the distribution of their products better.

Also not to be overlooked in the commonality between sales and security is the counterfeiting of a product and the investigation of any sales irregularities that may arise.

Aviation Department

Here again, the security department can be of great help in recommending proper aircraft alarms, giving personal security briefings for crews prior to foreign flights, and recommending corporate policy for aircraft security in regard to overseas flights. The security department alone has the resources and contacts to provide the above services, which would at best be fragmented if left to nonprofessionals.

International Department

In the international area, the security department not only acts in an advisory capacity, but may very well provide line-security operations by including an international security manager on the staff. Such a person would spend much time outside the United States working with the security needs of the corporation in various countries. This individual must have some inherent diplomatic skills and must realize that security must be handled differently in each country. He must be sensitive to the customs of security and police personnel in various countries and know how to steer a corporate investigation through the criminal justice systems and investigative processes of a particular country.

From a staff standpoint, the corporate security department can assist in providing overall security policy for traveling executives who range beyond the United States.

Corporate security people also generally handle counterfeiting of products on the foreign market and briefings and evaluations of terrorism and political unrest in countries of interest to the corporation.

Corporate Relations

During the time of a corporate crisis involving things such as kidnapping, terrorism, and natural disasters, the corporate relations department is faced with maintaining a close relationship with the media. By nature of the crisis, the management of such an event may very well become the province of the security department. For this reason both departments must work in harmony in the area of media relations, as imprudent statements to the press could compromise the actions of the security department. Oftentimes, the security department may be aware that local media coverage of a crime could affect the corporation, and thus it is necessary for security to work closely and quickly with the corporate relations department in planning what statements will be made, by whom, and in what context.

Credit Department

The security department often can help the corporate credit department in investigating bankruptcies, both voluntary and involuntary, in the sense of looking for hidden assets by debtors. Also ever-present is the possibility of "bustouts," which may be perpetrated by debtors under the guise of voluntary bankruptcies. Bustouts invariably are designed by organized crime or other illegal elements.

Legal Department

Corporate legal departments constantly are faced with the necessity of developing additional information that can be useful to them in various forms of litigation. This evidence can best be procured by the security department, whose investigative efforts generally will surpass even those of private investigative agencies used by many outside attorneys.

Insurance Department

As discussed in Chapter 9, Risk Management: A Total Integration, the security department can be of tremendous help with insurance matters such as the investigation of casualty and property losses within the corporation. In particular, it can make an ongoing contribution to corporate profits in its investigation of suspected workers' compensation claims that appear to be fraudulent or fraught with malingering.

Engineering Department

An engineering department may employ several hundred engineers whose sole job is to discover new types of products or enhance old ones. These are creative people prone to leaving blueprints, engineering notes, and other company-sensitive documents carelessly strewn about. The problem the security director faces is to protect proprietary corporate information, which is discussed in Chapter 11, while the chief engineer wants to get the most out of his or her personnel without stifling their creativity by insisting on strict controls over documents.

Distribution

The shipping, receiving, and warehousing departments may handle raw materials, parts, or finished products. The security manager may not only wish to enhance the physical security aspects of these operations, but also institute control systems as to the routing of these materials and the accountability for them. A balance must be struck, however, in that the security procedures cannot be so strict as to slow down the movement of these items unnecessarily.

Chapter 2

Organizing the Corporate Security Department

Any table of organization that can be designed for a corporate security department will depend, in large part, on the nature of the business, the number of locations, and the geographic territory covered. For instance, a company that is particularly susceptible to internal or external thefts, executive dishonesty, or other types of crimes against the company, must, of necessity, have a significant investigative function. Alternatively, companies engaged in heavy manufacturing and not particularly susceptible to thefts of finished products might very well have a heavy emphasis on plant protection and guard forces. Other companies, depending on the type of business, might have a need for both approaches, and this must be provided for in any table of organization.

In drawing up a table of organization, the company must decide to whom the top security professional will report. The ideal reporting situation would be for the top security official to report to the CEO. Healy and Walsh, in their book *Principles of Security Management*,[1] state that in organizations that have well-managed security programs, the security executive usually reports to a senior executive who is not more than three steps down from the chief operating officer. This would seem to make the security executive too far removed from the top executives of the corporation. In the authors' opinion, the director of security should never be more than two steps below the CEO. As Healy and Walsh correctly point out,[2] the top officers of the corporation must be interested in the security program, and their support is absolutely essential if the security department is to succeed. Top executives cannot pay lip service to the security department but instead must become personally involved so as to show all levels of management that the program is supported at the top of the organization.

[1]Richard J. Healy and Timothy J. Walsh, *Principles of Security Management* (San Carlos, CA: Professional Publications Inc., 1981), p. 28.

[2]Ibid., p. 25.

TABLES OF ORGANIZATION

The organization of any new security department will depend greatly on the role that top management envisions for it within the corporation. More often than not, tables of organization for a new department will not be drawn up beforehand but will come along sometime later as the department evolves in structure and scope. Rather than being preplanned, they often will be reflections of how the department has been set up or changes that have been made in older departments. Be that as it may, a table of organization is important not only for other members of the corporation but also for key members of the security department who can, at a glance, appreciate their jobs and functions in relation to those of others.

Each corporation has varying needs and unique aspects that will, in part, dictate the type of security organization needed. Such factors include the size of the company, whether it operates on a nationwide or international basis, the number of operating locations, the size and nature of the operating locations, the number of guard forces in the field, whether the company business lends itself to numerous investigations, and whether the nature of the business is such that only physical and perimeter security are necessary.

In Figures 2–1, 2–2, and 2–3, we attempt to give you some idea of how a security department may be organized. Note that all three figures reflect a centralization-type operation, or a modification thereof, rather than a decentralized department.

Figure 2–1 illustrates the security organization of a corporation with sales in 1984 of $900 million. It is principally an apparel manufacturing company, with a limited number of specialty apparel retail stores. Note that the complete risk management approach has been used in structuring, this department. Safety and insurance functions are coordinated, where indicated, with the security function of the company. Safety and insurance functions also are on the same line level as the second highest ranking member of the security department. Also note that although the regional security managers have a certain amount of autonomy, they do perform certain safety duties on behalf of the corporate safety function. The regional managers also have a dotted-line, or functional, supervisory relationship with the various guard forces that are in use within the manufacturing section of the company. This was set up this way originally because the security department felt that regional people were spread too thin to be effective in the day-to-day supervision of any guard force. Therefore, this supervisory function is left to someone within line management who then shares in the dotted-line relationship with the regional security manager.

Although not specifically shown on the chart, the chief investigator

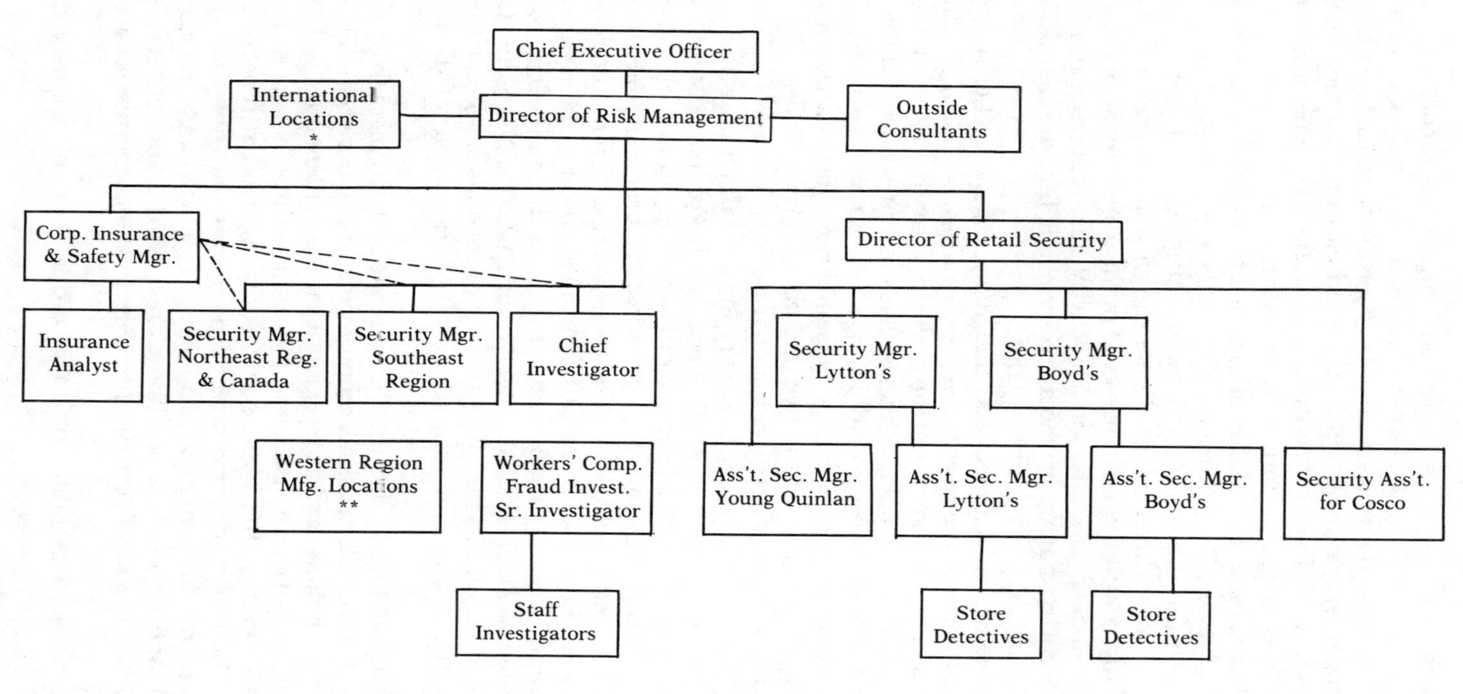

Figure 2–1 Corporate Risk Management Department Table of Organization.

*Handled personally by director of risk management
**Handled personally by chief investigator

and his investigative staff provide full investigation support services throughout the corporation, including both manufacturing and retail. In particular, the investigation section also coordinates closely with the insurance department to investigate suspected cases of workers' compensation fraud. Note that in this organization, the two entry-level positions are staff investigator and store detective.

Figure 2–2 presents the table of organization of the security department of McKesson Corporation, a $4 billion plus company in 1982. Note that this corporation does little manufacturing and has no retail stores. Its more than three hundred operating locations are made up principally of distribution centers involved in the warehousing of drugs, liquor, and chemicals. The director of security has, reporting to him, five regional security managers who are responsible for administration of security within their respective regions.

At one time necessity demanded that the company be heavily involved in investigations, but over the years the nature of security within the corporation has changed, and now the primary focus is on loss prevention. The company acknowledges that current security stresses a systems approach wherever possible and minimizes the use of guards. Also, day-to-day security operation is dependent on line management that is supervised and coached by the regional security manager. Given the size of the corporation, these five regional security managers become almost equivalent to a director of security for a small corporation.

The security organization of the Apex Small Appliance Manufacturing Company, with 1981 sales of $2 billion, is shown in Figure 2–3. This hypothetical corporation is engaged entirely in the manufacturing process, and although it has its own distribution centers, it has no retail stores. Because of the size of its manufacturing locations, a heavy commitment to guard forces is needed, and in effect, the major locations have what amounts to their own security departments. Note that the plant security manager has his own investigator, who is supplemented, if need be, by the national investigative staff operating out of the corporate office.

As in Figure 2–1, although the department is centralized from the corporate level down, dotted-line relationships exist between the regional security directors and the regional vice presidents, as well as between plant security managers and plant operating managers. In a decentralized company, the plant security manager often reports directly to the plant operating manager. This means that the plant operating manager has his own private police force, which can be misused or underused, and also is in a position to restrict the flow of security information from the local security force up to the corporate security office.

Note in the various tables of organization that the security de-

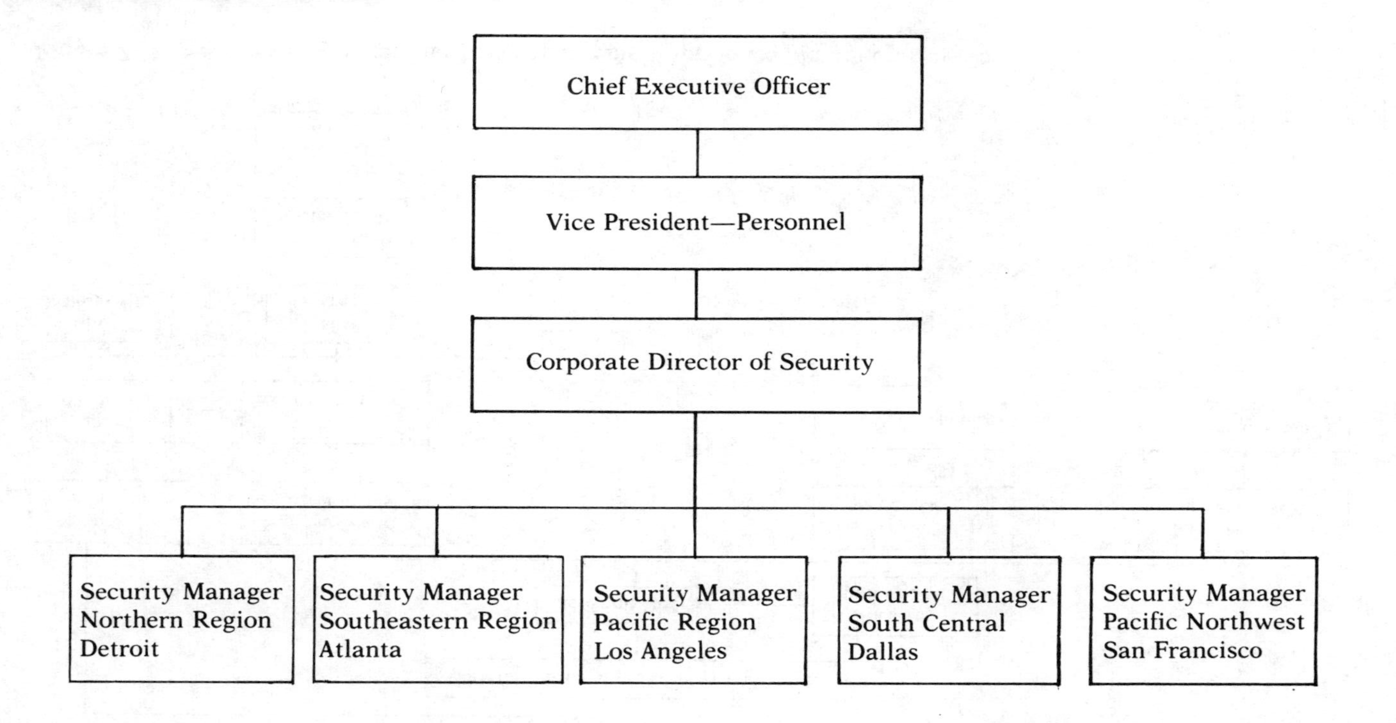

Figure 2–2 Corporate Organization Chart. The Foremost-McKesson Corporate organization chart shows Foremost-McKesson's two-tiered approach to security management. Corporate policy and procedure are set by the corporate security director in San Francisco. Responsibility and authority to implement the programs at specific plant locations are vested in the five regional security managers, who report directly to the corporate office. Reprinted with permission of *Security World*.

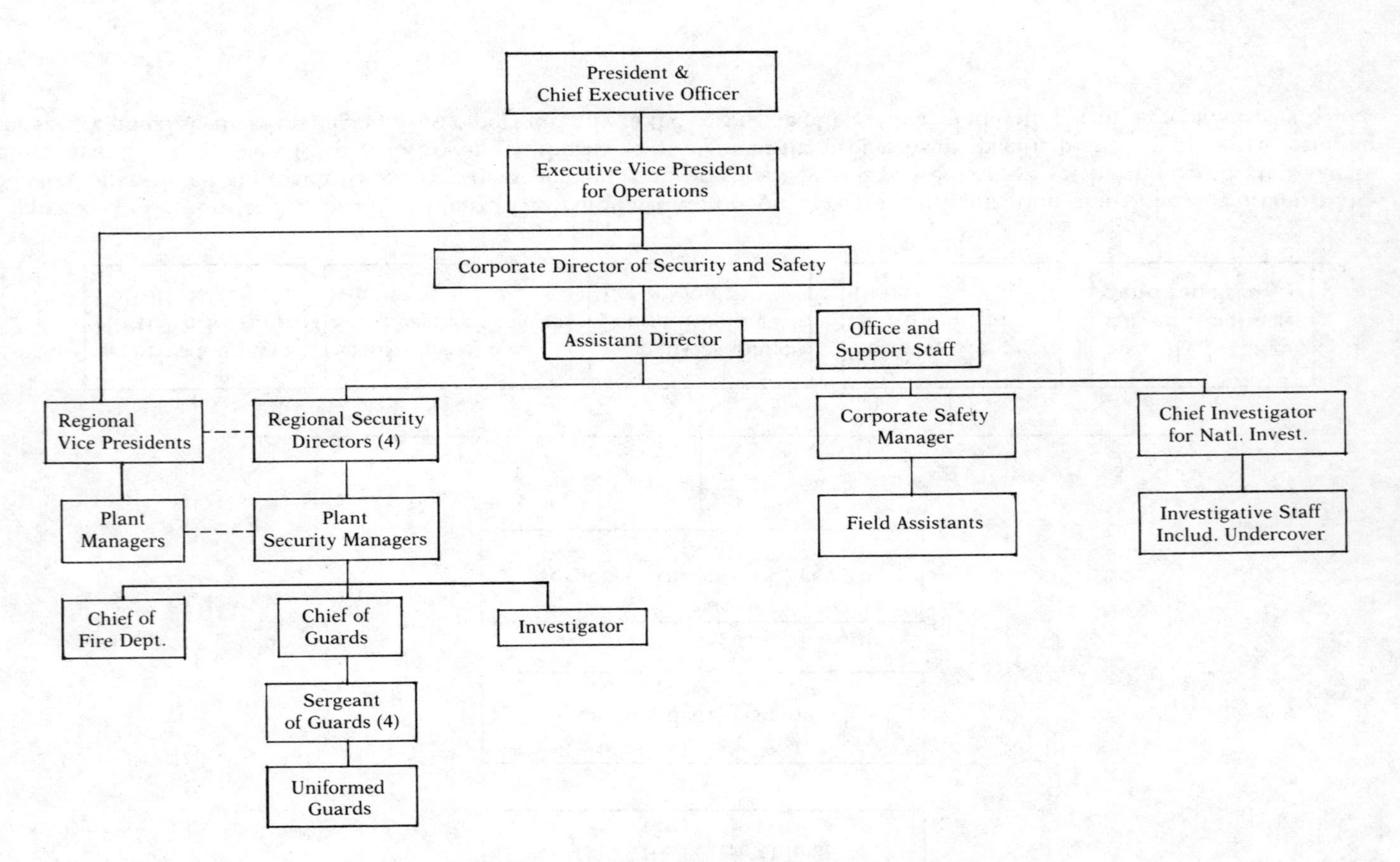

Figure 2–3 Security Organization Chart: Apex Small Appliance Manufacturing Co.

partments tend to be organized on a corporate or centralized basis rather than on a decentralized basis. There are many pros and cons and many differing points of view about the desirability of centralization versus decentralization. These various views are worthy of extensive discussion.

CENTRALIZATION VERSUS DECENTRALIZATION

Within the spectrum of major U.S. corporations, it is the authors' feeling that possibly 50 percent of corporate security departments are set up on a decentralized basis. The trend in recent years, however, has been for more departments to become centralized, with the head of security reporting to a top corporate executive.

In many companies where top management has not stressed the concept of good security, there has been a tendency for field and operating personnel to hold on to the old concept of decentralization and to require field security personnel to report to a line executive rather than the corporate office. This is quite common in large retail companies where the head of security in a large store will report to the store manager. Perhaps even the regional security chief will find himself reporting to a regional vice president. A number of arguments can be made against this practice and in favor of a centralized system.

Although it may be possible to establish broad directives and policy statements in a decentralized department, it is impossible for the corporate security chief to fine-tune individual performances within his department under a decentralized plan. Also, it is a common occurrence for local security personnel to be reluctant to pass along sensitive information to corporate headquarters.

Under a decentralized system, one can find a greatly reduced ability on the part of security personnel to conduct investigations where local executives may be targets. Security under local management makes about as much sense as having internal auditors report to field vice presidents! Although the corporate security chief may very well decide to acquiesce in the supervision of local guard forces, he never should acquiesce in the handling of investigations on the local level. Corporate security must reserve the right to control, direct, and participate in all investigative matters.

In the event that local guard force operations are passed along to local management for supervision, corporate security, in order to protect the best interests of the corporation, should monitor their activities and reserve the right of veto over the selection of security agencies. In other words, corporate security may set up standards of guard performance, which are then monitored on a daily basis by local personnel. Rather than let any operating location become involved in an unscrupulous or illegal agency, or one that features dishonest management, the right of veto is a must.

To give the reader an idea of how all this may be accomplished, assuming that the corporate security director has the necessary authority and leverage, a company with various store chains could easily appoint the security manager for the chain and keep such a manager on the corporate payroll. His salary may or may not be charged back to the operating division, depending on individual circumstances. The important fact is that the manager is kept on the corporate payroll and that his pay raises are then handled at a corporate level, as is his performance rating. In turn, the assistant security manager, various store detectives, and other security personnel could be placed on the local payroll under the direct supervision of the corporate manager, who is in complete charge. This has worked well in various companies, but it must be approached with the understanding that security for that particular store is a working partnership between the corporate security manager, who is stationed there, and the company's operating head.

The retail industry is replete with examples of security personnel who have been discharged or otherwise forced to leave a company because of their attempts to handle investigations of high-ranking retail executives. Experience has shown that there is a definite tendency on the part of local management not to report problems that require internal investigation.

The following two cases clearly illustrate why the concept of centralization is far superior to that of decentralization.

St.Louis: On a routine review of charge-account balances, the corporate security manager, who was stationed in this area and who headed the complete security department for a retail chain, discovered credit balances of approximately $6,000 each, belonging to five brothers who owned a construction company. This construction company had an exclusive maintenance contract with the retail company and also had handled the construction of new stores, renovations, and so on.

Under a decentralized plan, the security manager would have been powerless to investigate and would have run a certain risk even in passing this type of information on to corporate headquarters. Under the centralized plan, the information was passed along, and an extensive investigation revealed that the construction company was passing kickbacks to the president of the retail company and that the brothers who were partners in the construction company had violated federal income tax laws. This case never would have surfaced as promptly as it did were it not for the fact that the security manager was a corporate employee.

Atlanta: A few production workers in a manufacturing plant were found to be falsifying production records to gain more individual rates of pay. The discovery was made by the internal auditing group but was passed over by management, who attempted to minimize the problem and discharge the offending employees. At this point, the corporate security manager, who was based in the area, stepped in and blocked these discharges until he could make a full investigation. As a result of the investigation, approximately eighteen offending employees were discovered and prosecuted. The prosecutions largely resulted in court-ordered financial restitution to the company. The company benefited directly from this approach in the recovery of funds. At the same time, local management was unable to minimize the problem and prevent it from becoming what they considered an embarrassment.

Throughout the entire security industry, many corporations are applauded for the success of security departments that operate on a centralized basis. It is well established in the security profession itself that the only way to do a good security job and make a profitable contribution to the corporation is to have the security people on a centralized basis. They are then immune from intimidation and retaliation by local management, who may not appreciate security's contribution because of their own feelings of embarrassment.

Chapter 3

Strategic and Operational Management

All corporate staff departments are called upon to analyze their functions within the corporation and to answer the question "Why do we exist?" Security departments usually have been excluded from this process by claiming to be different or by throwing out horror stories about internal or potential losses. The chief security executive should welcome the assignment to analyze the security function in order to send out a clear message why the department exists. Such an analysis also will answer the question "Can the department be more effectively organized?" From this type of introspection, the director can then develop an effective organizational system and a long-range plan. Here is a suggested outline for developing a security department analysis:

1. How do we define security in our corporation? What is the scope of the responsibility?
2. What evidence suggests the need for a security function within the corporation?
3. Does our program deal with symptoms or causes? For example, are we uncovering employee dishonesty without eliminating basic reasons for its existence?
4. Do we have a long-range goal to protect the assets of the corporation more effectively and preserve the moral values of our business?
5. If we do have a long-range target, let's define it as clearly as possible.
6. Given the target, do we have a plan of action to ensure reaching the target?
7. What areas require the highest priority in the security function—reducing inventory shrinkage, improving employee screening, lowering burglary rates, lessening internal theft, or improving fire prevention?
8. How do the security needs of the various company groups differ? Can they be prioritized for security services?

9. What alternatives are available for servicing the security needs of the corporation and the individual groups? Do these include reorganizing the internal security department, using outside consultants with a smaller internal group, eliminating the security function, and/or insuring losses?
10. Are existing methods possibly incompatible with a positive program of employee relations? Can these factors be reconciled? What are the trade-offs?

This outline is not all-inclusive, nor would it fit all corporations, but is should provide a starting point for a director to begin a careful analysis of the security function.

Most company stockholders want the chief security executive to have the attitude that a major part of his job is to provide the best security to the corporation for the least amount of money. That presents a continuing challenge to any security director because corporations seldom are static. The above exercise of analysis is one example of strategic planning that sets the stage for developing a mangement style, plans of action, policies, and procedures.

ORGANIZATION PLANNING

Organizing is an integral part of management. It means arranging an orderly way of accomplishing objectives by developing patterns of activities to reach goals as efficiently as possible. While organizational patterns may vary considerably, with centralized or decentralized management controls being used to solve similar loss problems,[1] the manager is charged with identifying, grouping, and structuring the activities of his staff to achieve specific objectives. The manager will do this by assigning activities, delegating authority to carry out these activities, and coordinating the activities.

To assist the manager, a staff must be chosen. This group of people is necessary to help the manager accomplish the chosen tasks. The staff should be trained, be properly compensated, and have specific and definite job requirements. To keep the positions filled, an inventory of qualified candidates should be maintained. Perhaps the most important function of a manager is to coordinate the activities of his or her staff. Coordination is the achievement of harmony in either individual or group efforts toward the accomplishment of the designated goals. Co-

[1]Richard S. Post and Arthur A. Kingsbury, *Security Administration: An Introduction*, 3rd ed. (Springfield, IL: Charles C Thomas, 1977), p. 735 (hereafter cited as *Security Administration*).

ordinating is arranging, setting in order, harmonizing, and bringing the tasks into proper relationships. A manager synchronizes the efforts of the employees, who in order to accomplish the tasks, must clearly understand the goals to be achieved.

Organization planning is an integral part of the total management process. Most authorities in organizational planning would agree with the following abbreviated definitions of terms:

Innovating Introducing new and better ways of doing things.
Planning Determining the results to be achieved and the action needed. Defining objectives and work plans.
Organizing Identifying and grouping work, delegating responsibility and authority, and staffing.
Directing Communicating, motivation, developing a plan, training, and achieving teamwork.
Controlling Measuring work, comparing to standards, interpreting results, and taking correcting action.

The managerial function of planning, organizing, controlling, directing, and innovating should be thought of as a closed loop process.[2] In reviewing the closed loop process in Figure 3–1, we see that the parts are interdependent. For the management process to be most effective, all the parts must work well. One weak link lessens the results of the chain. It is also interesting to view the role of innovating, which should affect each of the other four components.

The security function traditionally has been mostly reactive. It must shift into an accepted management process if it expects the recognition and respect from other management disciplines. The management process described above would be an easy model to use in carrying out the objectives of a security function within most organizations.

Figure 3–2 analyzes and classifies security responsibilities and relationships and serves as a road map for organizational planning. Organizational matrices such as that in Figure 3–2 can take a variety of forms depending on the issue to be clarified. Issues might include who makes specific security-related decisions, priority analysis of responsibilities, and staffing requirements.

While organizational planning might not be the most important function of the security director, it is a significant management tool that will help the organization succeed.

---

[2]D. Yoder and H. Honeman, *ASPA Handbook of Personnel and Industrial Relations Editions* (Washington, DC: BNA Books, 1979), p. 3–78.

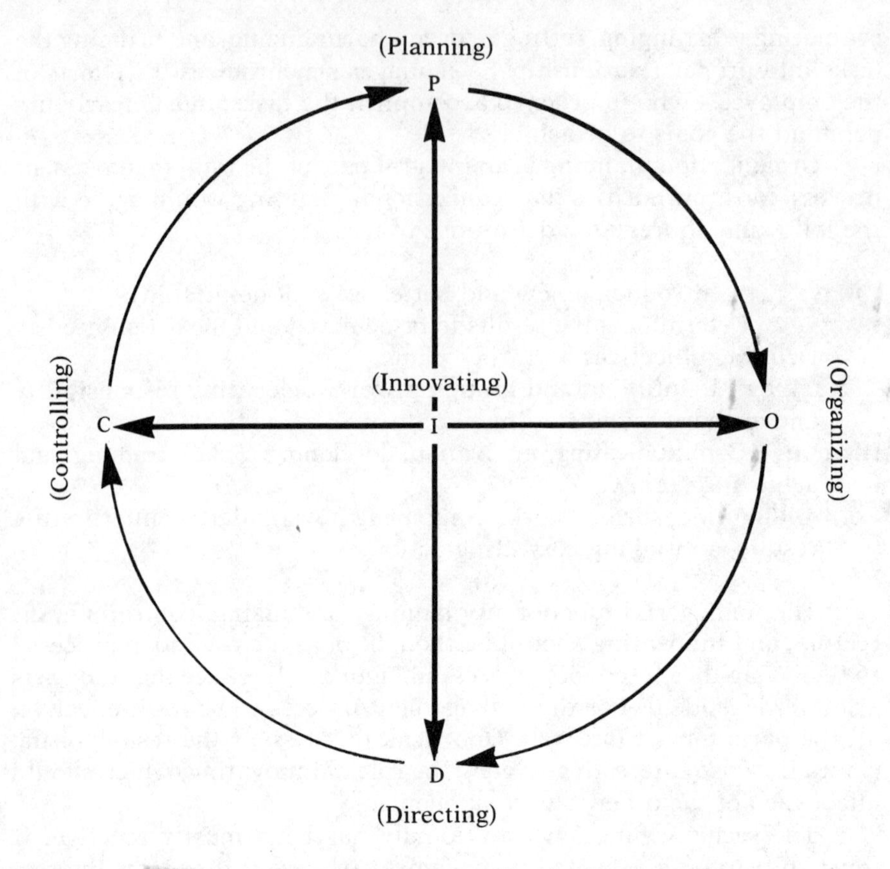

Figure 3–1 Management Cycle: ASPA Handbook of Personnel and Industrial Relations Editions.

MANAGEMENT AIDS IN PLANNING

Two widely used acronyms for basic management functions are PODSCORB (Planning Organization Directing Staffing Coordinating Reporting Budgeting) and POSTBECPIRD (Planning Organizing Staffing Training Budgeting Equipment Coordination Public Information Reporting Directing).[3] "There is nothing more vital to the long-term success of a security program than strategy and planning."[4] Planning can be defined as a scheme or program for doing or arranging something

[3]Philip P. Purpura, *Loss Prevention,* p. 26.

[4]Post and Kingsbury, *Security Administration,* p. 655.

Decision of Action Areas	Corporate Security HQ	Regional Corp. Security	Operating Co. Security	Operating Management	Other
A. Physical Security	I	II			
B. Investigations	I	III			
C. Security Clearances		I			
D. Budgeting/Staffing	III				
E. Policy/Procedures	IV			IV	

Figure 3–2 Degrees of Responsibility (i.e., authority, action, accountability). Code: I—Primary, no notice required; II—Primary, must notify before action; III—Must consult with prior to action; IV—Joint responsibility.

with selective objectives and goals that are formulated beforehand. Plans guide managers in their use of personnel, equipment, resources, and money. A plan helps a manager to prepare for later preformances.

There are many types of plans—short term, intermediate, long term, strategic, tactical, and so on. A wide range of devices assist a manager in planning. One is a calendar on which the manager records things to be done on specific dates. Another is a suspense or "tickler" system. In this system, the manager utilizes a box of 3-by-5 cards, which are divided chronologically by day and month. If, for example, a manager decided that fire extinguishers should be checked regularly at four-month intervals, he would insert three cards—one for each month—labeled February 15, June 15, and October 15th and would indicate the work to be done on them. If a manager had a report due by July 25, he would insert a 3-by-5 card under that date with the proper notation. Naturally, the manager would review these cards on a regular basis.

A third method for aiding planning is a Gantt chart, which schedules by affixing time values to each needed activity in the total project. This chart emphasizes work-time relationships and through graphic charting points out the importance of scheduling and time values. The chart normally is horizontal from left to right and can measure progress against time.

Another aid in planning is the Program Evaluation and Review Technique (PERT).[5] This technique is more appropriate for massive, complex, and nonrecurring tasks. (Some investigators have attempted to use PERT charts for involved fraud cases.) In utilizing PERT, the manager must formulate all the different activities that make up the overall project or program. An activity represents the work or process required to accomplish an event. Only activities consume time; events do not. Each activity measures time to determine how long each separate and respective step will take. In using this method, one starts at the left with the first event and goes on to the right to the last event or ending. Activities are represented by arrows and events by circles, and the length of time for each activity is noted on top of the arrow. In noting the time required for an event and to help estimate, the manager can list three times: the shortest possible time in which an activity can be completed, the average time for completion, and the maximum time. An event is accomplished when all activities leading up to it are completed. Also useful with the PERT system of planning is the use of Critical Path Methods (CPM). This involves the longest path and sets the time limit to complete the overall program or project.

---

[5]Ronald S. Burke and Lester R. Bittel, *Introduction to Management* (New York: McGraw-Hill, Inc., 1981), p. 118.

MANAGEMENT BY OBJECTIVES

Management By Objectives (MBO) is a tried and true method of planning in which employees or groups of employees are asked to state objectives to be reached in the course of a particular time frame (usually one year). Each objective can be broken down into additional objectives. If an objective is to reduce accidents, one can break it down into reducing accidents in the transportation area, the machinery area, the warehouse area, and so on. These objectives can be short term or long term and specify what the employee or group expects to do. MBO helps the manager avoid duplication of effort, improve coordination and direction, and set priorities.

The term management by objectives was introduced nearly thirty years ago by Peter Drucker in his book *The Practice of Management,*[6] and it is thought to be the most influential concept ever generated by Drucker. It shifted the entire focus of management thought from supervision of activities to observation of the results of actions. Output or productivity, rather than work efforts or inputs, became the areas to measure. MBO seminars are still popular among management personnel, and numerous articles and books have been written on this subject. Literature on the application of MBO to security management is, however, rather sparse. In *Management Decisions by Objective* George S. Odiorne gives this definition:

> In brief, the system of MBO can be described as a process whereby the superior and subordinate managers of an organization jointly identify its common goals, define each individual's major areas of responsibility in terms of the results expected of him, and use these measures as guides for operating the unit and assessing the contribution of its members.[7]

If your organization has committed itself to MBO as its management style, it would be easy to adopt that concept to the management of the security department. It would be possible, however, to use MBO even if the large corporation uses a less formal or no specific management style. The authors believe that MBO is easily adaptable to the security process. Under this concept, managers can be held responsible for results instead of a listing of activities. Moreover, MBO allows for a superior to have less day-to-day involvement with subordinates. Both have hammered out a set of objectives, so they understand and have agreed on the results to be obtained. The written document becomes a

---

[6]Peter Drucker, *The Practice of Management* (New York: Harper & Row, 1974), (hereafter cited as *Management*).

[7]George S. Odiorne, *Management Decisions by Objective* (New York: Prentice-Hall, 1982).

road map that can quickly review and measure specific progress. As with all road maps, there will be detours and unforeseen events that will cause revisions of the original document. Neither party should view the style or the document as being carved in stone. Not using a road map can be frustrating or even disastrous, however, because it is difficult to tell where you are going or know when you have arrived.

Too many security departments are predominantly reactive in their management style. This is a carryover from early law enforcement styles in which you constantly react to some action by investigation after the act or enforcement of specific laws. Even modern law enforcement personnel view themselves as managers, and many have adopted MBO as their style.

Who sets the objectives? It is best if the subordinate sets his own objectives, with the manager playing a coaching role. When the subordinate understands the process and has seen the broader objectives of the organization, he is more likely to buy into the concept and accept being measured by the results. Naturally, higher management has the authority to accept or reject the goals. Nevertheless, the subordinate is held responsible for participating in setting his goals. In *Drucker: The Man Who Invented the Corporate Style,* John J. Tarrant says, "The objectives of the individual are a function of the objectives of the larger unit of which he is a part."[8] The MBO process, if adopted properly, should encourage self-motivation, self-direction, and self-assessment, with the end result being a happier, more productive employee.

The MBO approach as modeled in this chapter places the supervisor in the role of a sounding board or coach who assists subordinates in achieving previously agreed upon results. Another productive aspect of using the MBO management concept lies in utilizing the Responsibilities-Indicators-Goals (RIG) document review as a basis for performance appraisal and salary review. This systems approach, described below, is a logical chain of events in which the employees set their own goals, with the results being objectively measureable and tied to performance appraisal and salary adjustments.

RESPONSIBILITIES-INDICATORS-GOALS APPROACH

Responsibilities are the major area in which the manager is expected to achieve results, and they usually are identified by reviewing where significant amounts of time are spent. In security staff positions it may be helpful to ask, "What managerial decisions do I wish to influence?" Responsibilities are listed in order of importance and are identified by

---

[8]John J. Tarrant, *Drucker: The Man Who Invented the Corporate Society* (Des Plaines, IL: Cahners Books, 1976), pp. 82–83.

nouns in brief tables, with qualifying adjectives omitted. Two examples are "Relationships" and "Self-Improvement." Minor responsibilities should be combined, and the list should not exceed ten major responsibilities.

Indicators are best thought of as yardsticks. Indicators are used to measure effectiveness in getting results in the key areas of responsibility. They are what a manager and his subordinate should look for in deciding how and when a responsibility has been fulfilled. One or more indicators should be listed for each responsibility, with five being the maximum. When possible, indicators should be measurable, be easy to use, and often use ratios or deviations from standards. It is permissible to use abbreviations and jargon when developing indicators such as the number of unreported incidents, response time, salary analysis, and head count deviation.

In developing goals, the indicators should reflect end results and have time frames. Goals should be achievable yet have some flexibility. They also should be quantifiable—for example, 20 percent maximum turnover per year, a revised security manual by the fourth quarter, or monthly status reports for the boss.

It is the authors' opinion that an MBO style of management utilizing an RIG document (see table 3–1) leads to increased job satisfaction in a security department. Professionals prize autonomy and desire opportunities to achieve, accomplish, and perform. Allowing the individual to set his own goals represents a commitment on his part. The dynamics of this type of working environment become a situation of an individual's goals being considered, along with those of the supervisor, to assist and support the individual. Interaction is ensured with this process because there is a scheduled follow-up or accounting, usually on a quarterly basis.

To illustrate the MBO concept as applied to security management the authors have developed an RIG document for a hypothetical security manager (see Table 3–1). The document also can be used as a planning and controlling device. It is strongly suggested that the supervisor review his RIG document with each subordinate to show that this is a systems approach to managing the function so that the subordinate can see how his objectives fit in with the department and total organization. It also is helpful to prepare work plans for each objective as a control device that answers who, what, when, and how the objective will be accomplished.

POLICIES AND PROCEDURES: THE CORPORATE SECURITY MANUAL

Nearly all corporations have a range of policy and procedure manuals covering in detail how the business should be conducted in specific

Table 3–1 RIG Document

R *Responsibilities*	*I* *Indicators*	*G* *Goals*	*Target Date*
Administrative Budgets	1. Actual vs. Budget	1. Determine expense—budget plus or minus 5% total budget	¼ review
	2. Actual vs. Prior year	2. Maintain travel expense at not m/t 10% over prior year	Mo. review
	3. Actual vs. Prior year	3. Maintain capital expense budget at not m/t 6% prior year	¼ review
Staffing	1. Head count deviation from authorized	1. Check head count variance—Zero	Mo. review
	2. Existence of succession plans	2. Identify one candidate as backup for each key manager	¼ review
	3. (# and %) turnover	3. Maintain no more than 10% turnover annually	Annual
	4. Time to fill vacancies	4. Make sure no authorized position open m/t 30 days	Ongoing
Security Clearance	1. Statistical reports	1. Develop and distribute ¼ statistical info. on new hires processed	30 days
	2. Consistency of program	2. Conduct all clearances prior to hire	¼ review
	3. Statistical reports	3. Make no exception to clearance procedure for units on the program	Ongoing
	4. Review current employee printouts	4. Make sure no "not recommended" hired unless cleared thru appeal procedure	Ongoing
	5. % "not recommended" statistics and quality control	5. Keep rejection at not m/t 25%	¼ review
Loss Prevention	1. Survey schedule	1. Give ⅓ of all facilities initial survey each year during next 3-year cycle *(prioritize)*	½ review

	2. Follow-up reports to key management and staff	2. Ask director to obtain home office support on most serious vulnerabilities; give appropriate feedback to staff on field surveys	Ongoing
	3. # alarm complaints	3. Reduce alarm complaints to not m/t 5 per quarter; replace equipment or alarm contractor when necessary	¼ review
	4. # of facilities added to corp. locking program	4. Keep 90% of all facilities on corp. locking program	End of 3d qtr.
	5.	5. Maintain 100% compliance with all security regulations; make sure no licenses lost or suspended due to security breaches	Ongoing
Investigations	1. # of investigations not performed	1. Investigate all suspected or proven losses and ensure dismissal/prosecution/recovery	Ongoing
	2. Time lapse	2. Respond promptly to all investigations and within 12 hours on more significant losses	3 days
	3. # similar repeat investigations	3. Perform postmortems to I.D. cases, then design countermeasures and test to prevent repeats	30 days
	4. Staff critique of investigation reports at semiannual meeting	4. Perform all investigations to highest degree of professionalism	¼ review
	5. Complaints by legal audit or sr. management	5. Conduct all investigations in legal and ethical framework in compliance with corporate policies	¼ review
Special Projects (short term)	1. Knowledge of operating company plans	1. Have ¼ reviews with each op. co. concerning closings, acquisitions, relocations, additions, and labor contracts	¼ review
	2. # of unreported incidents	2. Make sure no loss or avoidable embarrassment to co. due to lack of security involvement	¼ review

Table 3–1 *(continued)*

R *Responsibilities*	*I* *Indicators*	*G* *Goals*	*Target Date*
	3. Response time	3. Achieve security involvement early enough to affect plans	¼ review
	4. # senior management special requests	4. Respond to all special security requests from sr. management; clear thru boss prior to taking action	¼ review
Staff Development	1. % turnover	1. Achieve 20% maximum turnover per year	Annual
	2. Salary analysis	2. Keep all key managers at salary grade midpoint between 2nd and 3rd year of service	Annual
	3. # on bonus plan	3. Phase in key staff to bonus program	Annual
	4. Training programs	4. Conduct 2 in-house training seminars per year; Send each key manager to one outside training seminar	Annual
	5. Management development plans	5. Conduct performance appraisals and career counseling	Annual
Innovations	1. Existence of special studies	1. Conduct feasibility study to improve records and statistical data storage	End of 2d quarter
	2. Manual revisions	2. Revise security manual	End of fiscal yr.
	3. Addition of int'l security program	3. Develop total security program for international division	End of 3d quarter
Relationships	1. monthly dept. report; ¼ RIG status report	1. Give status reports to boss	Mo. and ¼ reviews
	2. # of reviews with boss	2. Review RIG and coaching session with boss	¼ reviews
	3. Frequency of meetings	3. Plan communications meeting with each op. co. senior management	¼ review

	4. Existence of contacts favorable to co.	4. Act as liaison with police, regulatory agencies, and security product/service reps.	¼ review
Personal Development	1. # seminars attended	1. Attend 3 annual seminars	Annual
	2. Contributions to profession	2. Get involved in professional association work a. give 3 talks to association b. hold office in one association c. write an article for professional association magazine	Annual
	3. Independent study	3. Read 2 books per year in business or security fields	Annual
	4. Health status	4. Hold weight and start physical exercise program	¼ review

functional areas. Too often the security function has been excluded from this process based on alleged security reasons. There is little evidence to support this reasoning, and the authors would encourage the writing and dissemination of a corporate security manual. In the event that there is truly sensitive material that should be guarded, the security director can color code those pages and limit distribution to a need-to-know group.

The size and complexity of many corporations warrants the development of corporatewide security policies but must at the same time encourage the development of policies that recognize the needs to each operating group. Corporate security policies should have an umbrella intent and allow for varying degrees of operating unit autonomy as might be appropriate for the respective organization.

It must be emphasized in opening statements, preferably authored by the CEO, that all employees observe the spirit and intent of the security policies. This consistency will facilitate employees productivity and positive attitudes toward the corporation, and it will minimize possible inequities among operating units relative to security-related practices. In all cases, a corporate security manual or comparable version developed by operating groups with corporate approval must be available in every location. Employees may review the manual during working hours at times convenient to the local manager, who is responsible for maintaining the manual. The intent is for statements of security policy to help management in the conduct of business.

Because of the complexity of the security function and its possible scope, the area of specific security procedures cannot be addressed adequately in this chapter. In addition to a corporate security policy manual, the authors suggest that security policy and procedures be developed as chapters within other policy manuals such as a personnel manual, internal audit policy and procedures manual, financial policy manual, risk management manual, operations manual, and general administration manual. Adding a security section to other department or functional manuals allows one to reach a broader audience and lends acceptance and credibility to security policies because they are now viewed as being part of the departments manual. Furthermore, this technique allows detailed security procedures to be written. Another key advantage would be the ability to cite these policies and procedures when seeking voluntary compliance with various weak areas found during a loss prevention audit or survey. The authors have found this to be a very effective technique as contrasted with a stand-alone corporate security manual.

To give the reader an idea of the major topic areas that should be included in a corporate security manual, the authors present the table of contents in Figure 3–3. This table has been taken from a major cor-

Figure 3–3 Security Manual Table of Contents.

Figure 3–3 continued

poration retailing division. It is the "bible" for all security personnel assigned to retail operations.

ROLE OF THE CORPORATE SECURITY OFFICE

The primary role of the corporate security office centers in the following:

determining overall corporate security objectives and plans;
establishing corporate priorities and allocating resources;
formulating policy and setting the character, style, and role of security within the corporation;
establishing the planning control and reporting systems;
monitoring operating groups' security performance.

Corporate security strategy could be defined as identifying the target area and then moving, through policy decisions, toward the target and eventually tackling it. An example of this might be the case of a national security director who wished to implement a nationwide polygraph program within his corporation. Undoubtedly, there would be pockets of resistance to such a program, and therefore the best strategy would be to implement the program, through policy decisions, in those divisions and areas that were least resistant. In this way, the director could save the most important and most resistant division until last and then be able to overwhelm such resistance by telling and persuasive arguments gleaned from the success stores of other divisions that have the polygraph program in place.

Other authorities have stated that strategy breaks down into different components, and using this approach to the corporate security field, we might find the following three points as being critical in the development of strategy:

1. Identify the funding available, then translate it, which means determining what type of budget the corporation will be willing to give the new security director, not only in the present year but also in succeeding years.
2. Determine which objectives are possible with the funding available. Again, this simply means deciding what can be done this year toward tackling the objective and what must be deferred until succeeding years.
3. Commit the resources of the department and of the corporation itself. This means determining what can be done toward tackling

the strategic objective with the work force and resources available to the director.

One area that should never be overlooked is using the resources of the corporation itself to accomplish these objectives. Oftentimes, the security director can utilize the sales department—through its sales representatives—the personnel department and its various local branches, and the research and development section's laboratory facilities. These sources often are available for no additional charge, if the situation is handled properly. They obviously are in a position to furnish information that might otherwise be difficult to obtain and also to assist the security director in many endeavors. Many directors are prone to tackle a project with the human resources available within their own department and seldom think of going to other major components of the corporation for additional assistance.

Security can and should play a significant role in realizing a corporation's commitment to deal with integrity, fairness, and responsibility toward all its constituents (investors, employees, customers, suppliers, and community/government segments). The business of the corporation, both domestic and foreign, should be conducted in accordance with the highest standards of corporate citizenship and in accordance with applicable rules of law and security policies. Each operating manager should be charged with full compliance with whatever government regulations and internal security policies are applicable to his responsibilities. This dedication to quality is so important that it should be tied to each manager's performance appraisal and subsequent salary review.

Chapter 4

Management Techniques

Jay Speckler and John Wicker write; "It is normally of more value for a corporation to achieve a grade A implementation of a grade D solution, than to have a grade D implementation of a grade A solution."[1]

The ability of the security department to achieve grade A implementations of even grade D solutions, is dependent on management, or, more specifically, the manager.

Not every great corporation has a top security department, and the top security department can often be found in other than the top corporations. In these top departments, one will always find a top leader—the manager or director.

Management can be defined in many terms. It means to direct or control the use of, to exert control over, to control the behavior of, or to make submissive to one's authority through discipline or persuasion. It also means to handle and direct through careful and tactful treatment. Other definitions include to administer the affairs of an organization or business, to manipulate, to contrive or arrange, or to supervise. It means to succeed in doing or accomplishing. Depending on your point of view, management may mean any of the following:

> "The force that runs an enterprise and is responsible for its success or failure;
>
> The performance of conceiving and achieving desired results by means of group efforts consisting of utilizing human talent and resources;
>
> Getting things done through people;
>
> Planning and implementing;
>
> A resource used by everybody to achieve goals."[2]

---

[1]Jay Speckler and John Wicker, "Internal Consulting Groups: Catalysts for Organizational Change," *Management Review*, November 1980, p. 24.

[2]George R. Terry, *Principles of Management* (Homewood, IL: Richard D. Irwin, Inc., 1977), p. 4 (hereafter cited as *Principles*).

A more encompassing definition is that "management is a distinct process consisting of planning, organizing, actuating, and controlling, performed to determine and accomplish stated objectives by the use of human beings and other resources."[3]

Management is an activity that makes specific things happen purposely and, with luck, successfully. It is accomplished by the efforts of others, with the efforts of others, and through the efforts of others. Management is not passive. It is taking action and getting things done. It is making every action and decision contribute to a carefully chosen goal. Management is devoting one's attention to the most pressing issues and influencing the behavior of one's own staff, other employees of the corporation, and visitors.

In protecting assets, a security manager's purpose is to prevent loss of life, property, and information or ideas. This means protecting tangible and intangible corporate assets against loss from disasters, crime, fire, accidents, and other causes. To accomplish this, the security manager will work with people—members of his own staff, other employees of the corporation, visitors, or people outside the corporation but involved in its business. The security manager also will work with money, machines or equipment, and other resources and materials with the objective of preventing loss on a cost-effective basis.

One should keep in mind that the old hierarchical or pyramidal business structures are being labeled by today's management experts as no longer workable because they lack a circular fashion or networking horizontal linkage. Naisbitt states that modern business is more globalized than heretofore, and its major resource is information.[4] Institutions in the future will be organized according to a management system based on networking. The new management system will be more informal and have more equality. Its communications style will be lateral, diagonal, and bottom-up, and its structure will be cross-disciplinary. By the late 1980s, 80 percent of total management will be under the age of 45. Naisbitt also feels that employees will contribute to the solution of operational problems, and committees—not hierarchical staffs—will make decisions.

THEORIES OF MANAGEMENT

The new corporate security manager will have to deal in a workplace where employees will be better educated, be more aware of due process

---

[3]Ibid.

[4]John Naisbitt, *Megatrends: Ten New Directions Transforming Our Lives* (New York: Warner Books, 1982), p. 198 (hereafter cited as *Megatrends*).

rights, speak out more, and want more privacy. They will be more litigious, desire to know more, and want more participation in management situations. This will be contrary to the authoritarian, top-down management style.

There have been many theories of management, and some of them include the following:

The autocratic theory is based on absolute power. The employees are obligated to follow management's orders. They are prodded and not led, which does not develop their human potential. There is negative motivation, and management does the thinking while employees do what they are told.

In the custodial theory the managerial orientation is toward tangible benefits for the employees. These include pensions, insurance, medical benefits, and salary increases. The aim is to make the employee happy and contented. The employee is not, however, motivated to produce to his or her full capacity or capability. The employee relies on the company for security.

The supportive theory is an enlightened approach. Here the employee is afforded a supportive work climate and thus can grow in skill and performance, take on additional responsibility, and strive to contribute to the organization.

Herzberg's work motivation theory breaks down the job into two different categories. The first category is called the hygiene or maintenance category and has factors such as pay, benefits, working conditions, job security, and interpersonal relationships. Dr. Herzberg believes that employees expect the things that are in the first category (hygiene) and that genuine work motivation comes not from these things but from the second category (motivators)—the job itself, which gives motivators such as responsibility, recognition, advancement, growth, and achievement.[5]

X, Y, AND Z THEORIES OF SECURITY MANAGEMENT

Some of the most talked about theories are Douglas McGregor's Theory X and Theory Y.[6] In Theory X, the security employee works as little as possible; is resistant to change; has little ambition; is self-centered,

---

[5]Charles A. Sennewald, *Effective Security Management*, 2nd ed. (Stoneham, MA: Butterworths, 1985) (hereafter cited as *Effective Security 2e*), p. 120.

[6]Ibid., p. 117.

passive, and indifferent; and wants to avoid responsibility. This employee, with his lack of ambition, is not motivated by doing the job but rather by financial incentives. This employee does not object to being led or directed.

The more enlightened approach, which gets better results, is Theory Y. This humanistic approach to job motivation recognizes that employees do not dislike work. They find work natural and will expend physical and mental efforts at their jobs. These employees are capable of assuming responsibility, have ideas, are ambitious, have potential for development, and want to do a good job. In this setting, management provides an environment where the employee can exercise control and achieve.

A recent attention-getting management style is the Japanese Theory Z.[7] Theory Z suggests that Japanese companies have a special way of managing employees so that a Z company culture exists. The company has a commitment to its workers that includes humanized working conditions, long-term employment, long-range staff development, consensus decisionmaking, and attention to human relations. It also deals in trust, intimacy, and close personal relationships, and it assumes that the worker's life is whole (rather than just nine-to-five). It also touts MBWA (Management By Walking Around), a self-explanatory term.

THE SECURITY MANAGER

One authority describes managers as having two functions: strategy formulation and strategy implementation.[8]

The following question also is asked: "Do managers spend more time with people or with reports?" In security, it has been well established that people time must have priority over paperwork time. Security, after all, is a people-related endeavor and is at best only supplemented by data, reports, and the like. It is the ability of the security director or manager to sit down with a division or other field officer and, in a face-to-face effort, be persuasive and gain that executive's support and participation in a particular security program that is in the planning stages.

Nadler and his associates also raise the question "Do managers

---

[7]William Ouchi, *Theory Z: How American Business Can Meet the Japanese Challenge* (Reading, MA: Addison-Wesley Publishing Co. Inc., 1981), p. 195.

[8]David A. Nadler, J. Richard Hackman, and Edward E. Lawler, III, *Managing Organizational Behavior* (Boston: Little, Brown, & Co. Inc., 1979), p. 261.

spend more time taking initiatives or reacting to the initiatives of others?[9] Obviously, a progressive security manager will take the initiative rather than sit back and wait for things to happen to which he can respond.

What better performances are the members of the security department capable of, and what improvement in security results will these better performances make possible?

Most of the important problems a business faces arise from the desires, attitudes, and behavior of employees. To help and properly motivate the employees, a manager should be a good leader who will guide and direct the employees through example, persuasion, influence, and communication. This is an interpersonal aspect of managing and is a tool to help the manager direct and cause the employees to follow a particular course of action. Part of managing is making decisions. No decision can be made, however, until the manager has clearly identified the problem(s) involved. To do this, the manager must obtain complete information about the apparent problem and should do this by utilizing facts. These are answers to the questions what, when, where, why, who, and how. Once the manager gets the facts, he should analyze them. After the facts have been established, the manager can then determine plans and proper solutions to the problem. The manager should choose the best solution plus alternate solutions and then arrange courses of action for accomplishing the solution. Once the plan has been put into effect, the manager should check its progress and continually measure performance against the established goal.

The manager must control the activities of his staff. This is directing, commanding, regulating, and exercising authority over the activities and programs. Controlling is measuring and correcting the activities and deviations of the employees to conform to the selected plans. Control can be exercised by direct or indirect supervision and through other procedural devices.

In developing good criteria for the qualifications of a corporate security manager, we find that Drucker gives an excellent description:

> There is tremendous stress these days on liking people, helping people, getting along with people, as qualifications for a manager. These alone are never enough. In every successful organization there is one boss who does not like people, who does not help them, and who does not get along with them. Cold, unpleasant, demanding, he often teaches and develops more men than anyone else. He commands more respect than the most likeable man ever could. He demands exacting workmanship of himself as well as of his men. He sets high standards and expects that they will

---

[9]Ibid.

> be lived-up to. He considers only *what* is right and never *who* is right, and although often himself a man of brilliance, he never rates intellectual brilliance above integrity in others. The manager who lacks these qualities of character—no matter how likeable, helpful, or amiable, no matter even how confident or brilliant—is a menace and should be judged "unfit to be a manager and a gentleman." What a manager does can be analyzed systematically. What a manager has to be able to do can be learned (though perhaps not always taught). But one quality cannot be learned, one qualification that the manager cannot acquire but must bring with him. It is not genius, it is character.[10]

Drucker states that there are five basic operations in the work of the manager.[11] Paraphrasing these operations, we find that they are as follows:

1. Objectives. The manager must set objectives for his or her department. Along with this, it is necessary to determine the goals in each area of the objectives and what has to be done to reach these goals. The objectives then must be communicated to the subordinates whose performance is the key to attaining the goals.
2. Organization. A manager analyzes the activities, decisions and relations needed. He classifies the work and divides it into manageable activities. These are then further divided into manageable jobs. People are then selected for the management of these aspects of the jobs to be done.
3. Motivation and communication. A manager creates a team out of the subordinates who are responsible for various jobs. This is done through the manager's practices and his own relationships with his subordinates. Much of this is done through people decisions on pay, placement, and promotion. This is a constant communication process to and from subordinates, to and from the manager's superior, and to and from other colleagues.
4. Work measurement. The manager must establish methods of measuring the performance of the organization and of every person in it. This comes about through analysis, appraisals, and interpretation of performance. As in all the other areas, the manager is constantly communicating the meaning of these measurements and findings to his subordinates' superior and colleagues.
5. Management development. A manager must be able to develop people, including himself. To allow subordinates to stagnate in

---

[10]Peter Drucker, *Management*, p. 402. Reprinted with permission.

[11]Ibid., p. 400.

their career development is a disservice to the company, the subordinates, and the manager himself.

SPAN OF CONTROL

Years ago, management held that the span of control should be a minimum of three and a maximum of seven employees. Drucker contends that what counts is not how many people report to a superior but rather how many people who have to work with each other report to a superior.[12] The important factor is the number of relationships under the manager rather than the number of people per se.

Drucker's philosophy is that the more interacting relationships that occur beneath a superior and between subordinates, the fewer the number of people who should report to the manager (certainly not more than eight to twelve). Alternatively, Drucker maintains that in a decentralized organization where each subordinate operates independently of the other, the number could easily run to several hundred subordinates reporting to one superior.

In the typical corporate security department, however, the relationships among subordinates are often not only desirable but necessary to provide a team approach and adequate manpower coverage in difficult cases. This would suggest that a span of control should be limited to somewhere in the area of seven or eight persons.

Most authorities agree that it is difficult, if not impossible, to alter the personality of adults. If we can accept this premise, then it becomes obvious that we should steer clear of attempting personality changes in favor of concentrating on how to make subordinates more effective in their career endeavors.

In determining a manager's objectives, Drucker favors the idea of each subordinate writing a "manager's letter" twice each year.[13] He feels that in this letter to a superior, each manager first defines the objectives of his superior's job and then his own job as he sees them. Drucker feels that the subordinate should then state the performance standards that he believes are being applied to him. He also should list the things he feels that he must do to attain the goals, including things that his superior and the company do to help him and to hamper him. Finally, according to Drucker, the subordinate should outline what he proposes to do during the next year to attain these goals. If the superior accepts this "manager's letter," it becomes the charter under which the subordinate operates.

---

[12]Ibid., p. 412.

[13]Ibid., p. 438.

Style of management is very individualistic, developed through experiences, and tempered by the traditions of the employing company. Because of the great diversity in the loss prevention field, security management cannot be easily defined. Corporations differ in their environments but have similar problems. The following descriptions of security managers reflect their individual styles or approaches.[14]

> Manager number one tries to manage by participation and coordination. She tries to anticipate problems and make sure that everyone affected by a problem understands the problem. She is flexible in problem solving and participates in its solution. She tries to project a positive attitude that a solution for the problem can be found. She keeps her people informed, asks for their input, explains her decision, and encourages her subordinates to look for ways to improve their jobs. She recognizes her employees' contributions and tries to provide an environment where people will enjoy coming to work.
>
> Manager number two encourages communication and decision-making on the part of his staff, and he tries to supervise as little as possible. He feels that problems arise because people are reluctant to address the issues. He looks for ways, other than short-term satisfiers, to solve problems and displays constant awareness and recognition of each employee's performance.
>
> Manager number three delegates authority and encourages his people to work together on a problem, which is participative management. He believes that everyone's input is better than only one person's ideas and does not tolerate sloppy work. He welcomes new ideas and motivates his staff by giving them the opportunity to develop through initiative.
>
> Manager number four strives for perfection and is sales-oriented. He tries to sell needed changes by explaining the reasons for them. This manager does not dictate but supervises through guidance and inspiration. He motivates by setting an example, treating people courteously and giving bonuses and salary raises.
>
> Manager number five has loose supervision, as his staff are professionals. He believes that his responsibility is training the staff.
>
> Manager number six uses OST (Objectives, Strategies, and Tactics) as the framework for his managerial style. He believes in a lot of communication and effects this through weekly, monthly, and

---

[14]Mary Alice Kmet, "What Is a Security Manager?" *Security Management*, May 1979, p. 6.

quarterly meetings at which goals are refined, redirected, and reported. He is willing to listen and motivates by recognizing achievements, by giving responsibility and authority to his employees, and by providing a way for them to grow professionally and financially.

George R. Terry also promulgates some guidelines for managerial success:[15]

1. Know the company's goals.
2. Select effective subordinates and group members carefully.
3. Delegate by letting subordinates decide issues within their respective spheres of operation and make sure each group member is assigned work best suited to him.
4. Check to make sure results being obtained are satisfactory, carefully evaluate what is achieved, and consistently evaluate group members.
5. Motivate group members.
6. Develop good communication, learn to speak and write effectively, and see situations from another's viewpoint.
7. Strive to obtain good interpersonal relationship and strengthen human relations skills.
8. Minimize conflicts among group members.
9. Set high standards or proposed levels of achievement.
10. Become effective in decisionmaking.
11. Adopt a questioning attitude to discover and use new ideas.
12. Be a leader by getting involved in the action.
13. View management as an opportunity to influence others favorably.
14. Spend time on matters that are really important.
15. Plan and follow through on progress.
16. Express personal feelings and understand the feelings of others.
17. Look for the best in others.
18. Encourage members to assume responsibility.
19. Appraise his or her own self and performance honestly.
20. Keep cost expenditures at a minimum with the service required.
21. Increase personal overall knowledge.

The manager of the future will not be confined to any managerial parochialism and will coordinate a multiplicity of disciplines.[16] He will have to be flexible and responsive to change and must continually up-

---

[15]Terry, *Principles of Management,* p. 10.

[16]Ibid., p. 609.

date his education through refresher courses, in-service courses, university classes, and professional periodicals. The future security manager must be alert to new ideas and techniques and have empathy with specialists due to technological changes. This manager will work in an environment that places less emphasis on hierarchical structure and more on equalitarian efforts.

Chapter 5

Staffing

Two major elements necessary for the existence of a corporate security department are equipment and staff. This chapter will be devoted to the most important resource: staffing. M. Scott Myers has said, "The purpose of the staffing function is to find, attract, and utilize qualified people in such a way that their talents will find expression in the successful pursuit of organizational and personal goals."[1]

RECRUITMENT

Basically, recruiting presents three options to the national security director:

1. Recruiting the entry-level position.
2. Recruiting experienced personnel from the outside.
3. A combination of the above.

In any case, you must recruit against standards that should appear in a detailed job description. (See Appendix 1 for examples.)

One of the keys in building a dynamic, goal-oriented security department is selecting the right people to staff the positions. Too often this is done by visceral feelings with little objectivity. To improve this critical process, the authors recommend a selection worksheet as shown in Figure 5–1. As an example, if the position were for a regional loss prevention manager, the starting point for evaluating the candidates would be to review the appropriate job specifications with an emphasis on what results must be achieved. The next step would be listing the skills, knowledge, experience, and traits that are needed to get those results. The rating scale could be from 1 (low) to 10 (high). This process is of great help because:

[1] M. Scott Myers, *Every Employee a Manager* (New York: McGraw-Hill Inc., 1970).

Goals	Skills	Knowledge	Experience	Traits	Candidates A	B	C	D	
Survey 85% of all locations next fiscal year	Time management Persuasion	Security generalist in hardware, policy, and procedures	3 to 5 years in security surveys 1 to 3 years independent field work	Tenacious Even-tempered Self-disciplined	7	8	5	6	
Add 10 locations to corporate locking program	Persuasion	Product knowledge	One year locking devices experience	Tough-minded Aggressive	5	9	6	4	
Contribute two items per quarter for security newsletter	Time management			Creative Personable Is team-worker Takes initiative Self-confidence	2	5	4	8	
Reduce false alarms by 25% next fiscal year		Vendor relations Police relations		Creative Persuasive Tactful Follows through	9	3	5	7	
					23	25	20	25	Totals

Note: For this example, only a few hypothetical goals have been listed for this position.

Figure 5–1 Regional Loss Prevention Manager Selection Worksheet.

1. It eliminates the person who could not do the job (low scorer).
2. It identifies the most likely successful candidate (high scorer).
3. It puts personalities in the proper perspective as opposed to experience and skills.
4. It makes for more compatible and happier employees.
5. It makes use of the candidate's skills and experience.
6. It eliminates downtime to train high-potential but low-performance candidates.

If the department is large enough and of sufficient depth, the national security director will want to consider a policy of promotion from within wherever possible. Promotion from within provides a powerful incentive and motivator for younger security personnel, reduces turnover, and adds stability and expertise to the talents of the department. To pursue a policy of promotion from within, the security director must, of necessity, recruit for entry-level positions.

Recruiting Military and Police Personnel

A number of security directors have experienced mixed results in the hiring of retired military and police personnel. Many security chiefs hold to the view that they will not consider former police personnel with experience of more than six years, as anyone with longer police service probably has developed a law enforcement mentality that would be disadvantageous to security management objectives. Another problem encountered is that police personnel who have retired are looking mostly for executive security positions and are not willing to tackle the more mundane security jobs that ultimately would lead to an executive post.

Being a former law enforcement professional does not automatically qualify one for security management. That myth has vastly retarded the defining and growth of security management. Some law enforcement officers make good law enforcement managers, and most good law enforcement managers could be successful in business security management, but not all law enforcement officers should be considered as viable security management candidates. As in all disciplines, the candidate's experience and track record should weigh heavily in the hiring decision.

Retired military personnel have had some excellent training, which lends itself very nicely to the private security industry. This is especially true of people who have had military careers in the OSI (Office of Special Investigations, U.S. Air Force), CID (Criminal Investigation Division,

U.S. Army), and ONI (Office of Naval Intelligence). The one drawback encountered with military personnel is that occasionally, a military person who has retired from the service is not willing to put in the hard work and long hours that traditionally are part of the corporate security scene.

If the security chief can cope with the occasional drawbacks as presented by former police and military personnel, then the chances of finding worthwhile people from these sources is excellent. In general, if the person's former career showed continuing growth and success in progressively more important assignments, then it is safe to assume that those same traits could be transferable to a corporate security manager position.

In a company where promotion from within is ultimately desired, the director must, of necessity, utilize both entry-level recruiting and the hiring of experienced personnel. Neither one by itself is the answer, and in the initial stages there must be a blending of the two. To tackle immediate security cases, and to show results that are meaningful to the corporation, a security chief must have experienced personnel. Turnover, however, is significant within the security industry. As experienced persons drop out of the picture through normal attrition, the younger personnel who have been hired for entry-level positions have an opportunity to move up, forming the basis of a well-grounded security operation.

Recruiting from Colleges

Recruiting young people just graduating from college for entry-level positions has its drawbacks. It means that extensive on-the-job training must be provided for these people, and the security director also can look forward to a number of mistakes within the first three years of a recruit's employment.

If the security director does not wish to be plagued by occasional errors in judgment, and if the department is not of sufficient size to have a viable program of promotion from within, the director should look to outside recruitment of experienced personnel who have been with other companies. The recruiting and hiring of experienced and older personnel from outside presents some unique problems. Oftentimes, bad habits are perpetuated from one job to another. These are not easily broken and in some cases are impossible to change. Some experts also feel that at least 50 percent of the experienced personnel who are available "on the street" are rejects from other firms and have been failures in the security field. Fortunately, most of these rejects can be screened out of further consideration with the tools now available for that purpose. Among the tools recommended are in-depth interviewing, background investigations, polygraph testing, psychological profiles, and written honesty tests, all of which will be discussed in this chapter.

The ASIS has attempted to identify and list all the college-level schools in the United States offering degrees in security administration.[2] The major drawback to this list at present is that most of the schools are not four-year programs but rather offer two-year certificates or associate's degrees in industrial security. Those schools offering a four-year program leading to a bachelor's degree in industrial security or security management are simply too few to service the entire security field. The scarcity of schools offering a four-year security management program simply means that the security director must expand his recruiting efforts to schools offering a four-year program in criminal justice.

In any recruitment drive from any of the traditional four-year programs, a certain number of candidates will drift in from the criminology department. Although the criminology students are quite sincere and a number of them have made successful careers for themselves in the private security field, they do not come to the security director as well equipped as those students graduating from the criminal justice program. Criminology is, after all, a study area offered within the sociology department, and although it does address itself to causal and remedial aspects of crime, it is not slanted toward investigations and the management of day-to-day problems within the private security field. Alternatively, criminal justice students usually are better equipped because of their course background to absorb the specific training and disciplines found in the corporate security field.

Relations with the Placement Office and the Department of Criminal Justice

In any campus recruiting effort, two facets of the university must not be overlooked. Many students will have registered with the placement office and developed a set of credentials that can be readily examined by the recruiter. Also, the placement office will designate a time for interviews, will schedule same, and will provide a private interviewing office for the recruiter. The one drawback to this is that a number of good candidates often do not register with the placement office, and the placement office seldom has personal knowledge of any of these candidates.

The second part of the university that must not be overlooked is the department of criminal justice or security administration itself. By

---

[2]American Society for Industrial Security, 1655 N. Ft. Myer Drive, Arlington, VA 22209.

maintaining close relations with the department, the recruiter or security director can be made aware of outstanding students. Also, the department can assist the recruiter in doing a selling job on corporate security careers and, in particular, the corporation itself. Many students starting out as freshmen believe that they are headed for a career in police work. By having one or two of the members of the faculty occasionally mention the virtues of corporate security work, some students will be much more receptive to a career offering in that field as opposed to public law enforcement.

Selling the Company

The corporate security recruiter must realize that his biggest competitor is the public police field and, in particular, municipal law enforcement. Recognizing that most municipalities have twenty-year retirement programs and that police unions have pushed salary levels to all-time highs, the recruiter certainly has his work cut out for him in order to attract qualified personnel to the corporate security field. In recent years, this competition has been lessened somewhat by the fact that municipal departments have not been able to absorb the majority of criminal justice graduates and also by the fact that many graduating seniors cannot meet the rigid physical requirements set forth by municipalities. This is particularly true of people with slight handicaps such as poor eyesight. Many of these people, although not able to pass a rigid municipal examination, can and do make excellent corporate security people.

To be successful and overcome the sometimes wide disparity in starting salary levels, the recruiter must be able to sell his company to the candidate. Generally, young people are not interested in retirement and long-term disability programs as much as they are in salary levels. To overcome this discrepancy, the recruiter must be able to point out to the candidate that he or she will gain experience in corporate security work that might never come in a lifetime of municipal law enforcement. If the security department is an active one, with wide operating latitudes, this statement is quite realistic.

In selling the company, the recruiter must be able to point out career opportunities that are based on promotion from within. He must be able to point out specific salary increase schedules so that the candidate can look forward to pay raises at specific times. In offering career jobs, the recruiter must be able to outline specific career paths within the company, paths that will ultimately lead to an executive security position. Unlike the police field, which offers promotions based on ability plus time in grade, the corporate recruiter should stress the fact that age and time on the job play very minimal parts in promotion opportunities. This generally proves to be most appealing to candidates. Finally, it should be stressed that any deficiency in starting salary usually will be overcome within a few years and that those employees who exceed performance objectives will nearly always surpass the law enforcement counterpart. Simply stated, the opportunities for advancement are greater than in law enforcement. The recruiter should be able to illustrate examples to support this statement.

The Campus Interview

The importance of the interview cannot be overstressed. This is a time when the company itself passes the candidate's inspection, and it enables the recruiter to focus on the best possible candidates for the openings.

There is often a tendency to underestimate the intelligence of the typical graduating senior, and this can be a fatal mistake. Recruiters have been known to embellish and exaggerate the feats and accomplishments of their corporate departments. Many times graduating seniors come away from an interview of this type with nagging doubts about the sincerity and honesty of the department itself. There is nothing wrong with the recruiter attempting to point out the good features and desirable aspects of his department, but the recruiter must leave sufficient time to draw out the candidate in conversation so that the recruiter can determine the candidate's particular qualifications.

At the outset, the recruiter must be able to determine whether the candidate is willing to accept an entry-level position other than the executive post to which many graduating seniors aspire. Many companies have recruited graduating seniors for entry-level positions such as uniformed guards, store detectives, and undercover agents. These jobs require specific personal traits, and thus the recruiter must be sensitive to fitting the candidate into the proper slot. Many recruiters will take great interest in a candidate's family background or perhaps even the type of summer or part-time job the candidate has held. Candidates who earned 50 percent or more of their college expenses usually are mature and exhibit traits that help them succeed. If the candidate comes from a working-class family and has held temporary or part-time jobs that have required manual labor, the candidate probably is not averse to hard work and will diligently apply himself to new responsibilities.

Many candidates will take themselves out of the running, or will be eliminated by the recruiter, within the first fifteen to twenty minutes. More promising candidates should be allotted at least forty-five minutes, and the recruiter should have the placement office schedule the interviews accordingly. The recruiter also should leave ample time to return on a succeeding day for second and more in-depth interviews of those candidates who show the greatest promise.

The Second Interview

Most security directors are firm believers in at least two interviews, and for this reason, the interview given on a college campus should not be the only interview of the candidate. Every effort should be made to provide a second interview by another executive who will give his own perspective on the applicant's chances for success. Even more important, because it is a different personality and a different interviewer, additional questions probably will be raised that would not have been raised in the original interview. As a result, new and important information probably will be forthcoming.

It is recommended that the second interview be held off campus, preferably at one of the company facilities. This provides the recruiter an opportunity to utilize nonsecurity executives in either line management or staff personnel positions for additional interviewing.

Applicant Screening

A great percentage of security directors believe that all security applicants should be screened by polygraph tests prior to being hired. Unfortunately, it is a recognized fact that, like the police field, the private security field attracts a significant number of misfits, psychological cripples, confirmed thieves, and other undesirable personality types. The one examination that tends to identify more abnormalities than any other is a polygraph examination. There is little or no need for a polygraph examination of this type to deal with purely personal matters. Any such examination should, however, cover a review of the application form, drug usage, theft from former employers, school thefts or shoplifting, criminal convictions, unsolved criminal offenses, and discharges from former employment. Recognizing that approximately four out of every five rejections by polygraph will be based on admissions by the candidate himself, it is easy to visualize the tremendous amount of information that is generally forthcoming by using this technique.

Where a polygraph test is not possible due to legal restrictions, a written honesty test is the next best substitute. A number of security directors believe in administering both examinations. A written honesty test, such as the Reid Report (from Reid Systems, 233 North Michigan Avenue, Chicago, IL 60601), will give an accurate portrayal of an applicant's attitude toward honesty. Although this information is slightly different from past behavior patterns picked up by the polygraph, there is a high correlation between a person's attitude toward honesty and past behavior patterns.

The recruiter should make every attempt to use some type of psychological profile for the applicant. Keeping in mind that some security applicants are psychologically maladjusted, a good test is essential.

Two psychological tests are The Personal Audit (Clifford R. Adams and William M. Lepley, Science Research Associates, P.O. Box 5380, Chicago, IL 60680-5380) and the Minnesota Multiphasic Personality Inventory, MMPI (P.O. Box 1415, Minneapolis, MN 55440). Any psychological profiles determined through interviewing or testing, must be interpreted by a qualified professional.

Background Investigations

In corporations that do not utilize the polygraph or a written honesty test for screening job applicants, the security director should make every attempt to convince top management of the desirability of a background investigation. It is the authors' opinion that although a background investigation is generally not considered as reliable and fruitful as a polygraph examination, it is highly desirable and may be a substitute for the above. In a few companies, background investigations are used to supplement other forms of honesty screening.

The security director must be aware that in using any outside agencies to conduct background investigations, the person being investigated must be notified of the fact that he is being investigated and informed of the general parameters of the investigation. The candidate also must be advised that upon written request, he is entitled to know who was contacted during the investigation even though the candidate is not entitled to review the report or comments made by persons interviewed. This is mandated by the federal law known as the Fair Credit Reporting Act. In some states, such as New York, a release form must be obtained in advance from the person being investigated so that his credit history can be revealed by credit agencies. Without this release, the background investigation is limited to other public documents and interviews and does not include any credit history. A farsighted security director probably should obtain a release from the person being investigated, which would give the director the ability to check credit bureaus at some future date should a problem arise while the person is on the job.

If the credit bureau files are not deemed important for a particular job applicant, then the security director may use his or her own internal staff to handle the background investigation. In that case the director is under no obligation to put the applicant on notice that he is being investigated.

In conducting an in-house background investigation, economy is certainly a consideration. Most agency-type background investigations cost about $300 to $350 minimum. If the person has moved around the United States, that necessitates out-of-town checks, which makes the cost go higher. Obviously, the security director can bring in a background investigation for well under this cost if it is local in nature and if the director is able to use his own personnel. For further information on background investigations, refer to John M. Carroll's excellent text, *Confidential Information Sources: Public & Private.*[3]

The Job Offer

Other than for the director of security, an employment contract seldom is used. Nevertheless, some type of job offer will be made to a successful candidate, and to eliminate any misunderstandings, the verbal offer should be confirmed in writing with space for both parties' signatures.

Although the job offer will conform to individual company policy, the major points covered will include the following:

Starting salary
Performance review frequency
Reporting date and place
Headquarters for the job
Relocation expenses
Title
Eligibility for benefits program
Any probationary period
Any contingencies (security, physical, and so on)

TRAINING

Jobs in the private security field and especially corporate security that could be described as entry-level positions would be store detectives, guards, undercover agents, and members of shopping investigation

[3]John M. Carroll, *Confidential Information Sources: Public & Private* (Stoneham, MA: Butterworths, 1975).

teams. In hiring people for any of these positions, the security director is faced with decisions on how proper training should be administered and how to make it compatible with the entry-level position.

It goes without saying that the best possible training for any of these positions is on-the-job training coupled with proper in-house supervision. All the former education and specialized training courses will not teach the entry-level applicant about the particular company where he is to work. This can come only on an in-house basis, and this is what makes a new recruit a valuable member of a company's security department.

Basic Training

From the standpoint of formal courses, which of necessity are of a general nature, the Protection of Assets course offered by the ASIS is excellent, especially for beginning store detectives. This course is offered several times each year and provides a basic introduction to the various facets of private and corporate security. For newly hired guards, a number of states have passed regulations on formal classroom training in addition to minimum standards on firearms instruction, if the guard is to be armed. If guards are hired on an in-house basis, and especially in those states that do not require formal training of guards, it becomes incumbent upon the security director to devise his own formal guard-training program. To rely solely on coaching and on-the-job training leaves a company wide open to charges of negligence, which may be raised in a lawsuit. Again, if the guard is to be armed, it is even more important for the security chief to devise an acceptable and practical firearms training course for the new recruit. Not to do so is to place the corporation in an untenable position should something go wrong and legal proceedings result.

Undercover Training

For training new employees who are slated for undercover work, the authors suggest the joint training program set up for undercover agents by two corporations—Cluett, Peabody & Co., Inc., and McKesson Corporation (Appendix 2).

In 1971 McKesson was joined by Cluett, Peabody & Co., Inc., in an endeavor to conduct periodic joint training schools for undercover agents for both companies. Since 1960 the original training curriculum had been constantly improved and upgraded and eventually began to attract the attention of other companies. In 1979 Cluett and McKesson agreed to open the training program, on a nonprofit, break-even basis to other companies that had expressed a desire to participate. This availability to other companies has continued and not only includes private corporations but some security agencies as well.

Experience has shown that this formal training pays off for the company in the form of increased safety for the agent and increased chances of winning criminal prosecutions and labor arbitrations. In addition, it adds another dimension of professionalism to the security department. For the individual agent, we have found that those who do well at the school usually turn out to be very productive agents, while those who do poorly have generally not been successful after returning to their respective companies.

Most college graduates who embark on this training are willing to do undercover work, especially if they can see that it will lead to a higher position in the not-too-distant future. Occasionally, a student becomes so enthralled with his own ability at undercover work that he is content to remain in the position indefinitely. An outstanding agent who really enjoys his work can be worth more to his employer than even his immediate supervisor. Unfortunately, it is not possible to identify these unique persons in advance; only the true test of field undercover work can make that determination.

Another important facet of training for the entry-level position is that of moving and stationary surveillance. For a discussion of this subject, refer to the book *Employee Theft Investigation*.[4]

Medium-Level Training

Regional security managers, facility managers, chief investigators, assistants to those jobs, and other functional security managers could properly be termed medium-level, or middle management, personnel. Many training programs could be structured to accommodate the needs of such personnel, but the authors will discuss a number of points that they consider to be especially helpful.

On-the-job training for physical security and investigative aspects of the job is important. If the security manager is being recruited from the outside, he may come equipped with specific knowledge in these areas. If not, and the job requires such, then on-the-job training will have to be provided. In any large security staff, the security director, if he does not become involved with the training personally, will recognize that one of his people stands out above the rest as being knowledgeable and a potential trainer of others. This is the person to whom much on-

---

[4]J. Kirk Barefoot, *Employee Theft Investigation* (Stoneham, MA: Butterworths, 1979) (hereafter cited as *Employee Theft*).

the-job training should be assigned. It is not necessarily a job that outranks other comparable jobs, but it simply represents that individual on the security staff who is best equipped to give on-the-job training to others. In both physical security and investigative aspects, a number of good texts are available for outside reading.

Of note is a course offered periodically by the American Management Association (135 W. 50th St., New York, NY 10020) called Finance for the Non-Financial Executive. It is believed that this course is offered approximately four or five times each year in different parts of the country, and if a middle management security executive has no accounting background, this is a must for his development and training. Constructing budgets, issuing charge-backs and credits to other divisions in the corporation, understanding inventory adjustments, and performing other tasks dictate that security managers must have some familiarity with financial and accounting matters.

Another form of training, which could be administered by the security director himself, could be taken from the *Protection of Assets Manual*.[5] One method would be to assign specific chapters to your staff until those subjects applicable to your operation had been covered. By treating selected subjects as a training module, the director could use the manual for continuing training of his staff.

It also has been the authors' experience that a security executive who is well grounded in the material contained in the *Protection of Assets Manual* would have less difficulty passing the Certified Protection Professional (CPP) examination given by the ASIS. This examination is given at various times during the year throughout the country.

While being a CPP does not signify a certain level of training, the examination does require significant experience and knowledge. The preparation for this examination could be categorized as training. Most candidates attend a CPP review course in preparation for the examination, although it is possible to pass the examination by studying on one's own.

The Professional Certification Board was organized by the ASIS in 1977 to grant the CPP designation to any individual meeting established criteria of professional protection knowledge and conduct.

The certification of protection professionals benefits the individual practitioner, the profession, the employer, and the public. The evidence of competency in security protection furnished by certification will improve the individual, raise the general level of competency in the security profession, promote high standards of professional conduct, and provide evidence to management of professional performance capability.

---

[5]Timothy Walsh and Richard Healy, *Protection of Assets Manual* (Santa Monica, CA: The Merritt Company, 1983).

An increasing number of employers, seeking a professional to manage the organization's security program and to participate as a member of management, are placing a great deal of importance on the successful candidate's being a CPP. For example, "positions available" announcements in the *Wall Street Journal* and other publications often include requirements such as "Certification as a protection professional by the ASIS desirable" or "Must have certification as a CPP." This trend will become more evident during the next five to ten years, as employers and the public become more aware of the CPP program.[6]

As we have seen there is a trend toward the CPP designation being required, or at least preferred, for medium- and high-level security positions in business and industry. Several organizations have begun adding this requirement to specific job descriptions for security managers. The authors suggest that this generalist professional security designation either be held by candidates for medium- or high-level security management positions or that the candidate be willing to obtain the CPP credential within the first two years of employment. Many security practitioners believe that the CPP designation eventually will come to have the same degree of prestige to the security profession as does the CPA (certified public accountant) designation to the accounting profession.

High-Level Training

From time to time, the security director should attempt to keep abreast of the state of the art and make an effort to keep his skills as a manager and administrator honed to perfection. In the authors' experience, one of the better ASIS courses tailor-made for the top security executive was titled Advanced Security Management Course. It is now slated to be replaced by an advanced version of the Assets Protection course offered by the ASIS. This advanced course will undoubtedly have Assets Protection II as a prerequisite. The working and problem-solving sessions will be augmented by top speakers from various disciplines whose material will be put to use in solving problems assigned for each day. The former advanced security management course, covering the better part of five days, was undoubtedly the finest course designed specifically for security managers being offered at that time. Other training programs that would be beneficial to a seasoned security director interested in professional growth are the following:

---

[6]Professional Certification Board, ASIS.

Kepner-Tregoe[7]: This course teaches a logical fact-oriented rational approach to problem solving and decisionmaking rather than the creative or gut-instinct approach. Participants bring on-the-job situations with them to this week-long course, which is taught through a combination of lectures followed by case study and presentation methods. The information provided is designed to be used to improve results in the areas of problem analysis, decision analysis, and potential problem analysis.

Situational Leadership[8]: This course uses video presentations, behavior models, case study analysis, group discussions, role playing, and simulations to explain effective leadership styles for improved performance and managing change.

Dimensional Management Training[9]: This course for upper level managers is designed to help them analyze their own approach to handling people and those with whom they interact, thus helping them develop strategies to accomplish goals.

Influence Management[10]: This is an intensive three-day workshop for managers who usually work with others over whom they have no traditional or direct authority. Participants study and practice the following major concepts that affect performance and productivity:

1. Supporting and helping others as they perform their jobs.
2. Sharing power in the interest of the overall organizational goals.
3. Developing the art of encouraging others to trust him or her.

Each participant also receives confidential personalized feedback from the course management on how well he functioned in influencing others prior to attending the program.

Business Administration Courses

As corporate security work is performed for and on behalf of the profitability of the business, it is logical that training and educational background should encompass certain business courses. In addition to a

---

[7]Kepner-Tregoe, PO Box 704, Research Road, Princeton, NJ 08540.

[8]Leadership Studies Productions, Inc., 140 S. Hickory Street, Escondido, CA 92025.

[9]Psychological Associates, 8201 Maryland Avenue, St. Louis, MO 63105.

[10]Forum/Schrello, 555 East Ocean Blvd., Long Beach, CA 90802.

course or courses in accounting, other beneficial courses are personnel adminstration, labor relations, introduction to data processing, and logic. Introduction to marketing also would be worthwhile. One of the age-old conflicts in this field, especially in retailing, is a proper balancing of good security and marketing efforts. Without marketing, there would be no sales, and without sales, there would be no company or security department.

ASSESSING PERFORMANCE

Several years ago at a company meeting held in the East for all corporate security personnel, the director of security, in consultation with his assistant, finalized a decision to terminate the services of an assistant security manager attending the conference from the West Coast. The assistant manager had not been doing an adequate job and had failed to progress as expected when he had been promoted into that position. He had been with the company a number of years, but had held the assistant security manager's slot for only about fourteen months.

After the decision had been made, the man's immediate superior, the assistant director, met with him and terminated his services. Needless to say, the assistant manager was shocked at this turn of events and requested to see and speak with the director of security. The main complaint, in talking with the director, was not that he had been discharged but that no one had ever told him that his job performance was unsatisfactory. He went on to state that had he known he was not performing up to the expectations of his superiors, he would have put more effort into the job, and he felt that he would have made a success of it. The director of security was quite surprised at this revelation, as he had assumed all along that the assistant manager had been given sufficient warnings and had received direction and counseling from his immediate superior. But there had been a total lack of communication relevant to job performance between the assistant manager's two superiors and the employee himself.

Although the above story is directly related to a security department, the same set of circumstances probably has occurred in numerous cases over the years in business and industry. This is why professional personnel people have attempted to foster in-service training programs and, more importantly, a formal appraisal and performance review of subordinates. If a situation such as the above were to occur under a formal performance review program, then obviously the reviewers should be the ones discharged rather than the deficient employee.

By starting at the top, the director of corporate security can, with his immediate subordinates, set the tone and proper procedures to be used in any annual performance review. A formal program, which should include a checklist, precludes the possibility of talking in generalities and forces the two sides to address themselves to specific traits as listed in the checklist. This procedure should then be carried down through the ranks to include the lowest level in the security department.

Appraisal Forms

In most corporations, the personnel department uses a standard appraisal form of its own design or perhaps of a commercial nature. These forms may not be entirely adequate for each job category in the corporate security department, so the director must be prepared to improvise his own specific appraisal forms, following as closely as possible the format of the master form issued by the personnel department.

To give the reader an idea of what these forms are like and the items contained therein, we present examples in Figures 5–2 and 5–3. Figure 5–2 is a specialized form used in the security department of one corporation. Note that the form calls for areas of rating that are peculiar to a security department in general and to this department in particular. Figure 5–3 is a regular corporate management evaluation form for all departments.

An adjunct to the appraisal form is one that can compare similar job performances on identical goals (as illustrated earlier in Figure 5–1). This is especially useful in identifying a candidate for promotion or eliminating or strengthening underachievers.

Note that a wide range of job or performance traits are covered, and in the improvised form (Figure 5–2), as shown for a corporate security department, very specific traits are addressed concerning security functions. Also note that in that form, the employee is asked to select several goals for completion by the following year. These goals should be outside the normal realm of his daily work and be designed to develop his career capabilities further. Also on the form is adequate space to record the results of these projected goals and to what extent they were completed for the previous year.

Self-Appraisal

Prior to the formal performance review and discussion between subordinate and superior, the subordinate should be mailed a blank copy of the appraisal form, which has been modified to enable him to do a self-appraisal. This forces the subordinate to review, albeit subjectively, his own performance for the preceding year. Although this may not be

Name____________________________ Position____________________

Location____________ Date of Hire________ Yrs.or Mths.in present position______

Explanation for Codes:

L.S. - Less than satisfactory	·*Fails to meet position goals or meets them in part; just getting by; improvements expected.*
S. - Satisfactory	·*Meets practically all position goals and in some instances exceeds them.*
B.S. - Better than satisfactory	·*Meets all position goals and in most instances exceeds them.*
O. - Outstanding	·*Exceeds all position goals and operates at sustained top performance*
N.A. - Not applicable	

EXECUTIVE ABILITIES

(Check unknown box whenever you have insufficient knowledge)

1. JOB KNOWLEDGE *(Consider the requirements of his job and compare them to his knowledge. Does he have specialized knowledge?)*

UNKNOWN ☐	SERIOUS GAPS IN KNOWLEDGE OF FUNDAMENTALS OF JOB ☐	HAS SATISFACTORY KNOWLEDGE OF ROUTINE PHASES OF JOB ☐	IS WELL INFORMED ON ALL PHASES OF HIS JOB ☐	HAS EXCELLENT KNOWLEDGE OF ALL PHASES OF HIS JOB ☐	HAS EXCEPTIONAL UNDERSTANDING OF JOB EXTREMELY WELL INFORMED ☐

2. INITIATIVE *(Consider his ability and willingness to do something when he sees that it needs to be done.)*

UNKNOWN ☐	A "SELF-STARTER" ORIGINATES PLANS — FOLLOWS THRU ACTS INDEPENDENTLY WITHIN SCOPE OF RESPONSIBILITY ☐	GOES BEYOND LIMITS OF ASSIGNMENT WHEN HE SEES THAT FURTHER WORK WILL PRODUCE A BETTER RESULT ☐	FAIRLY INTERESTED IN STARTING NEW PROCEDURES. NEEDS PRODDING TO SUGGEST OR DEVELOP NEW IDEAS ☐	SATISFIED TO PERMIT ALL FACTORS CONNECTED WITH JOB REMAIN "STATUS-QUO". VERY LITTLE ATTEMPT TO CHANGE THINGS ☐	DISPLAYS LITTLE OR NO INTEREST OR DESIRE TO DO MORE THAN CURRENT ASSIGNMENT ☐

3. JUDGMENT *(Consider his ability to grasp a situation, think clearly, and develop correct and logical conclusions.)*

UNKNOWN ☐	HIS DECISIONS OR RECOMMENDATIONS ARE WRONG MORE THAN RIGHT ☐	IS PRONE TO NEGLECT OR MISINTERPRET FACTS. OCCASIONAL ERRORS IN JUDGMENT ☐	JUDGMENT IS USUALLY SOUND AND REASONABLE ☐	HIS JUDGMENT RESULTS FROM SOUND EVALUATION OF ALL THE FACTORS INVOLVED ☐	OUTSTANDINGLY SOUND AND LOGICAL THINKER WITH AN EXCEPTIONAL GRASP OF SITUATION INVOLVED ☐

4. LEADERSHIP *(Consider his ability in organizing and obtaining the cooperation of others and in directing their efforts effectively.)*

UNKNOWN ☐	FAILS TO DIRECT EFFECTIVELY AND GAIN COOPERATION AND TEAMWORK ☐	MANAGES IN SOME INSTANCES TO OBTAIN EFFECTIVE TEAMWORK. MEDIOCRE IN DIRECTING OTHERS ☐	CAPABLE LEADER DEVELOPS ADEQUATE COOPERATION AND TEAMWORK UNDER NORMAL CIRCUMSTANCES ☐	A CONSISTENTLY GOOD LEADER IS EFFECTIVE UNDER DIFFICULT CIRCUMSTANCES ☐	OUTSTANDING SKILL IN DIRECTING OTHERS INSPIRES CONFIDENCE EVEN UNDER VERY DIFFICULT CIRCUMSTANCES ☐

5. COOPERATION *(Consider ability and willingness to work in harmony for and with others.)*

UNKNOWN ☐	EXTREMELY SUCCESSFUL IN WORKING WITH OTHERS ACTIVELY PROMOTES HARMONY ☐	WORKS IN HARMONY WITH OTHERS A VERY GOOD TEAM WORKER ☐	GETS ALONG WELL WITH MOST PEOPLE ☐	SOMETIMES INDIFFERENT TO OTHERS COOPERATES TO A FAIR DEGREE ☐	INCLINED TO CREATE FRICTION DOES NOT GET ALONG WELL ☐

JOB PERFORMANCE	RATING
1. Quality and timeliness of Security Inspections	
2. Quality and timeliness of Incident Reports	
3. Quality and timeliness of Investigation Reports	
4. Quality and timeliness of Activity Reports	
5. Quality and timeliness of Safety Reports	
6. Is handling of Expenses prudent and Reports timely?	
7. Highest possible quality of Polygraph Testing	
8. Highest possible Interrogation performance	
9. Thoroughness of Investigations (all types)	
a) Case Disposition Judgment	
10. Ability to organize self, office and work load (also planning)	
11. Care of assigned Company property	
12. Ability to adhere to rules, regulations and instructions.	
13. Originality of new ideas and procedures	

Figure 5–2 Corporate Security Department—Management Appraisal.

in conformity with his superior's ultimate rating, it does force him to think about his performance, and it also may very well cause the rater, or superior, to take into consideration factors that might not have come up otherwise. Experience has shown that after such a program has been in place for several years, the self-appraisals tend to be more realistic and more closely in line with the ratings that are ultimately made by the superior. Nevertheless, this whole process serves a worthwhile purpose. It further precludes the possibility that the superior or the sub-

JOB PERFORMANCE (cont'd)	RATING
14. Management Education and Relations	
15. Relations with others (subordinates, superiors, equals, public, police,etc)	
16. Loyalty to Corporate office	
17. Thoroughness of anti-shoplifting program	
18. Thoroughness of employee education in security	
19. Ability to select and develop personnel	
20.	
21.	
22.	

GOALS

A. Goals(s) last year for completion by this year:

___

___

___

Results:

___

___

___

B. Goal(s) set this year for completion by next year:

___

___

___

How will these goals be attained?:

___

___

___

OVERALL APPRAISAL

RATING SCALE				
	OUTSTANDING	BETTER THAN SATISFACTORY	SATISFACTORY	LESS THAN SATISFACTORY

Prepared by________________ Date__________ Reviewed by______________ Date______

Figure 5–2 continued

ordinate will make an omission like the one described earlier in this section.

CAREER PATHING

Career pathing has become an important responsibility of managers. Matching individual and organizational needs has always presented a

Cluett, Peabody & Co., Inc.

MANAGEMENT PERSONNEL EVALUATION FORM

Name ________ (Last) ________ (First) ________ (Initial) Location ________

Date of Hire ________ Birth Date ________

Present Position ________ Position Date ________

Position Grade ________ Present Salary ________ Range Quartile 1st ☐ 2nd ☐ 3rd ☐ 4th ☐

Amount of next to last increase ________ Date of next to last increase ________

Amount of last increase ________ Date of last increase ________

Amount of next scheduled increase ________ Date of next scheduled increase ________

FORMAL EDUCATION: Name of College ________

Years Attended ________ Degrees ________

High School (Circle One) 1 2 3 4

Factor Evaluated	Outstanding	Above Average	Average	Below Average	Not Acceptable
Job Knowledge					
Planning and Organizing					
Decision Making					
Judgment					
Motivation					
Ability to Communicate					
Ability to Innovate					
Flexibility					
Ability to Train					
Ability to Delegate					
Follow-Through					
Ability to Motivate					
Ability to Discipline					
Willingness to Discipline					

Employee's Strengths:

Employee's Weaknesses:

Major Accomplishments-Last 12 Months:

This employee is:

- ☐ Immediately Promotable
- ☐ Promotable in one year
- ☐ Eventually Promotable
- ☐ Probably not Promotable
- ☐ Should be Replaced

Overall Performance:

- ☐ Outstanding
- ☐ Above Average
- ☐ Average
- ☐ Below Average
- ☐ Not Acceptable

Recommendations for Employee Development:

Prepared by ________ Date: / / Reviewed by: ________ Date: / /

Figure 5–3 Management Personnel Evaluation Form.

DEFINITIONS

Ratings:

OUTSTANDING:	Obviously very superior - top 10%
ABOVE AVERAGE:	A clearly superior employee but not in the top group.
AVERAGE:	Completely adequate but does not stand out.
BELOW AVERAGE:	Barely Adequate
NOT ACCEPTABLE:	Candidates for replacement - bottom 10%

In applying ratings it must be remembered that employees should be compared with other employees in similar positions and with similar experience, not with the general population. If one hundred employees are rated, the distribution should be approximately as follows:

Outstanding	10 employees
Above Average	15 employees
Average	50 employees
Below Average	15 employees
Not Acceptable	10 employees

Rated Factors:

Job Knowledge: This includes technical knowledge, a knowledge of operations supervised, a knowledge of quality standards, and ability to meet performance standards.

Planning and Organizing: This includes the use made of a person's own time and that of his subordinates. Consider such factors as anticipating problems, visualizing results of decisions, and meeting deadlines.

Decision Making: This refers to the manager's willingness to make timely decisions and accept responsibility for their consequences.

Judgment: This refers to the track record of successful decisions.

Motivation: This includes personal ambition and dedication to the Company as evidenced by hard work, an inquiring mind, self-discipline and continuing self-improvement.

Ability to Communicate: Consider the ability to clearly and persuasively express concepts orally and in writing. Also consider the ability to grasp instructions and listen with an open mind.

Ability to Innovate: This refers to the ability to generate constructive new ideas in such areas as product development, development of new programs and policies, and the initiation of projects which impact directly and measurably on the business.

Flexibility: Consider the manager's ability to assess a changed or new business situation, reorient his thinking, and respond promptly and correctly.

Ability to Train: Consider the manager's ability and willingness to improve the performance of subordinates or peers by passing on knowledge, experience, and information.

Ability to Delegate: Consider the ability and willingness to select work for delegation, properly instruct subordinates, and accept responsibility for delegated work.

Follow-Through: Consider the ability and willingness to insure that delegated work is accomplished satisfactorily and on time.

Ability to Motivate: Consider the manager's ability to generate a sense of common purpose and zest for work in subordinates while maintaining discipline and imposing necessary standards of performance.

Ability to Discipline: This refers to the ability to criticize or discipline an employee constructively and dispassionately with resultant improvement in performance.

Willingness to Discipline: Consider professional toughness. Is the manager willing to face potentially unpleasant confrontations with subordinates.

Figure 5–3 continued

challenge to security managers. Most managers claim that they attempt to select applicants who are highly motivated, competitive, and aggressive. These same applicants have aspirations for personal and professional growth and usually will not remain long with any organization that fails to offer both short- and long-term career guidance. The applicant who has displayed traits consistent with upward mobility will respond well to an organization that believes in and practices career pathing. Managers who give this concept only lip service usually will have a high turnover rate. Managers who attract aggressive applicants by offering career pathing but fail to follow through will undoubtedly lose a lot of good talent.

Realistically, not everyone can become the chief security executive. The nature of organizations is similar to a pyramid, with the widest opening at the base and fewer positions available as one moves upward. Thus we encounter a dilemma. Our experience leads us to recommend that recruiting strategy be based on attracting both high-performance and high-potential persons. Those who are identified as possessing both traits should be moved along the career path as quickly as possible. Those who have a low potential but are high performers should make up the bulk of staff. This cadre of employees often has been referred to as the workhorses of an organization. High potential, low-performance employees should be avoided. Most security managers lack the highly sophisticated skills needed to develop this type of person, and seldom is such a choice successful. Maturity level usually is the barometer used to identify this type of person.

Having recruited the staff—a few of whom have high-potential and high-performance traits, along with the bulk who have low-potential and high-performance traits—you are now faced with the responsibility of developing career paths for these people. Quite often, meeting individual career needs is a matter of timing, and here the organizational needs will prevail. To give credence to your philosophy of career pathing, meetings should be held at least annually with each employee and perhaps quarterly with the high-potential high performers.

One technique that has proven very beneficial to the authors involves telling the staff that you intend to assist in their professional development in an aggressive manner with formal reviews at least annually. If at any time they feel that their career development needs are blocked, they should ask for a special conference to voice that opinion. If there is merit to their position, then you will begin working on new career paths for them—one being inside the organization but outside the security department, and the other being totally outside the organization. Perhaps one of the greatest contributions a chief security manager can make to the organization is to develop a reputation of being a training ground and feeder of outstanding managers to other departments. This also allows the chief security manager to make significant contributions to the security industry.

For another perspective on this general area, refer to the book *Effective Security Management*.[11] In particular, refer to Sennewald's philosophy on how to retreat if a mistake is discovered in a recent promotion.[12]

---

[11]Charles A. Sennewald, *Effective Security 2e*, p. 131.

[12]Ibid.

Chapter 6

Finance

Adequate financing of a modern-day security department is an absolute necessity. Without financing, nothing can happen. A corporation could very well have a security director, but unless he is given funds with which to work, it is impossible to recruit personnel, buy equipment, conduct investigations, and establish loss prevention programs. Represented in salary levels, financing determines the difference between high-quality personnel and run-of-the-mill security operatives who will never be able to raise the image of the department to the level that it deserves. Adequate financing also means the ability to take on a special or challenging assignment versus not being able to respond adequately when major security problems arise.

BUDGETING

Security World magazine states the following:

> [S]ecurity starts with a budget. If the dollars are not present for salaries, equipment, administrative costs and other expenses, then security will not exist. Similarly, if a budget is poorly planned and thought out, and if a number of important considerations and needs are overlooked in its preparation, then a security department may find itself short of the dollars needed for adequate operation or for emergency situations. Those dollars may be forthcoming, but every minute delay is another minute a security department is not operating at full potential. Like all other departments of a company operating in a competitive business environment, a security department must operate at peak efficiency. The security department is another investment—or cost—in doing business today.
>
> [T]hree basic approaches to developing a budget . . . are: Operating on a zero-based budget, operating as a standard revenue consuming department, or operating as a profit center.
>
> The vast majority of security departments in the country, however, operate as a simple and straight-forward revenue-using internal service department. In this framework, the need for, and the existence of, the department is accepted as a given within the company, and budgeting is

> done with this in mind. While costs must be explained or justified, the budget analysis is not as extreme as the "do or die" mentality that characterizes a zero-based budget.[1]

To give you an idea of how to plan a budget, a sample budget worksheet is shown in Figure 6–1.

Budget Contingencies

In the preparation of department expense budgets, security directors often find themselves in a quandary. First, there is the reality of the business world in which we find ourselves in competition for limited resources with other corporate staff functions who believe that they make as valuable a contribution to the corporation as we do. Second, the security director must accept that only a certain amount of resources is available and he never will get everything he wants. Finally, there is a tendency for security directors not to allow budget cushions that other corporate functions build into their projections. This probably is due to most security directors' highly developed sense of right and wrong, which makes it difficult for them to bend the rules or even slightly cushion the financial projections for their department. Unfortunately, other departments vying for the same resources do not play by the same rules. Occasionally, the economy tightens up or the corporate profits decline and all staff functions are advised to cut budgets for the balance of the year. This is where the security function often gets penalized for not having the same cushion that other departments have.

Having experienced these problems, the authors believe there is a solution that solves the problems without having to compromise your personal integrity through creative accounting. The starting point for preparing your future expense budgets is to write out your key objectives for each responsibility within your function, then seek your boss's approval that this document will be your charter for the next year. You can then put together a realistic budget to accomplish your objectives. Next you should identify discretionary items such as seminars, memberships, and donations that could be reduced without substantially affecting your goals and objectives. Such planning often can exempt you from drastic cuts in the middle of a fiscal year because when you present them to senior management, they decide that the security objectives should not be modified, and reductions are made on a well-thought-out priority basis as opposed to blanket reductions for all functions.

---

[1]Wayne Siatt and Brian Dusza, "Blending Basic Elements for Budget Solutions," *Security World*, December 1981, pp. 21–22.

Employees	Total	Jan.	Feb.	Mar.	Apr.	May	June
Salaries 1/1 15.1 (6/1 17.1)	180.3	30.1	30.1	30.0	30.0	30.0	30.1
Social security taxes	17.7	3.0	3.0	3.0	2.9	2.9	2.9
Group insurance	9.0	1.5	1.5	1.5	1.5	1.5	1.5
Retirement annuities	14.0	2.2	2.1	3.3	2.1	2.2	2.1
Savings plan	2.4	.4	.3	.6	.4	.3	.4
Travel and entertainment	77.0	12.9	12.8	12.8	12.8	12.8	12.9
Moving expense	8.2		7.0			1.2	
Seminars	1.1	.5	.2	.1	.1	.1	.1
Office supplies	3.0	.5	.5	.5	.5	.5	.5
Postage							
Telephone	12.0	2.0	2.0	2.0	2.0	2.0	2.0
Subscriptions and dues	4.9	.9	.8	.8	.8	.8	.8
Rent	5.9	1.0	1.0	1.0	1.0	1.0	.9
Building occupancy	8.3	1.3	1.3	1.6	1.3	1.3	1.5
Power							
Alterations	.7	.1	.1	.1	.2	.1	.1
Depreciation	6.0	1.0	1.0	1.0	1.0	1.0	1.0
Insurance	.8	.1	.1	.2	.1	.1	.2
Taxes	.3			.1			.2
Apportioned charges							
Company physicals	1.4	.3	.3	.3	.3	.1	.1
Professional services	20.0	3.5	3.3	3.3	3.3	3.3	3.3
Books and newspapers	.6	.1	.1	.1	.1	.1	.1
Outside investigators	3.5	1.0	.5	.5	.5	.5	.5
Equip. under $500	1.1	.2	.2	.2	.2	.2	.1
General	4.5	.9	.8	.7	.7	.7	.7
Total	382.7	63.5	69.0	63.7	61.8	62.7	62.0
Allocated	116.8	19.5	19.5	19.4	19.5	19.5	19.4
Net	265.9	44.0	49.5	44.3	42.3	43.2	42.6

Figure 6–1 Corporate Security Expense Plan—Six Month Budget Worksheet *(in thousands)*.

Some companies vary the budgeting process by having budgeting flow from the objectives, while other corporations have the objectives flow from a predetermined budget. For example, a corporation might say, "Here is x amount of dollars for the next twelve months. Tell us what you will be able to accomplish." Other organizations will insist on a "buy-off" (approval) of the objectives, then ask the security director to prepare a budget to obtain these goals. Others use some hybrid form—given less than x amount of dollars to accomplish all goals, the following must be deferred to the following year. It is important for the security director to understand fully the budgeting philosophy within his organization.

Unlike sales and marketing departments, which can pretty well program their activities in advance, it is impossible for a corporate security department always to anticipate the unexpected major case that may arise in any given fiscal period. A prudent security director always will establish a contingency fund to handle such a major investigation. The amount budgeted for such contingencies will depend largely on whether most investigative work is performed by the department itself or is farmed out to professional investigative agencies. At any rate, regardless of the method used, adequate planning must be undertaken in the event the situation should arise.

Monitoring the Budget

Most government agencies and some corporations monitor budget results by line item, while most corporations report all line items to department managers but only hold them accountable for bottom line variances. The latter process is advantageous and gives more latitude to the security director.

In most large corporations, the corporate accounting department will furnish a monthly review of expenditures, which will enable the security director to monitor constantly the performance of his department insofar as expenditure of funds is concerned.

Normally, these reporting or auditing functions will show actual line items such as salaries, social security tax, retirement annuities, travel and entertainment expenses, seminars, postage and telephone.

They will show the actual expenditure on each of these line items for the month in question versus the budgeted amount so that the security director can immediately determine whether he is over budget or under budget on any particular item. Also, there usually will be a cumulative total for the year-to-date, which can be compared to the cumulative total for the preceding year for each line item. (See Figure 6–2.)

	December		Year to Date—1982			Last Year
	Plan	Actual	Plan*	Actual	Variance	
Salaries	26.3	29.4	312.6	313.0	(.4)	300.5
Social security taxes	1.7	1.8	25.5	24.7	.8	24.1
Group insurance	1.1	1.6	14.2	16.3	(2.1)	17.5
Retirement annuities	1.9	2.0	24.2	24.2		25.5
Savings plan	.3	.3	3.9	3.9		3.7
Medical examinations	.3	.3	1.8	1.2	.6	1.2
Travel and entertainment	13.0	12.5	138.1	126.4	11.7	134.7
Moving expense			9.5	3.7	5.8	3.4
Seminars	.1		5.0	5.9	(.9)	
Office supplies	.5	.7	6.0	5.4	.6	4.5
Postage			.1	.1		.4
Telephone	1.9	2.2	21.8	23.0	(1.2)	19.2
Subscriptions and dues	.5		10.8	7.5	3.3	7.3
Seminars						2.2
Rent	1.0	1.7	12.6	13.3	(.7)	12.2
Building occupancy	1.0	1.1	10.6	10.9	(.3)	1.8
Power	.1		.8	.4	.4	.7
Alterations	.1	.1	1.4	1.4		1.7
Depreciation	1.1		9.9	9.9		10.2
Insurance	.3	.2	2.7	2.7		3.0
Taxes—commercial rent	.2	.1	.6	.7	(.1)	.6
Apportioned charges			.9	.5	.4	.8
Equipment under $500		.3	.7	1.5	(.8)	1.4
Books and newspapers	.1	.2	1.2	.5	.7	1.5
Outside Investigative Service	1.0		16.5	13.1	3.4	20.3
Legal and professional	10.0		65.8	.8	65.0	
General	4.3	(.4)	30.9	10.9	20.0	12.1
Consultant fees—external		.2		9.6	(9.6)	
Total	66.8	54.3	728.1	631.5	96.6	610.5
Allocated	24.3	1.4	203.0	148.0	(55.0)	99.2
Net	42.5	52.9	525.1	483.5	41.6	511.3

*Six months actual plus 6 months plan.

Figure 6–2 Corporate Security Year-to-Date Expense Plan *(in thousands)*.

This type of monitoring is of great help to the security director in determining where he stands at any given point in relation to the past, present planning, and actual performance. In this way, the director also can put into effect plans to reduce expenditures if he becomes aware that for several months in a row he is running over budget in relation to the grand total. It is quite common to see many corporate security departments slow down their activities toward the end of a fiscal period when the director is attempting to bring his department in close to predicted budget performance.

SECURITY AS A PROFIT CENTER

In an article in *Security World* magazine, the national security manager for Ace Hardware Corporation, George Harris, states:

> You have to consider both the direct and indirect costs of a security program in this sense. For example, consider a company with 100 million sales volume and a shrinkage factor of three percent, that means losses of three million annually. Assume the company spends one million dollars on security in a year and reduces shrinkage by two million dollars, that department has paid for itself and added one million to the company's revenues that was being lost before.[2]

In the article, Harris goes on to note that it may be difficult to get top management to accept that a department that has traditionally functioned as a revenue drain can be a profit center. "Doing that," he says, "becomes something of a sales function for the security director."[3] Harris continues:

> The biggest contribution a security department can make is in terms of reducing insurance premiums, particularly as they relate to Worker Compensation policies. Depending on the situation and the policy, one proven case of fraud can save enough money to keep an investigator active in the field for more than a year. These are things corporate management must be made aware of.[4]

It is the authors' opinion that in most corporations, especially those dealing with consumer products, the budgeting of a corporate security

---

[2]Ibid.

[3]Ibid.

[4]Ibid.

Table 6–1 Income Statement Hypothetical Apparel Company 1980

		$(000)
Net Sales		$20,000
Cost of Sales		16,138
Gross Profit		$ 3,862
Administrative Expense	$1,139	
Shipping Expense	597	
Selling Expense	901	
Operating Expense		2,637
Operating Profit		$ 1,225
Other Income & Expense		351
Income Before Taxes		$ 874

Helen Letcher, *Security Techniques to Prevent Theft, Six Action Plans to Double Apparel Profits,* American Apparel Manufacturers Association, 1981. Reprinted with permission.

function can be done as a profit center. This simply means being able to show the company the money returned to the bottom line of the financial statement each year that would otherwise be lost in theft and other criminal acts.

An excellent illustration of how theft subtracts from the bottom line of a profit and loss statement is made by author Helen Letcher of Canoe Manufacturing Company:

> Many top executives do not believe they have any problems until an inventory is taken and inventory shortages are discovered. Still other executives do not get upset about these losses because they are passed along to the consumer. A three percent inventory shrinkage is passed along to the consumer by adding an additional three cents to each dollar of the cost of the garment. This, too, can only go on so far because the price of the garment eventually becomes noncompetitive.
>
> Employee theft can no more be eradicated than burglary or murder, but it certainly can be curbed.
>
> Hypothetical Apparel Company (HAC) takes inventory once a year. Over the past 10 years, inventory shortages have been within parameters set up by management. At the end of 1980, a certified inventory was taken and an inventory shortage of $150,000 was discovered. Hypothetical Apparel Company showed a net profit of $874,000 [Table 6–1] which could have been considerably increased without this $150,000 inventory loss.[5]

[5]Helen Letcher, "Security Techniques to Prevent Theft, Six Action Plans to Double Apparel Profits," Arlington, VA: American Apparel Manufacturers Association, 1981. Reprinted with permission.

Inventory Variances

One of the very important barometers that a security director can use in attempting to portray his security operation as a profit center is the tracking of inventory variances. Before proceeding with this area, however, a word of caution is in order:

> Many business executives hold to a time-honored belief that inventory shortages are valid barometers of just how a company is doing in relation to internal theft. Many seasoned security experts, however, are quick to point out that while inventory shortages (occasionally referred to as variances) may be a primary and basic indicator of internal security problems, such shortages (along with overages) are subject to a wide range of variables. Any of these can influence the picture to such an extent that normal conclusions may often be completely invalid.[6]

Basically, variances in inventory usually can be attributed to one of three facors, or a combination of all three. These are: theft of assets by either insiders or outsiders; human error, such as a cashier inadvertently under-ringing sales; and poor records. The security director always should examine these possibilities before drawing the conclusion that internal theft or fraud is the sole factor of the inventory variance.

The cost-effectiveness of a corporate security program is not too difficult to measure. In the retail field, where security performances are judged on the basis of shrinkage percentage figures, it is easy to plot a downward trend of such figures, showing what is accomplished. To establish the true savings in such a situation, the actual loss of the first year can be projected for all succeeding years, even if the actual shrinkage goes down. In other words, the director would be showing the loss that would result without the existence of the security department. This is an easy way to establish the contribution security makes to the profit line.

Gross Profit Margins

In a number of companies today, book inventories are not maintained in the traditional way. Instead, these companies operate on an estimated gross profit basis. In the distribution field, because of the large amount of goods that are warehoused and distributed, upward and downward price changes are not necessarily recorded in the books throughout the year. Therefore, the company must operate on what is termed an esti-

---

[6]J. Kirk Barefoot, *Employee Theft*, p. 15.

mated gross profit. Estimated gross profits are arrived at by evaluating the actual gross profit percentages realized in prior years and are based on what an intelligent appraisal of the company's business indicates will be the amount of gross profit. Any inventory variances based on this system obviously are not as accurate as on a traditional accounting system, and therefore the security director also must look at gross profit trends, which are the actual gross profits recorded over a period of years.

In the manufacturing field, a similar estimate sometimes is referred to as a standard by which the company arrives at its gross margin of profit. In these situations, the basic accounting formulas that might normally be found in other companies have an added term known as cost of sales. Cost of sales in a manufacturing operation can be defined as all manufacturing costs incurred in finishing or producing a product. This includes raw materials, direct labor, and overhead costs. In wholesaling or distribution, costs of sales usually includes purchase price of the merchandise and any related transportation costs.

Where no proper records are being kept, price fluctuations or shortages in goods from the manufacturing unit to the warehouse are simply absorbed in the cost of sales accounting category. When this system is utilized, the only standard by which a company can judge its performance is an estimated gross margin or gross profit based on past performance.

Annual Crime and Security Activity Reports

Another important factor for the security director to utilize in profiling his department as a profit center is the compilation of annual crime and security activity reports. The basis of this type of reporting must be some kind of an incident-reporting mechanism that originates in the field. Most security activity and the generation of crime statistics begin with the reporting of crimes or other unusual happenings on an incident report form. This is much preferable to memoranda, as the incident report form, if well designed, will preclude the omission of certain information that is necessary to the security director. Examples of incident report forms are shown in Figure 6–3, which can be used for manufacturing and distribution, and Figure 6–4, which is designed for use in a retail operation.

In compiling an annual crime report, the director normally would list major divisions of the company and show the total amount of crime incidents or security activity for those divisions or operating companies. Typical categories to be considered for each company might very well include the following specific items:

INCIDENT REPORT FORM

(For use in all company locations except retail stores)

WHAT:
Theft
- [ ] Employee
- [ ] Suspected Employee
- [ ] From Employee
- [ ] Checks
- [ ] Embezzlement
- [ ] Burglary/Robbery
- [ ] Attempted

Other
- [ ] ____________

Shortages
- [ ] Transfer
- [ ] Receiving
- [ ] Delivery
- [ ] Money
- [ ] Myst. Disap.

Safety
- [ ] Accident
- [ ] Fire
- [ ] Glass

WHEN:
Date of report ____________
Date of incident ____________

WHERE:
Company ____________
Location ____________
City ____________
Phone ____________
Dept.: ____________

WHO (PERPETRATOR OR SUSPECT)
Name
Address Apt
City State

Color	Height	Weight	Build	Hair	Eyes	Comp

Dob Pob Age Sex
Emp
Address
City State
Position Length
SSN
Previous record

HOW (from the facts available describe fully HOW the incident happened or the method used. Time, place in bldg., etc.)

Description of Property	Value
Total	

REMARKS: (include any theory or supposition not revealed by facts. Also, names of witnesses or any other information which may prove helpful.)

Distribution
- [ ] Local Mgr.
- [ ] Plant Sec. Official
- [ ] Regional Sec. Officer
- [ ] Corporate Sec. office
- [ ] Other ____________
- [ ] Other ____________

Disposition
Suspended ____________
Ret. to duty ____________
Discharged ____________
Prosecuted ____________
Other ____________

Evidence at:
- [ ] Security Office
- [ ] P. Dept.

Evidence # ____________
- [ ] Returned to stock
- [ ] Other

Report prepared by ____________
Title ____________

CLIP 3 REV. 5-79

Figure 6–3 Incident Report Form for a Manufacturing Company.

INCIDENT REPORT FORM

FOR USE IN ALL CLUETT RETAIL STORES DIVISION, COSCO, AND EMPLOYEE STORES

WHAT:

THEFT
- ☐ Shoplifting
- ☐ Other Customer Fraud
- ☐ Employee
- ☐ Suspected Employee
- ☐ Credit
- ☐ Checks
- ☐ Burglary/Robbery
- ☐ From Employee

OTHER
- ☐ Mysterious Disappearance
- ☐ False Alarm
- ☐ ____________

SHORTAGES
- ☐ Transfer (Unresolved)
- ☐ Distribution (Unresolved)
- ☐ Money

SAFETY
- ☐ Accident-Injury
- ☐ Fire-Smoke
- ☐ Glass Breakage
- ☐ Water Damage

WHEN

Date of Report / /

Date of Incident / /

Time of Incident ☐ AM ☐ PM

WHERE COMPANY

STORE STREET ADDRESS

CITY | STATE

PHONE (AC)

WHO ☐ Employee ☐ Customer ☐ Vendor

Name

Address | Apt.

City | State

Color	Height	Weight	Build	Hair	Eyes	Comp

Dob | Pob | Age

Emp

Address

City | State

Position | Length

SSN

Previous record

HOW (For Shoplifting)

First observed
- time
- place
- by

Approached
- time
- place
- by

Searched
- by
- cash on person

Time left store | Purchases made

Dept	Quan	Description of Merchandise	Unit Price	Value
			Total ▶	

DESCRIPTION OF INCIDENT

FOR ACCIDENTS THE FOLLOWING QUESTIONS MUST BE ANSWERED
1. Kind and extent of INJURY or DAMAGE to equipment, property or mdse.
2. CAUSES such as UNSAFE ACT or CONDITION.
3. WITNESSES and their address/phone 4. REMEDY to prevent recurrence.

DISPOSITION ☐ Suspended ☐ Ret to Duty ☐ Discharged ☐ Released ☐ Prosecuted ☐ Hospitalized

WHERE | BY WHOM

MERCHANDISE AT: ☐ Security Office ☐ P. Dept. Evidence # ____________ ☐ Returned to stock ☐ Marked out of stock

REPORT PREPARED BY | TITLE | NUMBER OF ATTACHMENTS ☐

DIST	RETAIL STORES DIV. (VIA OPERATIONS)		COSCO (VIA AREA SUPERVISOR)		EMPLOYEE STORES (VIA COORDINATOR)	
	W- CO. PRES.	Y - DIR.RET.SEC.	W - OUTLET STORES DIR.	Y - DIR. RET. SEC.	W- PLANT MGR.	Y - DIR. RET. SEC.
	P - CO. SEC. MGR.	G - STORE FILE	P - AREA SUPERVISOR	G - STORE FILE	P - EMP. STORE COORD.	G - STORE FILE

Figure 6–4 Incident Report Form for a Retail Operation.

Safety Inspections
Security Inspections
Man-days Investigation
Bomb Threats
Vandalism
Burglary, Robbery, and Attempts
Internal Thefts and Attempts
External Thefts and Attempts
Embezzlement
Check and Fraud Cases
Thefts from Employees
Miscellaneous
Suspected or Known Crime Losses
Admissions
Merchandise Recoveries
Cash Recoveries
Insurance Settlements
Number of Employees Discharged
Total of All Types of Prosecutions

In retailing, there appears to be a need for specialty information that is peculiar to the retail industry. Therefore, an annual crime report for various retail operations might very well have the following categories and subcategories:

Miscellaneous Items
- Safety Inspections
- Security Inspections
- Man-days Investigation
- Bomb Threats
- Vandalism
- Miscellaneous Incidents
- Miscellaneous Known Losses

External Thefts and Attempts
- Burglary, Robbery, and Attempts
- Losses—Burglary/Robbery
- Recoveries—Burglary/Robbery
- Frauds—Including Checks and Credits
- Losses—Frauds, Checks, and Credits

Recoveries—Frauds, Checks, and Credits
External Prosecutions
Number of Shoplifting Incidents
Suspected or Known Shoplifting Losses
Admissions—Dollar Amount
Shoplifting Recoveries
Shoplifting Apprehensions
Shoplifting Prosecutions

Internal Thefts and Attempts
Number of Incidents—Excluding Embezzlements
Embezzlements
Suspected or Known Losses
Admissions—Dollar Amount
Merchandise Recoveries
Cash Recoveries
Insurance Settlements
Number of Employees Discharged
Number Referred for Prosecution

All this information should be kept for each year, and one of the pages of an annual crime report should show a reflection of the past five or six years of security activity. In other words, the earlier listed categories would be shown on a separate sheet for the year in question, along with the same number for the preceding five years. Each year the crime report is done, an earlier year is discarded in this summary.

The security director also should present a compilation of security by specific personnel within the department. Not only does this act as a check on activity by location or division, but it also gives the individual security agent information to retain regarding his own activities on an annual basis. Suggested categories to be recorded are as follows:

Location Visits and Inspections
Number of Location Visits
Number of Security Inspections
Number of Safety Inspections

Man-days
Investigation
Training
Supervision
Court Preparation and Court Days
Personal and Property Protection
Shrinkage Control
Floor Coverage

Number of Persons Handled
  Polygraphed
  Interviewed and Interrogated
Number of Apprehensions
  Employees
  Shoplifters
  Customer Fraud

Evaluating the Program

In addition to giving the security director good statistical information about the performance of his department and any trends that may have developed, the annual crime and security activity report also can be used, along with inventory variance trends, to help maintain the profile of a profit center for the security function.

Experience has shown that a well-run corporate security department eventually will have less and less investigative work to do as pockets of thieves are eliminated. This is generally reflected in the record keeping under admissions gained from employees in any given fiscal year. In other words, assuming that the security department is operating at peak efficiency, the totals on admissions eventually should begin to decrease over a period of time. Of course, there will be some fluctuations in the trend as the unexpected major cases develop, but overall the trend should be downward. This downward trend also would hold true in categories such as suspected or known crime losses, merchandise recoveries, cash recoveries, and insurance settlements. In the latter two instances, however, the trend is more long term, as many cash recoveries and insurance settlements come through in subsequent years covering major investigations that took place one, two, or even three years prior.

In summary, the annual crime and security activity report should tend to corroborate the downward trend in inventory variances (shortages) and the two combined should give the security director ample ammunition to use in his attempt to be looked upon as a profit center. The director should keep in mind that the ultimate goal is not the generating of large statistics on admissions, merchandise, and cash recoveries but the eventual elimination of as much crime as possible in the corporation, which, in turn, actually decreases the statistics. As time goes on and more crime is eliminated, the security director can increasingly turn his attention to more positive aspects of the total job—mainly loss prevention, including security education programs.

FINANCIAL GAMES TO BE PLAYED

In many corporations, the security director must be alert to dishonest or unethical financial practices in which certain executives may engage.

One factor commonly overlooked by corporate executives is the so-called return on investment (ROI). If a particular executive can over-inflate his merchandise inventories to receive kickbacks from vendors, this would of course be reflected in higher purchasing costs and reduced ROI. His inventory turns would be far less than corporate standards, and the return on the investment of that inventory would be severely diminished.

Another, more intricate, practice sometimes encountered in the retail field is the handling of markdowns. In this context, when merchandise is reduced in price, a so-called markdown is taken. That is, the price is marked down, but it is also recorded in the inventory books of the company. If, for some reason, the merchandise is reduced but the markdown is not recorded in the books, this would result in an inventory shortage. Alternatively, usually after a sale, markdowns are marked up by putting through a markdown cancellation. If the markdown cancellation is not properly recorded in the books, and the price of the merchandise has increased, then a department or store manager has created an inventory cushion, which can be used to cover other shortages or inventory variances.

Another technique that can be used in the retail field is to get a large shipment of merchandise from a vendor close to the closing of the fiscal period. Even though the merchandise is received, it is not put onto the books until after the close of the fiscal period. It is physically counted as inventory, however. An unscrupulous manager has once again created a comfortable inventory cushion that can cover shortages and also have a direct effect on his personal bonus. A practice such as this can be detected by internal auditors or ultimately discovered by security personnel in conversations with other employees.

Chapter 7

Loss Prevention

Perhaps the most important role the security function can play is that of preventing losses. While that may not appear very profound today, it took decades for security managers to accept and vigorously embrace the loss prevention concept as their number one priority item. We all tend to grasp those skills that we do best and are most comfortable with. Traditionally, the security function usually was staffed with former law enforcement persons, whose primary role continued to be enforcement of our laws and dealing with violations.

When the change in emphasis occurred is hard to establish, but surely the past twenty-five years have been a period of evolution for the security industry, and few, if any, modern security managers would object to ranking loss prevention as their number one responsibility.

SECURITY INSPECTIONS

The forerunner of what we refer to as security audits, or loss prevention surveys, was security inspections. This concept originated from military and police organizations and was primarily designed to give an official critical appraisal or review of the current status against established standards. The technique of conducting the security inspection usually consisted of using a security checklist. The checklist was designed to be answered "Yes" or "No," with a comments section to expand on the items checked "No" (Appendix 3).

Although many corporate security departments continue to use such a checklist as the cornerstone of their loss prevention programs, there is a multitude of problems with this approach. All questions appear to be given equal weight. There is little motivation for managers to act on the document, and no specific response is indicated. Too often, the managerial response to a security investigation report is "So what?" Those in staff functions who write critical reports on operating management might easily get the reputation of being the ones who go in after the battle to shoot the wounded. It should be no surprise that these same managers seem to get selective deafness to security recommendations with capital expenditures.

While most questions on a security checklist might appear to be valid to the security practitioner, they are often viewed by field managers as being nit-picking or totally lacking in value.

For example, the question "Are all full cases of merchandise unopened?" might appear to be a good inventory or housekeeping-type question, but it has little impact on security. It is necessary for the security person to explain the purpose of such a question as being one of the many barometers used to measure potential internal theft problems. The observance of a full case and several open cases of the same product with merchandise missing could be an important indicator of internal theft. Therefore, security must instruct managers on the logic behind the question. Of course, in this example, security also must be educated in the operational logic and logistics of the particular type of business so as not to interpret incorrectly the meaning of finding several open cartons of the same product. It could be that individual salespersons have entered the full-case area, opened cartons, and removed items to inspect a new product, add to their sample line, or for other legitimate business reasons. In any event, a two-way dialogue is needed prior to establishing specific checklist questions. While an acceptable explanation might eliminate a negative answer to a specific question, the answer also could unveil an equally dangerous practice that needs tightening, such as limited access control or improving accountability. The point is that to be credible in designing specific checklist questions, you must be knowledgeable about the industry, its risks to various losses, and commonsense, cost-effective solutions to lessen or avoid the losses. The responsibility for initiating this education process falls on the security practitioner and should be viewed as an excellent opportunity to win over operating persons to his point of view in a nonthreatening environment.

LOSS PREVENTION SURVEYS

We prefer the term loss prevention survey to other descriptive terms such as security audit because the former, by definition, implies a meaningful purpose for conducting the survey—that is, to prevent losses. For senior business managers whom you hope to impress with your report, the term loss prevention survey is catchy and equates to cost-avoidance, which is interpreted as improving profits without increasing revenues.

The security executive must recognize that he is competing with other staff who are not only writing their own surveys for senior management but also believe that their function is just as important as everyone else's. At the bottom of this information funnel is the senior management or the field line management, who have the authority to act or spend, if necessary, in order to carry out security recommendations. Those staff managers who make poor use of other managers' time soon find their reports given very little attention. Comments such as "No violations to existing company policy were found in this section" or filler-type statements have little purpose and only hurt your credibility. The audience for your report usually performs a fast skim to try to find out why the report was written, what needs correcting, and what recommendations will rectify the problems.

To get some action on a report, it has been helpful to use a cover sheet that has the three words LOSS PREVENTION SURVEY in 3/4-inch bold letters. Moreover, the lettering is much more effective if it is bright red to get immediate attention. No matter how often the incoming mail is shuffled, the bright red lettering is an attention grabber and should get read first. Included on the cover sheet should be the facility location, the date the survey was performed, and the name of the security person who performed the survey.

One of the principal differences between the survey approach and that of the security inspection is that the survey lends itself easily to a narrative form of writing. Instead of comments that usually are terse in nature, the survey usually is structured in sentence and paragraph form and tends to be more positive.

In the survey, the writer attempts to explain his reasons for recommendations and how corrective action will either avert a loss or possibly even add to profits. Figure 7–1 shows examples of the report-writing style used in the survey approach.

Of course, to produce the type of report mentioned above, it is still necessary for the inspector to work from a checklist. Not to do so would ensure that any such survey would contain significant omissions. Such a checklist is shown in Appendix 4. (Courtesy of McKesson Corporation of San Francisco, CA.) A checklist for electronic data processing centers and a safety inspection report are included in Appendixes 5 and 6. (Courtesy of Cluett, Peabody & Co., Inc., New York, NY.)

At least one national security director has observed that it may not always be possible to utilize the survey approach in initial inspections or surveys of facilities. A survey, by its very nature, is highly dependent on the writing skills of the inspector and also the fact that the inspector must be tuned in to the business approach and cost-effectiveness of recommendations and corrective actions. In other words, relatively new security inspectors cannot be expected to put together a survey-type report with the same skill and business style as a more seasoned pro. Therefore, the security inspection checklist may be appropriate in the initial stages of a beginning corporate security depart-

STATEMENT OF PURPOSE

This Loss Prevention Survey was conducted at this time as part of the Corporate Security Department's continuing program of review to determine the means by which company merchandise and property may be protected against loss.

DISCREPANCIES AND DEFICIENCIES

1. The physical truck check in during the afternoon is accomplished by the loader. During the morning, the check out is done by one of three production workers who also load trucks during the same time frame and leave their positions in the production area to accomplish this.

2. There is no protection against the elements for the ingoing or outgoing checkers at the main gate.

3. The main gate is open basically at all times during the working day, limiting control of the trucks returning or leaving the production area.

4. The refurbished water cooler storage building is open at all times, day and night.

5. Gates located on the south side of the production area are not locked.

6. Check out of loaded trucks is accomplished using a salesman's load sheet. The checker refers to the load sheet and compares same to the truck load.

7. The night loader works from 2:00 P.M. to 10:00 P.M. without any supervision after 6:00 P.M. offering an opportunity for diversion of product and/or water coolers and the possibility of being injured without any assistance being available.

Figure 7–1 Loss Prevention Survey Example.

ment, and as maturity and wisdom increase, the security director may then be able to move toward the survey approach.

ACCEPTANCE AND COMPLIANCE

After the loss prevention survey or security inspection is completed, it becomes incumbent upon the security department to gain acceptance and compliance with the report. The security manager always should attempt to discuss the report, if at all possible, with local operating management prior to his departure from the scene. Although some things within his report may give rise to disagreement with local management,

DETAILS

OPERATIONS

It was also noted during the Loss Prevention Survey that the refurbished water cooler storage building is open at all times with no access control whatsoever. It is feasible and very possible that a driver could pull his truck next to the building, enter the refurbished water cooler storage area, load whatever amount of water coolers he felt like, and leave by the gate which is also open located at the south central portion of the area. Locking this building and restricting the keys could prevent this happening as well as locking the gate at the south central portion of the production area, giving the key to a supervisor who could open the gate when necessary.

Check out of loaded trucks is accomplished using the salesman's load sheet. Recommend that the checker take a blind or independent inventory of the truck both when it returns in the afternoon and in the morning when it departs on the route. This independent inventory should not take a great amount of time and could be compared to the loader sheet by management to prevent overloading and/or diversion of product or water coolers. As previously mentioned, the production workers in the morning load and check trucks. Strongly recommend that one person be responsible for checking the loaded trucks upon departure and the trucks which return in the afternoon or evening.

Figure 7–1 continued

the fact that it is discussed personally with them before being passed along to a higher authority means that the security manager will gain a certain respect for the way in which he operates, as the local operating manager will then know exactly where he stands in relation to the recommendations.

During such a discussion, the security manager should base his recommendations on logical arguments. His recommendations should be couched in terms that assume that management has the proper attitude toward security, even though they may not. After gaining local agreement with the operating manager, the security individual should attempt to gain a commitment from local management as to target dates for completion of specific corrective action. All these acceptances and agreements, along with the target dates for completion, should be included in the written report for a higher authority to see. This helps to ensure that local management will comply with the recommendations.

Certain operating managerial types will always be resistant to security recommendations. They are by nature anti-security and, because of this, it will be very difficult to work with them. In this case, appeals for compliance should be routinely directed toward the person's superior—possibly a regional manager or a regional vice president. Depending on the relationship involved, this appeal for help from above can be directed by the regional security manager or perhaps the director of security himself. Here again, the approach must be positive in nature and assume that it is a foregone conclusion that compliance will result. The manner of communication should be such that negative responses to the recommendations would be highly unlikely. A typical statement that could be used in a written communication would be along the lines of this: "If any of the items in this report are in question, please advise and we will discuss. Otherwise, we will assume that corrective action will be taken within the very near future."

At least one corporation has found it desirable to combine security topics with those of a safety nature. Here, local committees are called safety-security committees, and from time to time security subjects will be included in monthly meetings. Results of a recent loss prevention survey also can be included on the agenda, as well as results of a safety inspection. An example of such a safety inspection is shown in appendix 5 (courtesy of Cluett, Peabody & Co.). The important thing, however, is the fact that any such educational meeting should be held on a regular basis, whether it be with employees or supervisors. By doing so, you instill in the group the idea that they are an integral part of the security-safety effort at that operating location. The results of this are increased benefits for the corporation as a whole and enhancement of the loss prevention concept.

EMPLOYEE EDUCATION

Employee education is an absolute must in retailing, where employees routinely deal with the public and with various types of criminal law perpetrators who are not employed by the company. Employee education also is highly desirable in the wholesale and distribution field, and although desirable in the manufacturing sector, it is not always practical because of the size of manufacturing plants and the large number of employees working therein. In this case, the educational effort should be directed toward the supervisors of such manufacturing plants. From time to time, the security department may be instrumental in putting out items for educational purposes, and which may, in fact, be directed toward employee supervisors. As an example, we reproduce a portion of an educational piece taken from the *Supervisor's Bulletin*:

Develop Proper Attitude

The supervisor who wants to increase profits and cut costs through good security . . . must have the proper attitude—he must think of himself as a member of management, and be as concerned with the preservation of assets and profits as top management is.

Why is attitude so important? "Workers sense a supervisor's attitude toward security in the same way they sense his attitude toward absenteeism, lateness or any other area covered by company policy—by what he does about it," [J. Kirk] Barefoot observes. That's why the supervisor has to set the moral tone. He has to be completely scrupulous, which means more than simply *not* stealing; more than just catching thieves. It means demonstrating a genuine, active respect for company property and developing that same respect in his men. His attitude, reflected in his actions, is what's going to most deeply affect the attitudes and actions of his subordinates.

Use Controls

While your day-to-day attitude will be picked up by your subordinates, that's not all there is to good security. You also have to exercise control over manufacturing, storage, packing, deliveries—every aspect of your department's operation.

Good controls, says Barefoot, are preventive. They function to minimize theft; not to catch someone after a theft—when it's too late.

Use an aggressive approach to the proper storage of stock and materials, Barefoot recommends. If something is not where it belongs, don't just shrug your shoulders. Have it put back in the right area and find out *why* it was in the wrong place and who put it there. You might not get all the answers, but your employees will remember that you asked. They'll begin to feel more responsible for the stock and materials because they know that *you* feel responsible for them.

Good housekeeping is another way to control loss prevention, Barefoot declares. "Whenever I've found pilferage of any kind, the housekeeping has been poor," he says. "If employees see that the supervisor doesn't care about filthy, unsanitary or unsafe conditions, they figure there's a pretty good chance he probably doesn't care about anything else."[1]

The *Supervisor's Bulletin* was used during the 1970s for all supervisors within Cluett, Peabody & Co. Inc. A film that lends itself to manufacturing and distributions is *Mission: Loss Prevention.*[2]

The corporate security office should be charged with the responsibility of providing educational materials for employee or supervisor meetings. For retailing, three excellent films have been found to be very

---

[1]*Supervisor's Bulletin* (New York: Bureau of Business Practice, Inc., 1974). Reprinted with permission.

[2]*Mission: Loss Prevention* is available from Saul Astor/Management Safeguards, New York.

appropriate for the retail sector. The first, *Sticky Fingers,*[3] concentrates on the problem of shoplifting and credit card fraud within the retail department. The second, *The Ten Billion Dollar Rip-Off,*[4] deals with employee theft itself. And the third, *Who, Me?*[5] addresses itself to prevention of losses not caused by criminal acts.

RELATIONS WITH REGULATORY AGENCIES

Depending on the nature of the corporation's business, the security director may very well become involved in relations with certain regulatory agencies. As an example, if the security director is employed in the drug industry, he may have certain relationships with the Drug Enforcement Administration (DEA). Additionally, if his job is broad enough and includes the area of plant fire protection and safety, he may have relations with the local fire department, insurance carriers, and the Occupational Safety and Health Administration (OSHA). In some cases, such as the chemical industry, he also may develop relations with the Environmental Protection Agency (EPA).

It is not within the purview of this text to attempt to visualize each and every relationship that may exist between government and a particular corporation and in which the security director would play a role. Nor do the authors intend to delve into the complicated relationship between corporations that do national security work and the Department of Defense (DOD). DOD regulations and procedures are voluminous and have been well covered by other authors in the security field. Rather, it is the authors' intention to comment in general on some of these agencies and to suggest a possible posture for the security director that could help improve such relationships.

In the manufacture and wholesale distribution of controlled substances, companies are inspected regularly, and their handling of controlled substances is proscribed and controlled by the DEA, which is a branch of the U.S. Department of Justice. Any company would be well advised, if it was so engaged in this field, to approach these relationships with an attitude of cooperation and a certain amount of openness. In any type of regulatory agency, certain respondent companies often will develop a reputation for evasion, noncompliance, and an adversary posture. This type of attitude only serves to make inspectors even more

---

[3]*Sticky Fingers* is available from Aptos Film Productions, Los Angeles.

[4]*The Ten Billion Dollar Rip-off* is available from Gallerie International Films Ltd., North Hollywood, CA.

[5]*Who, Me?* is available from Anne Saum & Associates, New York.

stringent in their approach to an inspection and, in the long run, probably results in more punitive action toward the corporation.

In the drug industry, investigation matters often have a dual interest to both the corporate security directors and the DEA, and a spirit of cooperation is essential in these instances. If the government agency is of the opinion that the corporation is not sincere and is always assuming an adversarial role, then there is little or no incentive to cooperate in any joint investigative effort, and any investigation may very well be to the detriment of the company rather than the benefit of both the corporation and the government agency.

If the security director also has the safety and fire responsibilities for the corporation, then a relationship with the local fire department is absolutely essential. Most fire departments will respond to invitations to participate in drills on corporate property and even bring their fire fighters into the plant to familiarize them with the location of fire hoses, shut-off valves, and so on. Further, the training of a fire brigade or emergency organization can be greatly enhanced by the participation of the local fire department. Most rank-and-file employees have little or no training in fire fighting and do not even understand proper techniques to be used with fire extinguishers and hoses. The participation of the local fire department in these exercises is essential to have the best possible loss prevention organization.

Although they are not regulatory agencies in the true sense of the word, various insurance companies may have a financial impact on a corporation. Again, if the security director's responsibilities include safety, then he probably will become involved in inspections of the insurance carriers both toward personal safety and plant safety. Occasionally, some of these organizations' recommendations are not practical from a financial standpoint, and only a cooperative dialogue can moderate the demands of insurance company inspectors. Here, of course, the security director must be keenly aware of a cost-effective recommendation versus one that may be desirable but not cost-effective.

In summary, the best posture for a security director to have with any inspection or regulatory agency is to show openness and a spirit of cooperation and practical compliance. A lot of this can be accomplished through the existence of various manuals and written policies generated by the security director and distributed throughout the corporation. Most inspectors will be greatly impressed by the existence of such manuals and directives, which tend to show that the corporation is striving to comply with laws and regulations and to be a good corporate citizen.

Chapter 8

Investigations Management

Of necessity, the investigations manager or security director must be well grounded in the art of investigation. If he is not knowledgeable in this area, he will remain in the dark as a result of shortcuts and shoddy investigation performances by either his investigators or outside agencies. For this reason, it is imperative that any corporate security department have a top executive who is knowledgeable in this area. Without one, the department never will attain the level of investigative sophistication that is otherwise possible.

The investigations executive must remain detached and totally objective while the investigative staff pursues its target. He must be able to balance the ramifications of the investigation, if any, against the best interests of the corporation. Many times, the fallout from an internal investigation does more damage to internal corporate relations and executive morale than the results, even if the investigation turns out to be successful. In the corporate world, there are many occasions when it is more prudent to defer an investigation than to proceed and create a situation such as the proverbial bull in a china shop. For an in-depth discussion of investigative techniques, especially those useful against blue-collar thieves, refer to the book *Employee Theft Investigation.*[1]

On many occasions, the investigations director will have to make a decision about whether to handle the investigation on an in-house basis or to refer the work to an outside agency. Many factors will help decide this issue, such as the competency of the manager's own in house investigators versus those available to him from outside. It is the authors' belief that the bulk of security agencies generally do not possess the same degree of talent that a corporate staff might have. There are, however, a few very elite outside agencies that might have a higher level of expertise than an inside investigator and that generally prefer to specialize in high-level or executive crime. Agencies of this type generally do not wish to become involved in run-of-the-mill employee theft or other types of lower level fraud.

---

[1]J. Kirk Barefoot, *Employee Theft.*

In the event that an outside agency is selected to perform the investigative function, the investigations manager still should maintain tight control, as his department and his superior's reputation remain on the line regardless of who is doing the work.

CORPORATE HEADQUARTERS LIAISON

In any investigation of note, other corporate executives invariably will be brought into the picture on a need-to-know basis or will otherwise be aware of the situation as it develops. The more persons in the corporate office who know of an investigation in progress, the more need there is for the investigations or security director to maintain a good liaison with the other interested corporate departments. This also includes the top executives of the corporation, whose backing is absolutely necessary if an investigations program is going to be viable.

Corporate executives, as a group, tend to become impatient or anxious to hear reports of the progress of an investigation, and for this reason, someone from the corporate security office is needed to act as a liaison with these people. A buffer is essential at the corporate level to prevent executives from trying to contact investigators in the field to learn of progress on a particular case. The investigations director is the only logical person to decide what information can be released and what the timing of such a release will be.

INVESTIGATIONS DISPOSITION

The security or investigations director also is in the best position to recommend the disposition of investigations and offenders who may be the target of such investigations. If he is experienced in the field of investigations, he will know what elements of proof are needed to win an industrial theft arbitration case. Specific union contract language, general labor law, and National Labor Relations Board (NLRB) rulings notwithstanding, the investigations manager, working with a labor relations specialist or company lawyer, is in the best position to evaluate the quality of the evidence and the testimony in dishonesty cases. He also can effectively recommend the disposition of dishonest executives, should they be the target of an investigation.

In those companies that occasionally, or routinely, file criminal charges, the investigations or security director can be especially helpful in knowing what kinds of charges may be filed. Oftentimes, investigators in the field may not be aware of the variety of charges from which to choose. This also holds true occasionally with district attorneys in some of the more rural areas of the United States. The investigations director, knowing his criminal law, can be immensely influential in steering a proper course in this tricky area.

EXECUTIVE CRIME

There is little question about the fact that widespread executive crime only fosters crime and other forms of misbehavior in the lower levels of a company. For many years, experts have realized that if blue-collar workers perceive their immediate executives to be dishonest, they feel that there are no barriers to engaging in their own form of dishonesty. Unfortunately, these perceptions often are not accurate but only appear to be so on the surface. Nevertheless, if a company is to remain relatively free of internal crime, the moral tone has to begin with the top corporate executives and then filter down into the blue-collar ranks.

Sex and Expense Reports

Many security directors have made it an unwritten rule never to investigate the sexual behavior or the travel and expense reports of top executives in the corporation. One could make a strong argument that both these areas can be controlled by strong superiors. There are several exceptions to this rule, however, and that is when a security executive is ordered to investigate such areas or if it becomes absolutely necessary as a means for opening the door to the investigation of another type of internal crime. Other than these two reservations, both authors urge that these areas be avoided in routine investigative work within the corporation. Note that some companies have compliance agreements with regulatory agencies or internal codes of ethics as part of their corporate charter. In such cases, a compliance investigation might be proper and could delve into these sensitive areas.

Need for Conclusive Evidence

In any investigation of a top-level executive within the corporation, the security department runs the risk of suffering in the end from the standpoint of departmental credibility and reputation. Generally, it is not possible to reveal the extent or conclusiveness of a particular executive's criminality. As a result, when an executive is terminated and his associates become aware of the fact that he has been a target of the corporate security department, invariably the security department suffers in its relationships with these associates.

For this reason, and also because of the fact that top-level management has a tendency to wish to be absolutely sure, the investigations executive will find a need for the most conclusive type of evidence when dealing with an executive. Without the most conclusive kinds of evidence, top management may be reluctant to terminate an executive and, in fact, may keep him on the payroll in a more restricted capacity. If this happens, and the executive is aware that he has been the target of an investigation, he will attempt to poison the reputation of the corporate security department with any associate who is willing to listen. Unfortunately, in these types of situations, the security department seldom is in a position to respond adequately and therefore must absorb the slander thrust upon it.

This problem can be minimized by reporting those outcome possibilities to senior management during the early stages of the investigation. Do not put senior management in the position of having to say, "I wish I had known my options before reaching this point."

Investigation of Foremen

A plant foreman is in a class by himself. He is generally removed from the blue-collar workers if he has any capability in his job as foreman. At the same time, he is not high enough on the corporate ladder to be accepted as a close associate of other corporate executives. For this reason, the investigation of a suspected dishonest foreman usually will be somewhat different from an investigation into the activities of dishonest blue-collar workers. If, by chance, the investigations manager is able to gather evidence against the foreman by concentrating on interviews of subordinates, this raises additional questions from a personal standpoint.

Experience has shown that foremen who are dishonest generally do not become involved with their subordinates or any dishonest superior. They are loners. The fact that subordinates can implicate their foreman in dishonesty implies that the foreman's relationship with the workers is too loose and careless. A foreman who has compromised himself with his subordinates cannot be an effective boss and should not hold the job in the first place. Investigative efforts probably will be more along the lines of surveillance and tailing rather than attempts to expose the foreman through the use of undercover agents or other employees, unless, perhaps, exit-type interviews are given to former employees.

Plant or Facility Managers

The investigation of plant or facility managers is not unlike that of foremen. There again, successful investigative techniques often utilize surveillance and tailing of such people. Moreover, the nature of a manager's theft often creates a paper trail that can be investigated extensively. The one thing that must be anticipated, however, is that the target of such an investigation might be "burned" and become aware of the investigation. The astute investigations manager will have planned for such an eventuality so that complaints to a regional executive will not reflect unfavorably on the corporate security department or top corporate management.

It goes without saying that untraceable license plates and investigator identities are a must. Many times, a local police department can be especially helpful in assisting in the integrity of such an investigation. Another investigative approach not to be overlooked is the possibility of developing a key informant within the office structure when a plant or facility manager is under investigation. Many cases have been made over the years because of information received from disgruntled secretaries, junior executives, and other office workers who are in a position to relate intelligence to the investigative staff.

Regional Personnel

Unlike investigations centering on plants and facilities where informants are a possibility, regional personnel often are much more difficult to target in an investigative effort. Seldom are regional personnel involved in dishonest acts involving local facilities. Rather, they tend to become involved in kickback schemes and other forms of white-collar crime. Oftentimes, investigative efforts into those sensitive areas, which were previously cautioned against, will become a necessity for the investigations manager to get an opening into the case. In addition to surveillance, background investigation and investigation into current modes of living may be indicated.

Not to be overlooked is the possibility of receiving assistance from the corporate auditing department. This resource definitely should be cultivated. Relationships should be developed to avoid turf problems and enhance mutual support and trust. Oftentimes, the auditors will have access to sensitive personal records, which if requested by the security department, would only alert the target of the investigation. An auditor's requesting and reviewing such documents generally is considered routine and arouses no particular suspicions.

THE CRIMINAL JUSTICE SYSTEM AND INVESTIGATIVE AGENCIES

Police Departments

In the 1950s and early 1960s, the inclusion of police departments in a corporate security effort was quite common. After the U.S. Supreme Court decision that placed certain restrictions on police officers' questioning of suspects (known as the Miranda decision) and excluded corporate or private security persons from the same restrictions, the participation of police departments and other law enforcement agencies was severely reduced. The role that a police department usually plays in a typical corporate investigation is that of unofficial advisor or observer of the events that take place. Private and corporate security people are not bound by the same restrictions as are police officers, unless a police officer is included in the investigative process. If this occurs, corporate and private security personnel must abide by the same ground rules as any police officer.

Generally speaking, it has been the experience of both authors that police officials are somewhat more receptive to working unofficially with corporate security personnel than they are with contract or agency persons. At any rate, the corporate security chief or investigations director must be alert to the fact that many police departments still have their local idiosyncrasies and that in any given community, certain persons or places may be completely out of bounds. In spite of this, most corporate security people have been able to forge good working relationships (albeit unofficial) with local police officials. This liaison certainly enhances the gathering of intelligence and the evaluation of information gathered during surveillances, stakeouts, and the like.

Many students of criminal law feel that corporate and private security personnel eventually must be placed under the same type of restrictions as police officers. The rationale here is that most persons in corporate and private security work have law enforcement backgrounds and thus maintain a certain working relationship with other law enforcement agencies. At least they are welcomed by them when first appearing for assistance. Until this happens, however, police departments probably will continue to be excluded, officially, from corporate investigations.

Sheriffs' Departments

Although there are many notable exceptions to the rule, many sheriffs' departments that retain a law enforcement function are extremely political in nature, and even the rank-and-file working deputies are political appointees. In this type of situation, it is generally wise for the corporate security director to seek out other law enforcement contacts. There have been many corporate cases over the years where a local sheriff viewed a gang of industrial thieves and their families as being his very important constituents. Needless to say, the type of help that is sometimes needed from law enforcement agencies is hard to come by in such a situation.

State Police and Other State Agencies

With a few exceptions, state police and other state law enforcement agencies generally are highly professional and free from everyday political influence. Furthermore, the degree of training given to some state police agencies surpasses even that of some of the better local police departments. It is rare indeed to read of a bribery or kickback scandal involving a state police organization.

Bureau of Narcotics and Drug Enforcement Administration

Of all of the federal agencies, the now defunct Bureau of Narcotics probably was the one with the most expertise in undercover matters and also one of the easiest for private or corporate security people to work with on cases of mutual interest. The Bureau of Narcotics eventually became the Bureau of Narcotics and Dangerous Drugs (BNDD), and finally its name was changed to the Drug Enforcement Administration (DEA). Although corporate security people seldom become involved with quantities of drugs that would be of interest to the DEA, this agency is readily approachable and makes a corporate security person feel comfortable working with it. In 1982 the DEA was brought under the jurisdiction of the Federal Bureau of Investigation (FBI).

Federal Bureau of Investigation

Dealings with the FBI have been an enigma over the years for many security directors. A common feeling among many corporate security people is that dealing with the FBI on an investigation of mutual interest is like a one-way street. The FBI accepts any and all information that the corporate security person has put together but gives little or nothing in return. In many cases, from a corporate standpoint, the corporate case takes precedence over any other outside considerations. When this happens, it is usually the desire of the corporate investigative director to accomplish his own goal in an investigation before having a law enforcement agency officially enter the case. This is sometimes not possible with the FBI, as they have been reluctant on many occasions to enter into such an unofficial understanding.

U.S. Secret Service

The Secret Service, in addition to its charge of protecting the president, also is responsible for investigation of violations of counterfeiting laws and certain crimes relating to the theft and forgery of government checks. Although corporate security departments seldom encounter cases in which they and the Secret Service would have a mutual interest, it is the general opinion of most corporate security personnel that the Secret Service is an easy agency with which to coordinate activities.

U.S. Postal Inspectors

Because of the broad possibilities of violations of U.S. postal laws, many security directors find that they can coordinate many of their investigations with postal inspectors and make a subsequent charge of using the U.S. mail to defraud. Many corporate crimes involve the mailing of certain documents, and this is all that is necessary to bring postal inspectors into a case. Most corporate security directors would agree that, historically, the postal inspectors have stood ready, willing, and able to assist corporate personnel in any worthwhile investigation. Furthermore, most postal inspectors generally recognize the needs and desires of a particular company and allow the corporate investigations director to proceed and conclude his own case before stepping in officially with charges of postal fraud.

U.S. Attorneys and Local Prosecutors

A security director often will find that a particular corporate investigation can be presented directly to a U.S. attorney or a local prosecutor. On some occasions, because of local protocol, the director may be referred back to a local law enforcement office to commence the proceedings, but in many cases the prosecutor will take the case directly. Only weighing all the facts and making a sound judgment will determine whether it is better to start the criminal case with a local law enforcement agency or to go directly to the prosecutor.

If the corporation has an operating facility in the local area, then it may be prudent for the investigations manager to initiate the criminal prosecution with a law enforcement agency rather than going directly to the prosecutor. Any law enforcement agency is apt to resent the fact that they have been passed over in such an approach and would later be reluctant to cooperate in any subsequent investigations that may arise.

Whether the investigations manager goes directly to the local prosecutor or initiates his criminal action through a law enforcement agency, he must decide early on which route to take in criminal prosecution. Should the security investigator sign a criminal complaint, or should the case be presented to a grand jury for possible indictment? Oftentimes, a corporate investigator may be pressured by a law enforcement agency to sign a criminal complaint so that a quick arrest can be made. Most corporate attorneys agree, however, that the action of a grand jury's handing down an indictment provides some type of insulation to the corporation.

In all probability, if prosecution is the policy of the corporation, both approaches will be used over a period of time. The authors simply wish to point out that there are certain advantages and disadvantages to either approach, and each case should be decided individually. A hard-and-fast policy of no criminal action except through the grand jury route would not be practical, but by the same token, a policy of always signing criminal complaints would be reckless. Obviously, there has to be a balancing of both approaches when a corporation is engaged regularly in criminal prosecution on a nationwide basis.

Chapter 9

Risk Management: A Total Integration

Risk management is the process by which a company identifies the areas of potential losses in its organization and then develop a plan to avoid or reduce those losses. It is a complex operation and in a large company may mean the expenditure of millions of dollars annually.

There are several methods of risk management. The first is eliminating the risk altogether. This may involve removal of flammable materials from an area. Another example would be the daily bank deposit of cash receipts rather than holding them on the premises overnight. In these cases, the potential loss is avoided by removing the major risks involved.

Another method of risk management is having someone else take the risk for you, usually in return for some benefit. This is called transfer of risk. The most common form of transfer is insurance, and the premium is the price paid for the transfer.

Retention of risk, or willingness to accept the cost of losses, also is used in risk management. If a loss is not covered by insurance, it is referred to as an unreimbursed loss. This type of full loss acceptance is not as common as partial loss acceptance, in which a company accepts losses up to a certain amount (insurance deductibles) or losses over a certain level (policy limits).

A company may actively undertake risk control, which calls for actions such as putting cash in a vault, posting a guard, or installing an alarm system. A total risk control program would include elements of security, safety, property conservation, environmental protection, and emergency planning. Because concern over potential loss is shared by several departments in an organization, the term risk management becomes meaningful. Large companies will have a risk manager, but in many cases this function will be the responsibility of the corporate security director.

EVOLUTION OF RISK MANAGEMENT

Although today's executives believe that insurance should be used only for protection against hazards that cannot be avoided through the use of various protection techniques, at one time insurance was used as the primary means of controlling losses. An insurance company representative would tour the facility to review conditions and would then recommend means of limiting risks and suggest the insurance coverage required by the enterprise. This practice often resulted in unrealistic corrective measures and needless or excessive insurance coverage, since insurance representatives were knowledgeable about insurance but not necessarily about the preventive aspects of assets protection or loss control.

It is now more generally recognized that prevention through risk elimination or control, rather than insurance policies, is the best means of protecting assets. In addition, it is recognized that regardless of the insurance coverage a company may have, full compensation for losses is virtually impossible. Avoidance of losses consequently has become the interest of most organizations. Insurance generally is recognized as the second line of defense against losses that cannot otherwise be avoided.

The insurance industry's requirement that a company protect itself from potential losses had a great impact on the development of corporate security programs. Management soon realized that implementing a comprehensive corporate loss control program not only greatly reduced insurance premiums but also was a cost-effective way to avoid risk. Insurance protects a company after a loss occurs, but it does nothing to prevent losses. A well-planned security program, however, often will prevent many types of losses from ever occurring in the first place.

CONCEPTS OF RISK MANAGEMENT

In any major corporation, there are natural adjuncts to the job of director of security. Over the years, there have been many instances of top security people being promoted out of their jobs into personnel, labor relations, corporate relations, and similar posts. In some companies, nonsecurity executives often are given the added responsibility of corporate security. Seldom, however, do professional security managers broaden their responsibilities by taking on other departments. This can be a mistake and may represent an underutilization of real executive talent.

The very traits and qualities that make up a top security administrator dictate that he also could be effective in other areas. Two such areas are insurance and safety. Together with security, they comprise the general area of risk management, a term that is seen and heard increasingly in the corporate world. A close examination of the use of this term reveals that it does not always mean the same thing to all people. In particular, it means one thing to persons associated with insurance, while it may mean something else entirely to those in corporate security.

Insurance Industry's Concept

In examining the various concepts of the term risk management, we find the more prominent concept held by the insurance industry. Here, the term has gained in popularity as corporations have attempted to assume more of their insurance risks versus the older tradition of assigning or placing the risks in their entirety with insurance carriers. This assumption of the risk has come about through self-insurance funds, the taking of higher deductibles, and the formation of captive insurance companies.

As corporations have moved more in the direction of assuming the risk, the traditional corporate insurance manager has been replaced by a director of risk management whose job it is to take on heavier responsibilities in assuming the various risks. He or his subordinates may be actively involved in the management of claims in the casualty area and, in particular, workers' compensation programs, along with other actions against the company, which traditionally take the form of civil lawsuits.

An additional area that may come into play under the purview of the modern risk manager is that of loss prevention. Here, the risk manager may or may not be attempting actively to manage the risk. Generally speaking, however, where efforts of loss prevention do exist under a modern risk management department, these efforts are directed toward the areas of employee and customer safety and fire protection.

Security's Concept

A newer use of the term risk management has come about from corporate security personnel who find themselves managing certain risks never encountered by insurance people. Examples of this would be the day-to-day considerations of executive protection and, of course, managing what, to some companies, may be the greatest risk of all—the problem of employee theft. Here, security personnel routinely become involved in the area of loss prevention.

In many companies today, fidelity insurance deductibles have risen to the point where, for all practical purposes, the day-to-day theft on the part of employees or outsiders is not insured and must be managed by the security department. Coupled with this is the impact that loss prevention efforts of a security department can have on merchandise inventories. Merchandise inventory variances frequently are classified as shortages, and although they are influenced by many factors, including dishonesty, they are almost never insured. The year-end physical inventory of any company involved in the manufacture, distribution, or retailing of merchandise has a tremendous impact on the profit and loss statement of that company for the year. This is not something that can be insured against, and therefore the security director is, in fact, managing what could easily be one of the largest risks that a company may face.

INTEGRATING THE RISK MANAGEMENT APPROACH

Some companies have attempted to integrate the risk management approach by bringing together the activities of the corporate insurance department, the safety department, and the security department. Charles Chamberlin, director of training for the Private Security Institute, recently wrote:

> To form functional cost-effective risk management programs, increasing numbers of security executives have combined their regular record keeping, safety inspection and fire prevention programs with insurance tasks. Risk management duties traditionally have included tracking and investigating workers' compensation, product liability, customer accident and property loss claims. But now, with shrinking budgets and inflated overhead costs, it may be financially sound to combine those tasks with safety, OSHA administration and security to form a single loss control department. . . .
>
> Who is better qualified to investigate fraudulent workers' compensation claims than security department investigators? What other department has the scheduling flexibility to provide credible witnesses for the myriad of hearings required by the workers' compensation boards, regulatory agencies and civil courts? Where else can fire safety, health hazards and insurance liability inspections be scheduled on a regular basis without the high costs of special training and scheduling changes?[1]

An examination of the functions of these various activities will show that they are interrelated in many ways.

---

[1]Reprinted by permission of Charles Chamberlin.

Workers' Compensation

Many companies are gradually assuming more and more of the risk by taking higher deductibles on workers' compensation coverage, all-risk coverage, and also fidelity insurance. They are attempting to manage these risks by different approaches. On workers' compensation claims, they have entered into an understanding with the insurer. Because of high stop-loss limits, one company insists that the insurer gain approval from the corporate safety manager before settling a workers' compensation case involving indemnity of more than $2,500 (not including medical and hospitalization expenses). The rationale behind this is that the corporate safety manager is the one person in the corporation who is closer to industrial accidents and has the best resources to develop insight into the people involved. By fixing the responsibility with the safety manager, he is given an opportunity to make significant inroads in the annual cost of workers' compensation.

Along with this is a new program, under the joint direction of the safety manager and the company's chief investigator, of investigating those workers' compensation cases that may be suggestive of outright fraud or malingering. One firm's program is now several years old. Results have been gratifying, and an evaluation would show the program to be extremely cost-effective. Already, a number of sizable cases have been reopened, and evidence of outright fraud on the part of the claimant has been presented.

The corporate safety manager also has access to regional security personnel for his safety program. This takes the form of periodic safety inspections in all locations. Follow-up for compliance is the same as in security inspections.

Insurance Considerations

In addition to the obvious functions of the corporate insurance department in the day-to-day dealings with the company's broker and various insurance carriers, the corporate insurance manager also plays an important role in this total integration concept. As various claims are received from the operating locations by the insurance department, it is important for the insurance manager to be able to identify those claims that could have a far-reaching impact on the corporation and should be referred to either the safety or security department for additional follow-up.

In some companies, another corporate department that plays a vital role in this integrated concept is that of plant engineering. This holds especially true in considering the requests for corrective actions put forth by the engineers of the property insurance carrier. Here, there is a blending of input between the corporate insurance manager, the corporate safety manager, and the manager of plant engineering, who has the ultimate responsibility of approving corrective expenditures over a certain limit. By working together as a team, these three individuals are in a much better position to negotiate with the property insurance carrier for a compromise solution to requests for corrective action.

Loss Prevention

In addition to performing certain routine safety functions for the corporate safety manager, the regional security personnel can be charged with managing the largest single uninsured risk that the company has—its inventory variances. This is done in a number of ways, including applicant screening for security-sensitive jobs. Many security experts concede that good security must begin with the proper selection of employees, especially those employees applying for sensitive positions.

Another effort at loss prevention is security inspections. Just as with safety inspections, each manufacturing and distribution location should undergo a thorough security inspection periodically. These inspections should include a review of personnel selection procedures, the monitoring of any guards or watchmen assigned to the location, key control, permanent access control, transportation security and other internal and external controls and security measures that may be necessary for a particular location.

In addition, the regional security manager also should monitor and attempt to work with the local safety/security committee, which may be present in many firms. These committees should meet on an average of once a month to discuss both security and safety matters. Although there may be several permanent members of the committee, companies should encourage local management to rotate production people on and off the committee so that a number of individual viewpoints can be expressed. Both the corporate safety and security departments can furnish material to these committees from time to time for discussion. Occasionally, either the regional security manager or the corporate safety manager should be included as a brief speaker on the agenda of that particular committee.

THE RISK MANAGEMENT MATRIX

The reader will immediately see the complexity in the various lines of interaction within the risk management function. A good explanation of how this risk management concept should work in a major corporation has been given by Peter Drucker.[2]

Drucker states that a manager has the task of creating a whole that is larger than the sum of its parts. He makes the analogy between a manager and the conductor of a symphony orchestra through whose efforts, visions, and leadership individual instrumental parts become the whole of the musical performance. Drucker also points out in this analogy that the conductor of a symphony orchestra has the composer's score and that he is only the interpreter. The manager, however, is both the composer and the conductor.

Drucker goes on to state that the manager's task of creating a finished product also requires that in every one of his acts, he considers simultaneously the performance and the results of the enterprise as a whole and of the many diverse activities in the enterprise that need to be synchronized.

Examining the matrix in Figure 9–1, note that accidents are generated by the operating location, and these may or may not result in

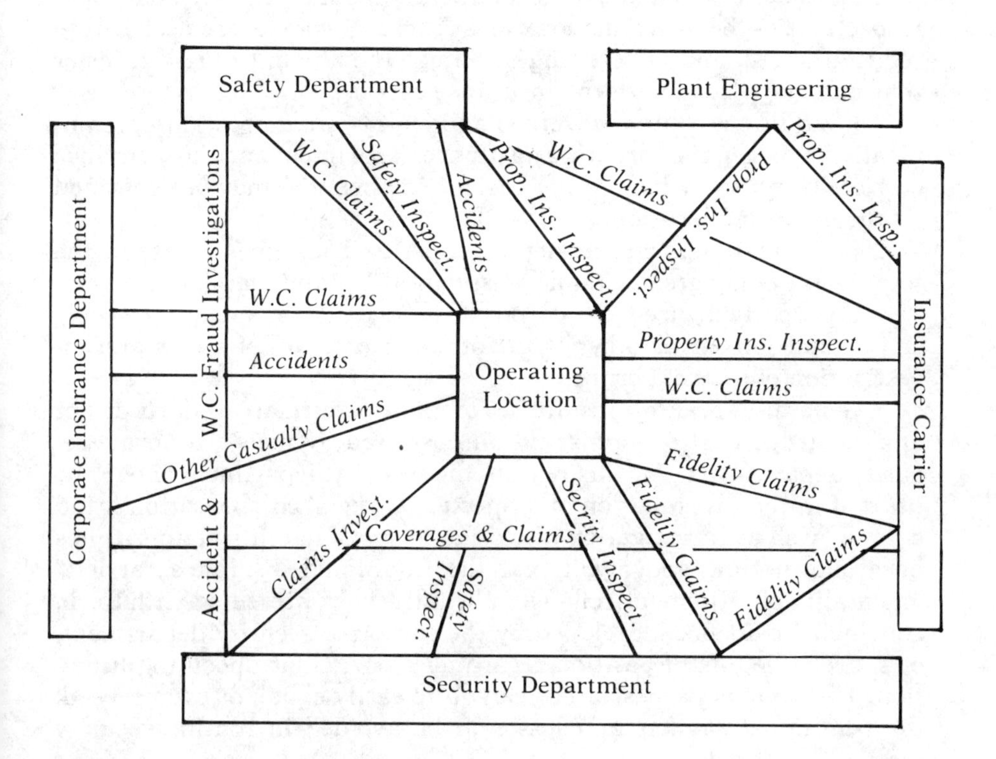

Figure 9–1 The Risk Management Matrix.

---

[2]Peter F. Drucker, *Management,* p. 398.

workers' compensation claims. At any rate, both the reports of accidents and the claims go into the safety department at the same time they are forwarded to the corporate insurance department. Also note that the safety department then proceeds to generate the workers' compensation claim with the insurance carrier and that there is interaction between the insurance carrier and the operating location on the same claim.

Property inspections are being conducted by the insurance carrier, as well as the corporate safety department, at the operating location. Note that the insurance carrier's communication on the property inspection reports is funneled back through the plant engineering department and then on to the operating location. As previously discussed, this puts a monitoring factor into the equation so that recommendations by the insurance carrier are reasonable and cost-effective. In the area of fidelity claims, we see that they are generated by the operating location and then handled by the security department before being passed back to the insurance carrier. The insurance carrier, in turn, interacts with the operating location in its claim handling in this area. Also note that the security department is conducting regular security and safety inspections of the operating locations. These, of course, are designed to reduce the risk and in so doing minimize the amount of risk transfer that must be placed with the insurance carrier.

In addition, routine coverage and claims are a constant communication between the corporate insurance department and the insurance carrier. This also includes other casualty claims that may be generated by the operating location.

If the matrix is administered properly, it becomes a case of the total result being greater than the sum of the individual parts.

If properly utilized, the corporate security department as a whole can extend into areas other than routine protection of assets and investigation of internal crimes.

Generally speaking, insurance company investigative efforts do not approach the level of sophistication possessed by many corporate security departments. For this reason, the security department should be utilized in the investigation of suspected workers' compensation fraud cases as well as investigation into other forms of liability claims. It has been shown time and again that the traditional insurance carriers' "mentality of settlement" changes abruptly when presented with fresh, convincing evidence, developed by the corporate security department, of a strengthening of position regarding a particular upcoming litigation. The savings in these areas can quite easily equal, or even exceed, the traditional savings and losses to be avoided in routine security matters.

Chapter 10

Legal Considerations

The United States has become a very litigious-intensive society, and every corporation faces potential vulnerability for a devastating financial loss due to mishaps, errors, or negligence, intentional or otherwise, by members of its proprietary or contract security staff. Therefore, the corporate security manager should be familiar with areas of potential litigation, which, if understood and handled properly, could go far toward forestalling corporate and personal liability loss.

The security manager should know whether those in his or her employ are legally classified as actual, sworn police or whether they are acting purely as citizens. If the employees are, in fact, sworn police officers, acting under color of law, and have been hired to work during their off-duty hours, then they must abide by the constitutional sanctions and rules that govern the activities of sworn law enforcement officers. For example, sworn police officers must operate under the sanctions imposed by the Fourth (arrest, search, and seizure) and Fifth (Miranda) amendments. Constitutional sanctions might apply to private security personnel under the following conditions:

1. when they act as agents for law enforcement agencies;
2. when they act in concert with law enforcement officers;
3. when they obtain evidence as agents for law enforcement employees to be used in prosecution;
4. when they act with deputized police powers;
5. when they act with limited police powers granted by a governmental licensing or regulatory body; and/or
6. when they are employed by a public authority.[1]

If the employees are not sworn police officers, the powers of authority that they possess are the same as those of all other citizens for that particular jurisdiction. And, whether working for a contract se-

[1]*Scope of Legal Authority of Private Security Personnel,* Private Security Advisory Council to the Law Enforcement Assistance Administration, U.S. Department of Justice, Washington, DC, June 1978, p. 3 (hereafter cited as *Legal Authority*).

curity agency or a proprietary (in-house) employer, ". . . security officers possess only the same power and authority of their employer and the power of an employer is exactly the same as that of any private citizen."[2]

PROBABLE CAUSE

The security director should be aware of the concept of probable cause as it relates to both sworn officers and private citizen security employees in the event that they make an arrest for a crime committed on or against corporate property. One definition of probable cause is "the existence of circumstances which would lead a reasonably prudent man to believe in the guilt of the arrested party; mere suspicion or belief, unsupported by facts or circumstances, is insufficient."[3] Citizens may make arrests under certain and varying conditions in specific jurisdictions. One should note that the standards for making a citizen's arrest may well be more stringent than those for sworn police officers to the extent that, in many cases, a felony must have been committed. Figure 10–1 will give you some idea of the varying statutory arrest requirements imposed by different states.

Probable cause is an absolute necessity when taking positive action such as making an arrest, and one should note that it also may be used as a defense in the event false arrest, malicious prosecution, or other charges are filed against the arrester or corporation.

For a compilation of state statutes spelling out specific requirements for arrest by private citizens, see *Protective Security Law*.[4]

MIRANDA WARNINGS

The constitutional sanctions imposed by the Fifth Amendment (Miranda rule) against self-incrimination apply to sworn police officers and not to private citizens. The information obtained in an interrogation by a private citizen security employee must be freely and voluntarily given. No pressures, such as force or duress, should be applied in an attempt to obtain information. "While the courts tend to scrutinize statements made to law enforcement officers more carefully than those made to private persons, it is the apparent trend of the case law to apply a general

---

[2]Arthur J. Bilek, John C. Klotter, and R. Keegan Federal, *Legal Aspects of Private Security* (Cincinnati: Anderson Publishing Co., 1981), p. 15. See also M. Cherif Bassiouni, *Citizen's Arrest: The Law of Arrest, Search, and Seizure for Private Citizens and Private Police* (Springfield, IL: Charles C. Thomas, 1977), pp. 3–8.

[3]*Black's Law Dictionary* 5th ed. (St. Paul, MN: West Publishing Co., 1979), p. 1081 (hereafter cited as *Black's Law Dictionary*).

[4]Fred E. Inbau, Marvin E. Aspen, and James E. Spiotto, *Protective Security Law* (Stoneham, MA: Butterworths, 1983), p. 236 (hereafter cited as *Protective Security Law*).

	Minor Offense											Major Offense														Certainty of Correct Arrest	
	Type of Minor Offense							Type of Knowledge Required				Type of Major Offense						Type of Knowledge Required									
	Crime	Misdemeanor amounting to a breach of the peace	Breach of the peace	Public offense	Offense	Offense other than an ordinance	Indictable offense	Presence	Immediate Knowledge	View	Upon reasonable grounds that is being committed	Felony	Larceny	Petit Larceny	Crime involving physical injury to another	Crime	Crime involving theft or destruction of property	Committed in presence	Information a felony has been committed	View	Reasonable grounds to believe being committed	That felony has been committed in fact	In escaping or attempting	Summoned by peace officer to assist in arrest	Is in the act of committing	Reasonable grounds to believe person arrested committed	Probable cause
Alabama				x				x				x										x				x	
Alaska	x							x				x										x				x	
Arizona		x						x				x										x				x	
Arkansas												x									x					x	
California				x				x				x										x				x	
Colorado	x							x								x		x									
Georgia					x			x	x			x											x			x	
Hawaii	x							x								x		x							x		

	Minor Offense											*Major Offense*														*Certainty of Correct Arrest*	
	Type of Minor Offense							*Type of Knowledge Required*				*Type of Major Offense*						*Type of Knowledge Required*									
	Crime	Misdemeanor amounting to a breach of the peace	Breach of the peace	Public offense	Offense	Offense other than an ordinance	Indictable offense	Presence	Immediate Knowledge	View	Upon reasonable grounds that is being commited	Felony	Larceny	Petit Larceny	Crime involving physical injury to another	Crime	Crime involving theft or destruction of property	Committed in presence	Information a felony has been committed	View	Reasonable grounds to believe being committed	That felony has been committed in fact	In escaping or attempting	Summoned by peace officer to assist in arrest	Is in the act of committing	Reasonable grounds to believe person arrested committed	Probable cause
Idaho				x				x				x									x					x	
Illinois						x					x	x									x						
Iowa				x				x				x									x					x	
Kentucky												x									x					x	
Louisiana												x									x						
Michigan												x					x				x			x			
Minnesota				x				x				x									x					x	
Mississippi			x				x	x				x									x					x	

Montana				x	x		x										x		x	
Nebraska							x		x								x		x	
Nevada			x		x		x										x		x	
New York				x	x		x										x			
N. Carolina*		x					x			x		x						x		x
N. Dakota			x		x		x										x		x	
Ohio							x									x			x	
Oklahoma			x		x		x										x		x	
Oregon	x				x						x		x							x
S. Carolina							x	x						x	x					
S. Dakota			x		x		x										x		x	
Tennessee			x		x		x										x		x	
Texas		x			x	x	x						x		x					
Utah			x		x		x										x		x	
Wyoming							x		x								x		x	

*Statute eliminates use of word arrest and replaces with detention.

Figure 10–1 Statutory citizen arrest authority. Report of the Task Force on Private Security, Private Security National Advisory Committee on Criminal Justice Standards and Goals, Washington, D.C., 1976, p. 397.

standard of voluntariness to all confessions—whether made to a police officer or not."[5] If a confession is obtained by private security personnel in a custodial situation with more than minimal or peripheral police participation, the private security personnel may be found to have acted as an extension of the police arm, and the confession can be suppressed if proper warnings are not given.[6]

In *People* v. *Jones*, two sworn plainclothes police officers were assigned to patrol a shopping center and entered a department store. Inside, they were informed by the store's security personnel that a man was under observation in the men's clothing department. Security officers pointed out the man to the police, but indicated that they did not "have anything yet." The police officers watched the man for five to ten minutes and then left the store.

Soon thereafter, the man under observation used wire clippers to cut the chains that ran through the sleeves of six leather coats, put the coats in a bag, and left the store. This was observed by the store's security staff, who followed the defendant while one of the security guards went to find the police officers. The guard informed the police officers that store personnel were about to stop someone and that their assistance was needed.

The defendant was stopped outside the store by security officers, who identified themselves and took the coats. When the police officers arrived, one of the security officers was holding the defendant against the wall, attempting to handcuff him. As the defendant stepped away from the wall, one of the police officers placed his hand on the defendant's shoulder, showed him his badge, identified himself as a police officer, and told the defendant to keep his hands on the wall and stay there. The defendant was then handcuffed and brought back to the store's security office by the police and store personnel. The police left the defendant at the security office and waited outside while store detectives questioned him.

Inside the office, the defendant was handcuffed to a desk by one hand and was asked to sign various items by the security officer. He was given a confession form and was asked to sign it if he understood it. When various paperwork was completed, the store detective turned the defendant over to the police for criminal prosecution. It was conceded that neither the police nor the store detectives had previously informed the defendant of his right to remain silent or to consult an attorney.

An appellate division court overturned the defendant's conviction based on the trial court's admission of the confession. The state claimed that there was no need to advise the defendant of his rights because the police participation was "minimal" or "peripheral." In affirming the appellate division, the court of appeals noted that the police were not merely anonymous observers but had actively participated in the arrest, identified themselves as police, escorted the defendant to the place of interrogation,

---

[5]John J. Burke, "Confessions to Private Persons," *FBI Law Enforcement Bulletin*, August 1973, p. 21.

[6]*People v. Jones*, 393 N.E. 2d 443, 47 N.Y. 2d 528 (1979).

and awaited the outcome of the questioning. This was, the court said, sufficient to create a custodial atmosphere, which the Miranda rule was intended to alleviate.

The corporate security manager also should be aware that in some instances, an employee has the right to union representation if called in for an interview where the employee reasonably believes the investigation will result in disciplinary action.[7] For a more extensive discussion of this rule, refer to *Employee Theft Investigation*.[8]

SEARCH AND SEIZURE

Fourth Amendment sanctions relating to illegal searches and seizures apply to sworn law enforcement officers and not to private citizens.

In the matter of *Burdeau* v. *McDowell*, 256 U.S. 465 (1921), McDowell was in possession of rooms 1320 and 1321 of the Farmer's Bank Building in Pittsburgh where he kept certain private papers. He was, however, discharged by his employer for alleged unlawful and fraudulent conduct in the course of business. In March, a company representative, with the authority of the company president, took possession of room 1320. At various times, a company representative, with a detective in charge of the room, took company papers and shipped them to an auditor in New York. The company representative also took private papers of McDowell's. To do this, two safes were drilled and blown open, the locks on his private desk were broken and forced open, and his files were broken into and abstracted.

In June, the company turned over a letter found in McDowell's desk to the U.S. Justice Department, which the government later wanted to use in prosecuting him. Claiming a violation of his Fourth Amendment rights, McDowell petitioned the district court for the return of his books, papers, memoranda, correspondence, and other data, which the court in turn found to have been stolen and ordered their return. This court also found that it did not appear that any government agent was involved in or a party to the taking of the papers.

The Supreme Court held that the Fourth Amendment protects against government actions and was intended as a restraint on the activities of sovereign authority. In its decision, the Court said the record clearly shows that no government official had anything to do with the wrongful seizure of McDowell's property and knew nothing about it until several months later. It also pointed out that McDowell had an unquestionable right of redress against those who illegally and wrongfully took his private property.

---

[7]*National Labor Relations Board* v. *J. Weingarten, Inc.*, 420 U.S. 251 (1975).

[8]J. Kirk Barefoot, *Employee Theft*, pp. 142–43.

The Fourth Amendment will apply if citizens act in concert with or at the behest of police, as seen in *Stapleton* v. *Los Angeles*, 447 P. 2d 967 (1969).

> Around midnight, one Bradford, an armed credit card investigator, and two other agents from different credit card companies, assisted the police in executing an arrest warrant for the defendant for credit card fraud. The police instructed Bradford and one other credit card agent to cover the rear of the house to prevent an escape, and they and the third credit card agent went to the front door with the warrant. Bradford entered the house after one of the officers requested him to do so and let him in through the back door. Bradford and the officers arrested and handcuffed the defendant. Bradford and the officers searched the house. Bradford asked if anyone had searched the defendant's car, which he had seen parked some distance down the street, and someone answered negatively. Bradford asked where the car keys were, and someone indicated that they were lying on a table. Another agent handed the keys to Bradford, who then went outside to the car to look for credit cards and/or merchandise purchased with the cards. Bradford said he was searching incidental to arrest and admitted he had no search warrant and had not been given permission for the search.
>
> Bradford searched the unlocked car and then unlocked the trunk. In the trunk, he discovered sixty cannisters containing a tear gas-like substance. In order not to disturb the "evidence," he closed the trunk and reported the discovery to the officers. One of the officers returned to the car with Bradford, opened the trunk, and retrieved the cannisters. The defendant was subsequently charged with possession of material capable of emitting tear gas, a violation of the penal code. The defendant's motion to suppress the cannisters was denied.
>
> The California Supreme Court found that the search of the car was clearly a joint operation by police and credit card agents. The court noted that the official participation in the planning and implementation of the overall operation was sufficient to taint with state action the subsequent acts of the credit card agents and thus ordered that the motion to suppress be granted. The court also noted that the police permitted action by Bradford, which probably constituted both a misdemeanor (tampering with a motor vehicle or its contents) and a trespass to personal property.

There are, however, many instances in which private citizens are involved in conducting searches mainly to stem the flow of stolen property or to protect life and property at corporate facilities, industrial sites, retail establishments, and the like. A search by private security personnel might be permissible under one of the following situations:

1. actual consent by the person to be searched;
2. implied consent via union or employment contract, or as a condition of employment;
3. in some instances, and then limited, as incidental to a valid arrest; and/or

4. in some instances, and also limited, to a valid detention.[9]

Numerous persons such as vendors, consultants, repairpersons, and customers visit private corporate property. Without consent, there may be no authority to search these people.[10] A consent must be given freely, voluntarily and knowingly. The following situations are examples of some search situations as conducted by private security personnel or private citizens:

X-ray scan of briefcase at airport, see *U.S.* v. *Henry*, 615 F. 2d 1223 (1980.)

Sensormatic devices on retail goods, see *Lucas* v. *U.S.*, 411 A. 2d 360 (1980); and *A.M. Parker* v. *Sears, Roebuck & Co.*, 418 So. 2d 1361 (1982).

Employee package search, see *Chenkin* v. *Bellevue Hospital Center*, 479 F. Supp. 207 (1979).

Spot check of parcels, see *Allums* v. *State*, 288 S.E. 2d 783 (1982).

Storage of goods at private warehouse, see *U.S.* v. *Roberts*, 644 F. 2d 684 (1980).

Cab of truck that delivered corporate goods, see *Commonwealth* v. *Leone*, 435 N.E. 2d 1036 (1982).

Shoplifter, see *People* v. *Zelinski*, 594 P. 2d 1000 (1979); and *U.S.* v. *Lima*, 424 A. 2d 113 (1980).

Stadiums, see *Nakamoto* v. *Fasi*, 635 P. 2d 946 (1981); *Jensen* v. *City of Pontiac*, 317 N.W. 2d 619 (1982); and *Jacobsen* v. *City of Seattle*, 658 P. 2d 654 (1983).

Abandoned property, see *U.S.* v. *Gomez*, 614 F. 2d 643 (1980); and *U.S.* v. *One (1) Piper Aircraft VIN 27-2593*, 520 F. Supp. 1023 (1981).

Where outsiders are to be searched upon departing company property, they must be warned accordingly beforehand so that their act of entering implies voluntariness of the subsequent search.

For interesting cases where private parties, acting as such and not for the state, were subject to the exclusionary rule, see *State* v. *Hyem*, 630 P. 2d 202 (1981); and Steven Fuller, "Private Security in the Courtroom: The Exclusionary Rule Applies," *Security Management*, March 1980, p. 38. For those corporations covered by the Occupational Safety and Health Act of 1970, the Supreme Court found in *Marshall* v. *Barlow's, Inc.* [436 U.S. 307 (1978)] that that agency's warrantless inspections were unconstitutional.

---

[9] *Legal Authority*, p. 15.

[10] John J. Sullivan, "Legal Authority of Security Personnel," *Security Management*, February 1973, p. 25.

TORT LITIGATION

Corporations have long suffered huge losses in tort litigation. A tort is a civil or private wrong, other than for a breach of contract, and has three elements:

1. The existence of a legal duty from the defendant to the plaintiff;
2. a breach of that duty; and
3. damage as a proximate result.[11]

The thrust of the cases involving security employees or their employers lies in two areas—negligence and intentional torts. Negligence, or the absence of due diligence, is "the omission to do something which a reasonable man, guided by those ordinary considerations which ordinarily regulate human affairs, would do, or the doing of something which a reasonable and prudent man would not do."[12]

Some examples of lawsuits involving negligence and security personnel follow.

Negligence in Hiring

This occurs when the employer hires someone he knows, or should have known, was unfit for the position sought, as in *Easley* v. *Apollo Detective Agency, Ind.*, 387 N.E. 2d 1281 (1979).

> Here, a woman entered her apartment, locked the doors, and went to bed at approximately 10:00 PM one evening. At about 4:00 AM the next morning, she heard footsteps in her apartment. She put on a robe, picked up a glass bottle, and went to investigate. She discovered a uniformed building security guard in her kitchen pointing a .357 magnum gun at her head. She threw the bottle in the air and began screaming. The guard brought the gun close to her head, told her he had used the passkey issued to him to enter her apartment, and said that he wanted to make love to her. She tried to get away, but he caught her and, pointing the gun to her head, said "If you do that again, I will blow your head off." He told her he wanted to rape her, and she threw up. He threatened to kill her, ran his hand over her body, and started to undress. After about an hour, she persuaded him to leave and then called the police. At a later criminal court proceeding, the guard walked up to her and said, "I am going to get you."

[11] *Black's Law Dictionary*, p. 1335.

[12] Ibid., p. 930.

In a civil suit, the lady received $20,000 in compensatory damages and $7,500 in punitive damages. In affirming the judgments, the appellate court noted in connection with the allegation of negligence in hiring that the guard company's background check responsibility was diffused throughout the company, that there was no record in the file that the guard's prior address had been checked, that there were no letters in the file as to checking the guard's out-of-state addresses, and that there were no marks in the file denoting that his references had been verified. Also, the guard did not take any intelligence or psychological tests, had only four hours of on-the-job training instead of sixteen, and was permitted to carry a gun at the outset of his employment instead of waiting for several months. The guard company failed to comply with a city ordinance requiring the licensing of "special policemen," and he was never asked to present his certificate of appointment as a special policeman. There were no copies in his file of a claimed training certificate or letter of recommendation. He had claimed to have worked for two other security companies before coming to Apollo, but Apollo never attempted to verify his licensing at either job. Nor did Apollo ascertain from these companies that the guard had been fired for sleeping on duty, was unreliable, was put on probation for nonperformance, had several complaints against him, and was not eligible for rehire. The appellate court affirmed the willful and wanton misconduct in hiring this guard, who was someone the employer knew, or should have known, was unfit. The court pointed out that a reasonably adequate investigation would have determined his unfitness and that Apollo's virtually nonexistent investigation exhibited a reckless disregard for the plaintiff's safety.

Negligent Entrustment

An example of this would be a case in which weapons entrusted to guards by the employer were used in off-duty shootings, as in *Horn* v. *I.B.I. Security Service of Florida, Inc.*, 317 So. 2d 444 (1975); and *Langill* v. *Columbia*, 289 So. 2d 460 (1974).

The defendant in the Langill case, age approximately 70 years, was hired by the Wackenhut Corporation as a bank security guard. He was issued a pistol and five live rounds of ammunition for use the following day. He was given no special or personal instruction in the use and loading of firearms. He had little or no experience in firing a weapon and was merely issued a guard manual, which contained some information on the proper handling of a weapon.

The next morning, the defendant, while dressing for work, partially loaded the weapon. At this time, two men came to his trailer residence to discuss some work to be done thereon. The defendant joined them outside and, during the discussion and without provocation, pointed the pistol at the two men and pulled the trigger, discharging a bullet that passed through one man, killing him, and lodged in the plaintiff's side.

The trial court rendered an adverse summary judgment against the plaintiff. The appellate court, after reviewing the record, found that a jury having an opportunity to review the facts may have determined that defendant Wackenhut Corporation was negligent in entrusting the newly hired guard with a pistol and five rounds of ammunition. Judgment of the trial court was reversed.

Negligent Supervision

The employer has the duty to supervise employees who are privileged because of their employment. This was established in *International Distributing Corporation* v. *American District Telegraph Co.*, 596 F. 2d 136 (1977), in which burglar alarm company employees bypassed an alarm system and entered protected property at will and looted same.

Negligence in Investigating

In *Davis* v. *Harris*, 570 F. Supp. 1136 (1983), delayed interviews of witnesses by a security investigator caused humiliation to a student who was later cleared.

INTENTIONAL TORTS

The second area of tort litigation is that of intentional torts. An intentional tort is a "tort or wrong perpetrated by one who intends to do that which the law has declared wrong as contrasted with negligence in which the tortfeasor fails to exercise that degree of care in doing what is otherwise permissible."[13] Examples of the different types of intentional torts that might affect security operations follow.

Defamation of Character

This is the use of false, base, or malicious words that prejudices or injures another's reputation. See *General Motors Corp.* v. *Piskor*, 340 A. 2d 747 (1975), where guards accosted a departing employee.

[13]Ibid., p. 1335.

Malicious Prosecution

This is defined as the bringing of criminal charges against a party without probable cause and with malice. See *Williams* v. *Boylan-Pearce, Inc.*, 317 S.E. 2d 17 (1984), where an employee was prosecuted although a search of the employee and her purse by security guards revealed nothing and the security investigation failed to check the jewelry inventory to determine whether anything was missing.

False Arrest and False Imprisonment

A purchaser paid for goods in a store and then transported them outside to his car. Store employees saw the goods in the car and erroneously concluded that they were stolen. The purchaser was then detained for shoplifting, and his car was searched. See *Robinson* v. *Winn-Dixie,* 447 So. 2d 1003 (1984).

Assault and Battery

In *Gonzales* v. *Southwest Security & Protection Agency, Inc.* [665 P. 2d 810 (1983)], guards took a wrestling match spectator into a small room in an auditorium and beat him.

> The plaintiff's suit against the security company and five guards arose out of injuries received while attending a wrestling match held in a civic auditorium owned by the city. The incident occurred as the plaintiff and a friend were leaving the auditorium and a woman accosted them for having thrown beer during the match. Security guards intervened and told the plaintiff and his friend to leave. Once outside the auditorium, the woman again accosted the plaintiff's friend, setting off a substantial disturbance. When security guards arrived, the plaintiff was a bystander. Nevertheless, guards threw the plaintiff to the ground, handcuffed him, and took him to a small room, where he was beaten, in part by the guard's nightstick. Throughout the incident, the plaintiff was apparently calm and did not provoke the guards. At the trial, the plaintiff was awarded $15,000.
>
> The appellate court affirmed this judgment, noting that the imprisonment and battering was in the course and scope of the guards' employment and incidental to Southwest's business. The court also ruled that Southwest provided the security personnel with uniforms, handcuffs, guns, nightsticks, and the authority to keep peace and that the beating was facilitated by instruments provided by Southwest. The court concluded that Southwest negligently equipped, trained, supervised, and retained the guards, and that Southwest's negligence was the cause of the

plaintiff's harm. The court pointed out that Southwest failed to investigate adequately the background and character of the guards before hiring them, that it did not adequately supervise the guards in general, and specifically this evening, that it failed to train them adequately in the use of weapons and that it failed to instruct its employees adequately in the proper methods of restraining and arresting individuals.

Trespass

Trespass is the unlawful interference with another's property, person, or rights. In *Souder* v. *Pendleton Detectives, Inc.* [88 So. 2d 716 (1956)], private investigators trespassed on the petitioner's property without his permission and peeked in his windows in a compensation case.

> The plaintiff was injured on the job. The workman's compensation insurer consistently denied his claims and hired the defendant to shadow, trail, investigate, observe, and secure information pertaining to the activities of the petitioner as well as to harass and invade his personal safety, comfort, and privacy. During May and June, two detectives observed, watched, trailed, shadowed, and eavesdropped on the petitioner. They used binoculars, took pictures without permission, trespassed on the petitioner's property without authority, and watched him in his house by peeking through the windows. The detectives also made known to the community that they were doing this. The trial court dismissed the action, but the appellate court reversed and remanded the case. The appellate court noted that the right to privacy is the right to be let alone and to live one's life in seclusion without being subjected to unwarranted and undesired publicity. This court also noted the right of insurance companies to investigate claims against them, provided the investigation was within legal bounds. The appellate court pointed out that the detectives, in trespassing on the petitioner's property, might have been guilty of a crime under the "Peeping Tom" statute, which provided for a fine of not more than $500, imprisonment for not more than six months, or both.

Invasion of Privacy

As this pertains to physical surveillance or shadowing, see *Pinkerton National Detective Agency, Inc.* v. *Stevens,* 132 S.E. 2d 119 (1963); by electronic means, see *Hamberger* v. *Eastman,* 206 A. 2d 239 (1965); by use of photography, see *McLain* v. *Boise Cascade Corp.,* 553 P. 2d 343 (1975); and by physical entry onto property, see *Gonzales* v. *Southwestern Bell Telephone Co.,* 555 S.W. 2d 219 (1977).

Harassment

As this pertains to constant telephone contacts, see *Housh* v. *Peth,* 133 N.E. 2d 340 (1956).

Outrageous Conduct

An example of this is a strip search of a female employee by a store manager in *Bodewig* v. *K-Mart,* 635 P. 2d 657 (1981).

AGENCY AND CONTRACTS

Agency is a relationship in which one person acts for or represents another by the authority of the latter and may be created by express or implied contract or by law and where one party delegates lawful business, with more or less discretionary power to another, who undertakes to manage that business and render an account to the delegator.[14] These relationships are: principal/agent; master/servant; employer/employee; and proprietor/independent contractor. Usually pay or another valuable consideration is involved, and the relationship exists for a specified period of time. Of concern to one charged with preventing loss relating to issues of company liability is the extent of the employer's right to select, direct the activities of, and discharge or remove the employee. Doctrines of imputing liability to the company for the wrongful act(s) of an employee are:

1. *respondiat superior,* or letting the master or principal answer for the wrongful act(s) of the servant or agent;
2. *vicarious liability,* which is indirect legal responsibility to the employer or principal for the wrongful act(s) of the employee or agent.

A question of concern to the security manager is whether the employee was acting within the scope of his or her employment—that is, the furthering of the duties owed to the employer—or engaging in activities not incidental or connected to the employment. Also, how much control does the employer exercise, directly or indirectly, over the activities of the employee? Following are some of the types of litigation in the area of agency.

---

[14]Ibid., p. 57.

Scope of Employment

In one case, a guard's assault of a patron was naturally incidental to and substantially arose out of an attempt to perform his security company's business. See *Gonzales* v. *Southwest Security and Protection Agency, Inc.,* 655 P. 2d 810 (1983). In another case, a rape/murder by a guard was not in furtherance of his employer's interest. See *Martin* v. *United Security Services, Inc.,* 373 So. 2d 720 (1979).

Respondiat Superior and Vicarious Liability

In one case, a rape by a guard was not in furtherance of the agency's business, and the security company was not liable. See *Rabon* v. *Guardsmark, Inc.,* 571 F. 2d 1277 (1978). In another case, a private security company was not vicariously liable for a willful and malicious fire set by an employee. See *Hoover Ball and Bearing Co.* v. *Pinkerton's, Inc.,* 500 F. Supp. 673 (1980).

Control over Employee by Employer

In one case, both a security service and a bar were served by a guard's armed presence and his shooting of a patron. See *Jax Liquors, Inc.* v. *Hall,* 344 So. 2d 247 (1976). In another case, an off-duty police officer acting as a bouncer was implicitly authorized to use force. See *Davis* v. *DelRosso,* 359 N.E. 2d 313 (1979).

Independent Contractor Hired by Proprietor

This applied to a case in which a corporation that had committed nondelegable and nonassignable duties of protection by contract to a private detective agency was able to seek indemnification from the detective agency. See *Hendricks* v. *Leslie Fay, Inc.,* 159 S.E. 2d 362 (1968). In another case, it was found that a grocery store exercised sufficient control over a contract security guard that it could be liable for the tortious conduct of the guard. See *Safeway Stores Inc.* v. *Kelly,* 448 A. 2d 856 (1982).

USE OF FORCE

On occasion, private citizens, including security personnel, use either deadly or nondeadly physical force. This is done to protect themselves and others, to protect or recover their property, or to prevent crime. This should be of great concern to the security manager, as he or she will hire others to protect corporate property. The user of force, and potentially the security manager and corporation, must justify not only the use of force, but also the degree used in each particular instance. The key to using force lies in what is a reasonable response under the circumstances presented by the threat. One must take into consideration the seriousness, danger present, and kind and degree of the threatened misconduct. The more serious threat allows utilization of a higher degree of force than a lesser threat, and, of course, one should not cause an escalation of the degree of force being used against him. Also, there is no need for any force to be used when the threat has subsided, except to make the apprehension.

One should consider that, generally speaking, life is worth more than property; that the law does not condone the use of unnecessary violence; and that you can use no more force than is necessary to accomplish your purpose under the circumstances. Other considerations to think about before using force include: determining whether the threat is real, imminent, or pressing and accompanied by the ability to carry it out; whether there are other alternatives to using force; how much time has elapsed since the incident occurred; whether the force to be used is for retaliatory purposes only; and who actually is the provocateur or aggressor. Remember that the amount of force used by your employee may be measured at a much later time by others—namely, a jury. Also note that many states have statutes covering the permissible limits on the use of force. Some cases relating to the use of force involving different conditions follow.

Deadly Force

In one case, the firing of a shot by a citizen could not be justified as the defense of an assault victim since the assailants were walking away when the shot was fired. See *State* v. *Ghiloni,* 398 A. 2d 1204 (1978). In two others, murder convictions were upheld for killings in adultery and car theft cases, respectively. See *State* v. *Nyland,* 287 P. 2d 345 (1955); and *Commonwealth* v. *Allen,* 276 A. 2d 539 (1971).

Use of Force to Prevent Crime

In one case, a murder conviction was upheld after the defendant shot and killed an unknown individual across the street who was "monkeying" around with windows at 2:30 AM. See *Commonwealth* v. *Chermansky,* 242 A. 2d 237 (1968). Another led to the adoption of the Model Penal

Code on Use of Force by the state of Massachusetts after a citizen shot a burglar of a drugstore across street. See *Commonwealth* v. *Kline,* 363 N.E. 2d 1313 (1970).

Self-Defense

No liability was imputed to an employer when an armed guard, after being suddenly attacked from behind, had his arms pinned to his sides, was beaten with his own club, and then shot his attacker. See *Price* v. *Gray's Guard Service,* 298 So. 2d 462 (1974). In this situation, the guard, who was authorized to carry a gun at a fair, was stationed at a gate that was not open to the public. This gate was reserved for exhibitors at the fair and for other persons connected with the fair. There was no facility at this gate for the sale or collection of tickets.

> One evening two big, strong young men, each about 5′11″ and 170 pounds, attempted to enter this gate. They were told by the guard that it was not open to the general public and that they could not enter there. A brisk conversation with curse words ensued, but there was no altercation. The two young men then entered the fair at an appropriate gate. When the fair closed, the two young men left and went toward their car. One of the men began talking about the earlier incident and told the other he was going "to whip his (the guard's) ass." They discussed the fact that the guard was armed. The young man insisted, however, that he "wanted to jump on the guy" and "knock him down."
>
> The two young men approached the guard, one from the blind side, grabbed him, and began hitting him. One took the guard's billy club away and began hitting him with it. They knocked off the guard's glasses and hat. Not knowing who his attackers were and with both arms pinned to his sides as he was being wrestled to the ground, the guard managed to draw his pistol and fire one shot, killing one of the young men.
>
> The trial judge granted a summary judgment in favor of the guard service, which was upheld on appeal. The appeals court (which was amazed that the suit was filed in the first place) noted that the guard was legally on duty, that he was legally authorized to carry a gun, that he was deliberately attacked by persons knowing he had a gun, that his arms were pinned, and that he was beaten with his own club. The court pointed out that the guard had no opportunity to retreat or to cogitate his next move. In this case, the guard acted in self-defense to protect his own life, which he believed was in imminent peril.

Defense of Property

This defense was used in a case where a scuffle occurred after a security guard had recovered some stolen blue jeans [*People* v. *Rickman,* 391 N.E. 2d 1114 (1979)] and in a case where a grocery store owner fired shots at an auto he erroneously believed contained robbers, which resulted in injury to an innocent third party [*Hatfield* v. *Gracen*, 567 P. 2d 546 (1977)].

Ejection from Premises

A business proprietor has the right to expel an abusive person who refuses to leave or persists in abusive conduct after being cautioned as long as expulsion or restraint is by reasonable force [*Griego* v. *Wilson*, 570 P. 2d 612 (1972)] and where the reasonable course was to call the sheriff's office rather than forcibly ejecting an abusive person [*Lantay* v. *McLean*, 406 P. 2d 224 (1965)].

Excessive Force

This ruling was used when a storekeeper set a dynamite charge in a cigarette vending machine in an attempt to protect monies therein and a child was killed as a result of tampering with the machine [*McKinney* v. *Wade*, 220 S.E. 2d 30 (1975)]; when a security guard committed intentional battery on the driver of a car allegedly parked improperly [*Cappo* v. *Vinson Guard Services, Inc.*, 400 So. 2d 1148 (1981)]; and when a third-party male, who had not entered a store, was slain in his car by the cashier's .357 magnum pistol after a teenaged female left the store without paying for two six packs of beer. The first-degree murder conviction of the cashier was affirmed in *State* v. *Wall*, 286 S.E. 2d 69 (1982).

> In the *Cappo* case, excessive force can be seen where the eventual plaintiff and three companions entered a restaurant parking lot that was for patrons only. A guard informed the plaintiff that if he was not patronizing the restaurant, he would have to park elsewhere. The plaintiff, who had been drinking, said it was his intention, along with his friends', to go to a nearby nightclub and told the guard he knew the owner of the restaurant, who had given his permission to park in the lot.
>
> Abusive language and threats ensued until the restaurant manager was notified and came out to settle the dispute. The manager tried to learn what the difficulties were so that he could resolve them. The plaintiff, in explaining the situation, called the guard an "old bastard." The guard then struck the plaintiff, causing him to fall to the ground and injure a bone in his left wrist.
>
> The trial court found that there was no question of liability, holding that abusive language was no excuse for the tortious conduct (intentional battery). The appellate court concurred, noting that "verbal provocation cannot excuse the commission of a battery upon a person." Also, because the guard was attempting to enforce parking regulations, the blow—al-

though probably sparked by personal insult—never became separate from the guard's employment. The plaintiff was awarded $7,500.

DEPRIVATION OF RIGHTS

Occasionally, the deprivation of a person's civil rights is caused by security employees. If the security employee is found to be acting under color of law (state authority), two federal statutes might come into play. Title 42, U.S. Code, Section 1983, provides for civil actions in federal court for the redress of grievances for the deprivation of rights. Title 18, U.S. Code, Section 242, provides for criminal penalties for rights' deprivation. The essence of these statutes deals with the misuse of power made possible only because the wrongdoer is clothed with the authority of state law. Sworn law enforcement officers are subject to these laws. Private security employees and private citizens may be subject to them if they are found to be acting under color of law or acting at the behest of or in concert with the police. Some examples are:

Under the first statute, a company detective was found to be acting under the color of law when he made an arrest by virtue of the authority given under the state Professional Thieves Act [*DeCarlo* v. *Joseph Horne and Co.*, 251 F. Supp. 935 (1966)], and a security guard was found to have acted under the color of law, as the state Private Detective and Private Security Agency's Act, combined with the statutory grant of police authority to approved security guards, reached the necessary degree of state control [*Thompson* v. *McCoy*, 425 F. Supp. 407 (1976)].

Under the second statute, it was determined that a private person could be convicted of conspiring to deprive a victim of civil rights if there were collaboration with police [*U.S.* v. *Lester*, 363 F. 2d 68 (1966)].

SHOPLIFTING

Shoplifting is nothing more than a specific type of larceny or theft and, because of the enormity of losses in this area, most states have enacted particularized shoplifting or retail theft laws. In addition, most states have "merchant's privilege" laws, which allow the merchant or his employee or agent a specific and limited ability to question, detain, or identify the shoplifter. These laws may give the merchant a rebuttable presumption (defense in a lawsuit) of such larceny or attempt if the merchant had reasonable grounds to believe the crime took place. Areas of concern to the security manager in these cases are: sufficiency of probable cause; degree of force used to detain; length and conditions of detention; depth of search after detention; and violation of store procedures by the employee.

PRETEXTS

The use of pretext interviews by security employees is risky, should not be tolerated, and may violate the security code of ethics, state and federal criminal and administrative laws, and a person's right to privacy. The utilization of this investigative technique deals with misrepresentation of identity, purpose, and whose interest is involved. The recipient of the pretext call or interview may be placed in a position of being unable to control the disclosure of the recipient's information. If security employees misrepresent themselves as city, state, or federal officials, they subject themselves to charges of criminal impersonation. The employee and/or employer also may become a defendant in an invasion of privacy lawsuit.[15] If you are licensed by the state, it is possible to have your license suspended for acts of dishonesty and fraud.[16]

POLYGRAPH

The polygraph, or lie detector, which records physiological changes in respiration, blood pressure, and galvanic skin response, has long been used as an investigative tool. The inadmissibility of the results of the test (as interpreted by the operator) in criminal cases to determine the guilt or innocence of the defendant was announced in 1923.[17] Some states have allowed its use through stipulations, or agreements, by both parties to the case. One state supreme court recently concluded in a twenty-six page opinion that although the act of polygraphy has advanced and does have a degree of validity and reliability, this did not persuade the court to permit unconditional admission of it as evidence.[18]

Many states prohibit or limit the use of the polygraph as a condition of obtaining or maintaining employment.[19] Should the use of the polygraph be allowed in a particular jurisdiction, a voluntary and knowing waiver or consent must be obtained from the person taking the test. Duress, force, or coercion in obtaining this consent will negate it.[20] As for polygraph use, approximately one-third of the states restrict or prohibit the use of it, one-third have standards for the operator, and one-third have no laws concerning its use.[21]

---

[15]Robert R. Belair, "Watch What You Say in an Interview," *Security World,* October 1981, p. 30.

[16]*Taylor* v. *Bureau of Private Investigators and Adjusters,* 275 P. 2d 579 (1954).

[17]*Frye* v. *U.S.,* 293 F. 1013 (1923).

[18]*State* v. *Dean,* 307 N.W. 2d 628 (1981).

[19]Inbau, Aspen, and Spiotto, *Protective Security Law,* p. 115.

[20]*Polsky* v. *Radio Shack,* 666 F. 2d 824 (1981).

[21]Bilek, Klotter, and Federal, *Legal Aspects of Private Security,* p. 37.

DUTY TO SAFEGUARD

A duty to safeguard occupants or visitors rests on owners or operators of certain properties, especially where habitation occurs. "Premises owners are increasingly being held liable for injuries intentionally inflicted by third parties unrelated to the victim or the premises owner."[22] This doctrine operates mainly in hotels, motels, and apartment houses because a special relationship exists, but it is extending to other areas. While a landlord is not always an insurer of his tenants' safety, suits may be brought if the terms of a contract were breached, if a statute were violated, or if negligence occurred. A landlord who has prior knowledge may have a duty to avoid the foreseeable risk of harm by providing adequate security because of a high and rising incidence of crime,[23] by repairing broken lighting,[24] or by providing adequate locks on doors.[25] This theory has been extended in some instances to parking lots in retail establishments.

Allegations in these suits have included that the owner failed to provide protection and security, that the location was in a high-crime area, that the institution provided less security than other similar institutions, that guards were negligent in allowing a dangerous condition to develop, and that similar crimes occurred on or near the location. Thus, the security manager should be continually alert to conditions on and around the premises under his or her care and maintain adequate security so as to prevent occurrences and suits of this type.

ALARMS AND ALARM COMPANIES

An alarm is designed to sense and detect a change in conditions and report this change. A timely and adequate response is necessary for this system to work. A security manager will, sometime during his or her career, deal with alarm companies. There may be a provision in the contract that the alarm company is not an insurer and that the liability of the alarm company is limited to a very small amount ($50 to $250) in the event that the alarm malfunctions. This may not sit well at corporate headquarters after a large burglary has occurred in which no one was notified and there was no response. These limitation clauses have been upheld,[26] absent other factors, so the security manager should

---

[22]Janet L. Brown and Delia A. Doyle, "Growing Liability for Premises Owners,'" *American Bar Association Journal,* March 1986, p. 64.

[23]*Kline* v. *1500 Massachusetts Avenue Apartment Corp.,* 439 F. 2d 497 (1970).

[24]*Kwaithowski* v. *Superior Trading Co.,* 176 Cal. Rptr. 494 (1981).

[25]*Garzilli* v. *Howard Johnson's Motor Lodges, Inc.,* 419 F. Supp. p. 1210. (1976).

[26]*General Bargain Center* v. *American Alarm Co., Inc.,* 430 N.E. 2d 407 (1982).

consider either trying to have the clause deleted or getting adequate insurance coverage. The alarm contract may contain a performance[27] or fitness warranty, and the security manager should be fully cognizant of what is represented. A telephone company may have no liability regarding the nonfunctioning of an alarm if the plaintiff's wires were disconnected by a burglar.[28] As for making alarm recommendations and response, police may have no general public duty to prevent harm to a store owner's property.[29]

An alarm company may be negligent by turning down an alarm's sensitivity level to a point where it will not detect entry,[30] by leaving a key to an ultrasonic system where an unauthorized person could get it and deactivate the system,[31] and by failing to employ a trustworthy and responsible person.[32] A misrepresentation by an alarm company may support a judgment against it.[33] In addition, one should not forget to check for false alarm ordinances that impose administrative fines.

> In the *Randall* v. *AFA* case, a jeweler entered into a written lease with an alarm dealer who agreed to install and maintain in the jewelry store an ultrasonic sound wave burglary system. This alarm system was designed to detect any motion inside the store and relay a signal to a central station, which would call the police. Over a six-month period, the system triggered many false alarms when the store was closed. The alarm company adjusted the system so that the false alarms ceased. An employee of the alarm company later inspected the system in response to the jeweler's complaint that the system was not working properly. Subsequently, the store was burglarized. After the burglary, an employee of the alarm company came to repair the system and, upon inspection, told the jeweler that the reason the alarm system did not pick anybody up was because it was turned down all the way. The jury found that the alarm company's negligence was the proximate cause in failing to detect the burglary and awarded the jeweler damages in the amount of $14,330.

Another alarm case follows:

> In *Pope* v. *Rollins*, a widow, age 60, who lived alone leased an alarm system that consisted of a master control unit, numerous battery-powered wireless transmitters, an outdoor siren, and a panic button to carry in her

---

[27] *Rinehart* v. *Sonitrol of Dallas, Inc.*, 620 S.W. 2d 660 (1981).

[28] *J. Meyer & Co., Inc.* v. *Illinois Bell Telephone Company*, 409 N.E. 407 (1982).

[29] *DeHoney* v. *Hernandez*, 595 P. 2d 159 (1979).

[30] *Douglas W. Randall, Inc.* v. *AFA Protective Systems, Inc.*, 516 F. Supp. 1122 (1981).

[31] *Central Alarm of Tucson* v. *Ganem*, 567 P. 2d 1203 (1977).

[32] *McGuire* v. *Arizona Protection Agency*, 609 P. 2d 1080 (1980).

[33] *Pope* v. *Rollins Protective Services Co.*, 703 F. 2d 197 (1983).

hand or purse. Three alarms were to be activated, namely: a high-pitched tone to be heard inside the house, a loud outdoor siren, and notification to the central station, which was to notify the city police and a neighborhood police service. She was told that the average police response time was three to five minutes and was assured that if the wires were cut, all the alarms would go off. Actually, if the wires were cut, the alarm would not go off. Also, there was evidence that the alarm company knew the burglars in the area were knowledgeable about this deficiency. The central station was, in reality, an answering service with no special access to the police and would not even notify the alarm company of an alarm call.

Upon returning to her home one night, she discovered cut wires. She ran screaming from the house and pushed her panic button. The siren, however, did not go off. Two burglars chased her, returned her to the house, threw her on the floor and held a gun to her head for twenty minutes while other burglars searched the house. The burglars rifled her purse and took her watch, a bracelet from her wrist, a pin from her scarf, and her wedding ring. A burglar ran his hands around her throat. A neighbor heard her screams and called the local police service. A security officer came to the home, made a cursory inspection of the premises, but did not find any evidence of the burglary. By the time he returned to the station, the prerecorded telephone message had been delivered because the burglars failed to cut this set of wires. The security officer then returned to the premises and found the victim.

The jury found that the alarm company had misrepresented the characteristics of the alarm system by stating that the system would provide safety and security from intrusion into her home, that the city police would be dispatched within three to five minutes (average response time was, in fact, twenty-six minutes), and that the outside siren would sound even if the wires from the master control unit to the siren were cut. The jury found that the alarm company caused confusion regarding the telephonic feature of the system, that it had been grossly negligent in the design and installation of the system, that it failed to warn the victim that burglars could disarm the system, and that it leased her a defective system. The jury awarded her $15,250 for loss of property, $150,000 for past and future mental anguish (mandatorily trebled under the Deceptive Trade Practices Act), and $150,000 in punitive damages.

DAMAGES

The object of a civil lawsuit pertaining to matters discussed in this chapter is for the person or corporation to recover damages. Damages are a monetary compensation recoverable by the plaintiff who has suffered some type of loss, injury, or detriment to his person, property, or rights through the unlawful act, omission, or negligence of the other party.[34] There are basically two types of damages: actual, or real, which

---

[34]*Black's Law Dictionary*, p. 351.

make good for or replace the real loss or injury; and punitive, or exemplary, which are over and above actual damages. Punitive damages result where the wrong was aggravated by malice, fraud, or violence or was wanton or wicked.

One example of actual damages is the case of a female employee versus the director of security, in which the woman sued for defamation and infliction of emotional distress [*Hall* v. *May Department Stores Co.*, 637 P. 2d 126 (1982)]. An example of actual and punitive damages occurred when a guard pulled a customer's colostomy bag, which was under the customer's shirt, resulting in prolapse of portions of the colon, which required eventual surgery [*Canty* v. *Wackenhut Corp.*, 311 So. 2d 808 (1975)].

> In the latter case, the customer had gone into a discount store to purchase a few items. At this time, because of surgery, he had a colostomy bag protruding from his body, and to cover this bag, he wore his shirt outside his pants. The man paid for his purchases and started toward the front door. He was stopped by a security guard who demanded to see what the man was carrying under his shirt. The man attempted to explain it was a colostomy bag. The guard, who failed to understand due to an inability to understand English, reached under the shirt, grabbed the bag, and pulled on it until it practically ripped off. This resulted in a prolapse of a portion of the colon protruding from the skin. Surgery was necessary to remove that portion of the man's colon. The jury returned a verdict of $50,000 for compensatory or actual damages and $180,000 for punitive damages, which was upheld by an appellate court. Punitive damages were left to the discretion of the jury and were dependent on the circumstances of the case, as well as on the demonstrated degree of malice, wantonness, oppression, or outrage found by them.

EDUCATION

The authors highly recommend that managerial security practitioners take courses in business law, which most colleges offer, and in private security law, which more and more institutions of higher learning are now offering. The objective of the security manager is to prevent losses. This is not particularly hard to do, provided he has an awareness of the problem areas and provides appropriate training and instruction to employees. To avoid a lawsuit for defamation of character, employees should be trained not to raise their voices so that third parties are able to listen to the conversation. To avoid a lawsuit for the intentional tort of battery, employees must be taught not to touch or impede the progress of people, no matter what the verbal provocation. If liability is to be limited in misdeeds by contract guards, management should relinquish control over them and have a hold harmless clause (see Chapter 13,

Control of Contract Security Services) in the guard contract. To avoid a potential problem of excessive force with weapons, employees should not be permitted to carry firearms.

The intelligent corporate security manager would be wise to keep abreast of legal developments affecting his or her operation. Subscribing to publications such as *Security and Special Police Update* by Americans for Effective Law Enforcement, Inc., 5519 N. Cumberland Ave., Chicago, IL 60656, and *Verdicts & Settlements* by Litigation Research Group, 651 Brannan Street, San Francisco, CA 94107, would be helpful in this area.

This chapter is not an all-encompassing view of all the laws and cases as they relate to the field of private security. This is a vast area covering federal and state constitutional, criminal, civil, and administrative laws, together with local ordinances. This chapter merely looks at some problem areas and hopefully provokes the reader to undertake further inquiry. The materials cited in this chapter are instructional and illustrative and are not to be relied on in all jurisdictions or situations. They are simply educational tools, and the security manager always should check with appropriate counsel concerning legal problems.

Chapter 11

Protecting Corporate Information

Today's corporate security director must contend with a shift from an industrial society, where the strategic resource was capital, to an information society, where the strategic resource is information.[1] New communications technology, coupled with satellites, has globalized the instantaneous distribution of information throughout our planet. John Naisbitt, in his prescient *Megatrends,* quotes Peter Drucker as saying that "the productivity of knowledge has already become the key to productivity, competitive strength, and economic achievement. Knowledge has already become the primary industry, the industry that supplies the economy the essential and central resources of production."[2] It is a rare company that does not have information of value,[3] and its loss may damage a business because of the costs to develop, process, and communicate this business information.[4] Company information is a valuable asset, and it should be valued and protected by its producers, handlers, and users, which is reflected in the fact that today many large companies have information management vice presidents or directors.

INDUSTRIAL ESPIONAGE

Industrial espionage is big business and costs U.S. corporations billions of dollars every year.[5] All businesses and industries are open to industrial espionage, and there are predictions that every large company will have

[1]John Naisbitt, *Megatrends,* p. 11.

[2]Ibid., p. 17.

[3]Brian Hollstein, "Keeping the Lid on New Ideas," *Security Management,* April 1984, p. 22.

[4]James A. Schweitzer, *Managing Information Security: A Program for the Electronic Information Age* (Stoneham, MA: Butterworths, 1982), p. 5.

[5]Robert W. Stewart and Michael A. Hiltzik, "Industrial Espionage Is Big Business," *The Best of Business,* Fall 1982, p. 96.

an industrial espionage department, which might be disguised as "market research" or "competitive intelligence."[6] Special schools to learn state-of-the-art industrial espionage have been set up for this "profession."[7] Domestic corporations in the United States specialize in finding and analyzing company and competitor information. They will conduct in-depth company studies; file for information under the Freedom of Information Act; conduct patent retrieval and certification, legislative and regulatory research, and government contract research; retrieve documents; conduct literature research; and make market studies. In addition, they will sell books with titles such as *How to Find Information About Companies: The Corporate Intelligence Source Book* and *Finding Company Intelligence.*

The types of corporate information that might require protection include the following:

Basic manufacturing data and processes
Design manuals
Plant operating instructions
Sample manuals, training manuals
Plant test results
Raw material specifications
Analyses
Technical report of experiments
Reports of production
Process evaluations
Engineering drawings
Flow charts
Production and process research
Research notebooks and techniques
Quality-control charts
Market analysis data
Cost, accounting, and pricing data
Profit margins
Distribution techniques

---

[6]Peter A. Heims, "Unethical, But Legal: Industrial Espionage Is Healthy in the UK (and Europe)," *Security Management*, November 1981, p. 10.

[7]Herchell Britton, "US Technological Superiority Is Threatened," *Security Management*, November 1981, p. 15.

Market strategies and sales
Customer, mailing, and discount lists
Budget forecasts
General know-how
Formulas
Plant capacity
Bid information
Cost-reduction methods.[8]

To have an effective corporate information security program, it is essential to have the backing of top corporate management. If top management gives only lip service to these vital security needs, even "the most aggressive asset protection plan is just so much wasted time and effort."[9] Having the crucial and necessary support of top management will allow the corporate security director to apply the traditional management cycle as it pertains to security of information.[10] The management cycle is outlined below:

I. *Planning the Security*
   A. Responsibility for security planning should be assigned to strategically and highly placed management-level personnel. Administrative responsibilities should be assigned to a security official who is in a position to avoid interdepartmental conflicts, and ultimate information security responsibilities should be assigned to line managers.
   B. The information security policy should be designed so as to provide guidelines and standards, and this should be in writing.
   C. An assessment and risk analysis of the company's most critical information assets should be made. Information can be obtained from members of top company management who are in a position to identify what deficiencies in information security would cause the greatest harm to the corporation.
II. *Implementing Security*
   A. Contingency plans should be made for all major destructive or irregular events due to loss of information so that restoration of business can be completed as quickly as possible. It is nec-

---

[8]Richard S. Post and Arthur A. Kingsbury, *Security Administration*, p. 577.

[9]Frank T. Roedell, "Selective Protection," *Security Management*, March 1982, p. 17.

[10]David A. Haeckel and Bruce B. Johnson, "Complete the Cycle of Information Security Planning: Information Must Be Viewed as a Management Concern," *Security Management*, May 1984, p. 54.

essary to prioritize and address responses to the most critical needs of the corporation first.

B. Periodic security surveys should be made to identify potential problem areas.

C. Security standards and controls should be developed.

D. Security can be enhanced by upgrading existing systems or installing new systems according to the standards set, and this should be done on a timely basis within the targeted dates and also within the confines of the budget.

E. Responsibility for ongoing security administration should be assigned so that current situations are monitored and evaluated to the extent that they affect company progress. Written procedures and reporting requirements would help in this aspect of the program.

F. Periodic security awareness training programs should be made available to corporate employees.

III. *Reporting*

A. Timely and comprehensive reporting of violations should be made to the responsible security official, who will then be able to follow up and enforce the standards.

B. Inasmuch as security violations may affect the entire business, management must be kept informed about these violations through progress and summary reports.

IV. *Evaluations*

A. Ongoing evaluations will be helpful in analyzing the progress made in protecting information and enabling the corporation to change allocation of its resources to accomplish the most cost-effective results. Budget, personnel, or devices may be increased or reduced in support of this program depending on the evaluation.

B. Regularly scheduled reevaluations of the program should be made, keeping in mind the changing business climate and new technologies.

A corporate security director should be aware of the fact that he or she, as business manager, may be personally liable for the protection of company assets, which include all vital company information, and that the penalties could include fines and/or imprisonment.[11] This liability may stem from violating the Foreign Corrupt Practices Act, and failure to utilize available cost-effective security methods to protect

[11]"Managers Are Liable for Information Protection," *Security World*, September 1984, p. 52.

computer information may in certain cases give rise to management liability should an adverse consequence occur.[12]

COPYRIGHTS AND PATENTS

There are several legal ways in which a person or corporation can protect information. The first is by utilizing copyright laws, which give the holder an exclusive privilege of printing, copying, selling, and publishing the copyrighted property. This is for a limited period of twenty-eight years, but an extension can be obtained. Copyright applies to literary property and artistic productions, including things such as music, choreography, drama, art, pantomime, sculpture, sound, pictorials, books, periodicals, lectures, and maps. It does not apply to ideas, procedures, processes, systems, concepts, principles, discoveries, or methods of operation.

Another way to protect information is by obtaining a patent, which is a grant of privilege or authority by the government and gives the holder a monopoly for the limited period of seventeen years. Patent searches are expensive, and the process of obtaining one takes a considerable amount of time, usually two to five years. A patent gives the holder an exclusive right to control the manufacture, use, and sales of the patented product. Patents relate to new ideas, discoveries, and principles such as machines, products, substances, methods, and improvements.

TRADE SECRETS

A third way of legally protecting information, which is becoming more popular, is through the use of trade secrets. Trade secrets are economically valuable to the holder, but they are equally valuable to competitors. To determine whether a trade secret exists, the corporate security director should work with department or program managers and the corporate patent attorney or legal staff because the director of security is not in a position to know all the trade secrets of a corporation.[13]

A trade secret may consist of any formula, pattern, device, process, or combination of information that is used in one's business and that

[12]Robert F. Johnson, "Judging Your Computer Liability," *Security Management,* August 1982, p. 25.

[13]William C. Dunlop, "Safeguarding Trade Secrets: One Company's Guide to Protecting Proprietary Information," *Security Management,* July 1982, p. 44.

gives that business an opportunity to obtain an advantage over competitors who do not know or use it. While there is no precise definition, some examples of trade secrets include confidential business information, technological know-how, intellectual property, recipes, techniques, methods, data, programs, customer lists, supplier lists, business forecasts, price lists, marketing surveys, advertising campaigns, and company strategies. It is a corporate intangible and a silent asset.

There are a number of reasons why people want to obtain business information. Today, information is a key corporate resource, and knowledge is a critical asset. Research has become more costly, and with the technology explosion, competition between corporations has become tougher. A company's very survival may depend on the information it has. There is more employee mobility today, more hiring of corporate employees by competitors, and a decline in corporate loyalty. There is also a decline in business ethics and widespread narcotics abuse, especially in high-tech companies. Corporations may be reluctant to litigate trade secret matters because litigation is expensive; they fear retaliatory lawsuits; in some instances, proof is difficult; the trade secret may be forced to be disclosed in court; and last but not least, relief may be inadequate.

Some of the objectives of trade secret law are that it encourages and rewards the independent innovator. It also prompts exploitation of the invention, fosters competition, promotes the sharing of knowledge and the efficient operation of industry, and gives the public the use of a valuable invention. Another objective of trade secret law is to maintain commercial morality and ethics.

While there may be no such exact thing as trade secret law, it is a combination of the law of torts, property, contracts, and equity as applied to a trade secret. In some instances, these branches of law may be separate, while in others they may be interdependent.

Some phrases used regarding the theft of multimillion-dollar trade secret know-how packages include unjust enrichment, misappropriation, inequitable or unauthorized use, discovery by improper means, disclosure or use without privilege, theft, bribery, stealth, deception, misrepresentation, and concealment.

Justice Oliver Wendell Holmes, Jr., in the 1917 case of *Dupont* v. *Masland*[14] stated that the starting point in trade secret law begins with confidential relationships. These relationships are those of the discloser (the corporation) and the disclosee (the employee). A reciprocal duty of trust and obligation between the two is created and requires good faith, especially by those entrusted with the confidence or trade secret. This obligation of good faith can be imposed by contract requirements. It

[14]244 U.S. 100 (1917).

should be noted that a trade secret is not a monopoly right and that the secret can be developed independently by fair and legitimate means, if there is no breach of confidence, through an honest discovery or reverse engineering. Congress has been silent about trade secrets, and state laws prevail.

Nine factors must be considered in recognizing a trade secret:

1. Has the secret been disclosed in a patent?
2. What is the extent of the information pertaining to the trade secret that is known outside the business?
3. To what extent has the secret been sought by lawful means through independent invention, research and development, honest discovery, and reverse engineering?
4. To what extent has the corporation taken security measures to guard the secret?
5. What is the value of the trade secret information?
6. How much effort has the corporation expended in developing this information?
7. How much knowledge concerning the secret did employees bring to the company?
8. How much knowledge concerning the secret did employees learn at the corporation?
9. What makes the secret unique?

Litigation is expensive and will come after the secret has been taken, so the best trial tactic is to avoid any litigation. This can be done to a great extent by utilizing preventive law through a paper trail of acknowledgments and documents and by having a careful, comprehensive corporate security program.

A defendant in a trade secret case (or the one who has taken and is utilizing the secret) will try to prove that the corporation had no security program or that the device was obtained through reverse engineering of the marketed product or by some other honest method. The plaintiff, or corporation, in a trade secret case must prove secrecy through the number of safeguarding methods it employed. The burden of proof is on the owner, who should document a systematic and comprehensive security plan to protect the secret. This, in effect, is an insurance policy in the event of litigation and will increase the corporation's chances of favorably resolving a lawsuit.

LEGAL COUNTERMEASURES

There are nine areas that a corporation may wish to consider as legal countermeasures to forestall loss in the trade secret area. Remember that legal relief may be unavailable if adequate security precautions have not been taken. Therefore, a comprehensive security program is essential.

1. *Physical Security.* A corporation may wish to fence the perimeter of its premises, monitor access, and restrict entry of persons to the property. Utilization of intruder alarms, closed-circuit television, and guards also are recommended. Hiding secret data from view and excluding group or visitor tours from secret areas are essential. Visitor control can be enhanced by utilizing a sign-in and sign-out log, which will show the name, address, and affiliation of the visitor, the person the visitor wishes to see, the reason for the visit, and the date and times in and out. This log information eventually could become evidence to establish a person's access to corporate secrets.

2. *Employee Knowledge.* Employees may need only fragmentary knowledge of a corporate secret, and information should be given only on a need-to-know basis. Dissemination of corporate reports can be restricted to those needing to know. Code symbols can be used in corporate papers, and identity of certain materials can be concealed through the use of coded containers. Portions of the corporate secret can be worked on at different locations by different employees. True parameters on instruments can be masked out and replaced with arbitrary indicia.

3. *Marking and Controlling Corporate Documents.* Responsibility should be assigned so that appropriate documents will be marked with an appropriate company legend indicating the document's confidentiality. The confidentiality of these documents should be reassessed from time to time. These documents should not be left unattended in open view on the plant floor or in trash cans. They should be locked up when not in use. A "clean desk" policy should prevail when the employees using the documents are absent. Confidential documents should be placed in opaque envelopes for transmission. Confidential documents and multiple copies thereof should be charged out, numbered, and recorded in a logbook. When there is no more need for the information, all materials connected with the document, such as carbon paper, typewriter ribbons, computer printouts, tapes, and disks, should be disposed of through some thoroughly destructive method such as shredding, mutilating, crushing, pulverizing, pulping, melting, incinerating, or chemically decomposing.

There are times when documents must be given to outsiders in the form of advertising, sales brochures, trade show handouts, press releases, trade journal articles, maintenance and training manuals, and speeches and reports. These should be screened by a knowledgeable company employee to make sure that trade secret information is not contained therein. At times, customers, vendors, consultants, or others may need specific corporate information, and it may be necessary to censor out as much information as possible. Also, after these other parties have accomplished their purpose, the documents should be retrieved and destroyed.

4. *Level of Security Necessary.* If the corporation takes no security precautions, there may be no protection for its secrets in a court of law. The corporation need not require absolute secrecy, have an impenetrable fortress, or take heroic measures to accomplish this purpose. A corporation must make reasonable efforts to protect a secret and must have a substantial element of secrecy so that it would be difficult for a third party to acquire the secret without resorting to some improper means.

5. *Inadequate Security.* Courts have held that there has been inadequate corporate security where visitors were not screened or restricted access; where the manufacturing process was routinely shown to suppliers, customers, and visitors; and where there has been an absence of locked fences, watchmen, restrictive signs, management information about the confidentiality of the material. Other examples of inadequate security are the practice of leaving documents laying around on the plant floor and in trash containers and free entry to the corporate facility. In one instance, a defense counsel entered the corporate property and took photographs of the premises.

6. *Confidentiality Obligations.* These obligations can be oral, but it is preferable to have them in writing and acknowledged by the employee, vendor, consultant, or other person having access to the information. It puts these people on notice, will help the corporation obtain legal relief, and will be an acknowledgment that would undermine the defense in a trade secret case. These documents should be short and understandable, and they should complement other security measures. They are documentation for court cases and insurance for maintaining or prevailing in a lawsuit. Examples of some of these documents are:

a. Agreements regarding confidential or proprietary information and inventions;
b. Confidentiality and nondisclosure agreements for current employees and current independent contractors;
c. Confidentiality and nondisclosure agreements for new employees and new independent contractors;
d. Confidentiality and nondisclosure agreements for visitors;
e. Letters detailing company policy regarding outside submission of ideas and suggestions;
f. Letters regarding disclosure to customers or prospective customers.[15]

---

[15]"Forms: A Paper Trail for Trade Secrets," *Security World,* August 1984, p. 85.

7. *A Corporate Climate of Confidentiality.* It is encumbent upon the corporation to make employees aware of the confidentiality involved in their work. This may be accomplished by indoctrinating new employees and by utilizing posters or house journals. Also, managers and supervisors should periodically remind employees of the confidentiality involved.

8. *Employee Debriefing or Exit Procedure.* When an employee leaves, company materials should be recovered and the employee reminded of his or her continuing obligation of confidentiality concerning trade secrets. A memorandum of interview with the terminated employee should record that this has been done. This should be followed up with a letter to the departing employee and, if the employee's new employment can be ascertained, a letter can be sent to the new employer pointing out the ex-employee's obligations. A signed statement should be obtained from the departing employee stating that company material has been returned and acknowledging the ex-employee's obligation of continuing confidentiality.

9. *Disclosure to Outsiders.* Certain corporate information must be given to people such as vendors, customers, contractors and subcontractors, licensees, franchisees, consultants, and business negotiators. Written commitments should be obtained from these people concerning the confidentiality of the information they are handling. These should obligate the recipient to return company documents and property promptly after they have been used.

Remember that a corporation that fails to monitor and enforce a comprehensive and systematic security program undermines its ability to prove in court that adequate precautions were taken.[16]

Some corporations seek criminal prosecution for the theft of trade secrets. This may present certain risks to the corporation to the extent that a public prosecutor and not the corporate legal staff will control the case. Some federal statutes that have been used are the National Stolen Property Act, Title 18, U.S. Code, Section 2314; Mail Fraud, Title 18, U.S. Code, Section 1341; Wire Fraud, Title 18, U.S. Code, Section 2511; and Conspiracy, Title 18, U.S. Code, Section 371.[17] Trade secrets have been found in federal courts to be goods, and their value can be established by expert testimony. The majority of the states have no special legislation to safeguard trade secrets, and general theft, larceny, embezzlement, or misappropriation statutes may be used. It may be

---

[16]Norman M. Spain, "Keep Secrets on the Q.T.," *Security Management,* July 1982, p. 49.

[17]Norman M. Spain, "Prosecution Options for Trade Secret Thefts," *Security Management,* September 1983, p. 59.

advantageous and necessary to hold explanatory trade secret seminars for appropriate law enforcement and prosecutorial officials.[18] This will create interest in the public sector, generate support for these officials, and assist them in any subsequent investigation and prosecution.

Insurance may be obtained for valuable documents such as maps, leases, mortgages, deeds, trust agreements, formulas, drawings, films, and corporate books and records.[19] This insurance will protect the owner against direct physical loss, and bonding may be obtained for dishonest acts of employees. The corporate security director in his or her efforts to reduce, eliminate, or transfer the risk of misappropriation of trade secret information should work with corporate or retained counsel to ensure that these secrets are properly guarded and to increase the chances of favorable resolution of any legal problems.

It is apparent that information is now the key resource of our business society and that it becomes more valuable each day. With this increasing value, the inclination and motivation for some persons to take that information correspondingly expands. The escape of this valuable and critical information can be instantaneous due to the ever-increasing speed of transmission and, because of satellite assistance, global distances are meaningless. Therefore, it is more vital than ever to ensure that proprietary information is appropriately safeguarded.

---

[18]"Do's and Don't's of Keeping Secrets," *Security World,* August 1983, p. 16.

[19]Cynthia Gale, "Insuring Valuable Documents," *Security Management,* August 1981, p. 113.

Chapter 12

Managing the Security Function of a Labor-Organized Company

Many things tend to frustrate the security director of a major corporation in the implementation of his security program. He often is faced with a shortage of funds, indifference on the part of top management, lack of cooperation from rank-and-file employees and supervisors, and incompetence within his own department. All of these, however, tend to pale when compared with the aggravation that results from attempting his security program in the face of opposition from organized labor. This is a factor that, if not handled properly, will plague the security director day after day and week after week. The modern-day security chief must develop the necessary skills to cope with organized labor and to make sure that his program can be successful even in the face of the union's opposition. Only by completely understanding the nature of the union and its strengths and weaknesses can a security director hope to achieve this goal.

HISTORY OF LABOR UNIONS

Although there are some instances of trade unions being in existence prior to the turn of the century, the real movement of modern-day unionism came about after World War I and began in the automobile and steelmaking industries. In many instances, working conditions were poor, hours long, and wages very low. The workers tended to band together for the purpose of collective bargaining with their employers to improve their lot. Many employers attempted to resist the formation of unions within their companies and resorted to labor spying through the use of undercover agents who were instructed to infiltrate the work force, attend union meetings, and report back to management on labor strategies that were being formulated. To utilize this information, many employers then resorted to physical force through their security departments or through the use of hired goons who were brought in to suppress picketing and other union activities.

As a result of all this strife, the U.S. government in 1935 passed the first of a number of significant labor laws. It was termed the National Labor Relations Act or the Wagner Act. This law, among other things, recognized the employees' right to collective bargaining, outlawed labor spying, and provided for the formation of the National Labor Relations Board (NLRB). The purpose of the NLRB ostensibly was to promote labor harmony by acting as a policing organization between management and labor. Many decisions emanating from the NLRB were inclined to be prolabor and antimanagement and, in fact, the NLRB over the years came to be recognized as prolabor at the expense of the employer. This probably came about because members of the NLRB were appointed to their posts by politicians who were indebted to organized labor for their elective successes. For this reason, many decisions of the NLRB, which would otherwise be looked upon as labor law, have been appealed into the federal court system by various corporations with some notable success.

PRESENT-DAY REALITIES

For the past fifteen years, the membership in national labor organizations has been declining. No longer are workers easily swayed by union rhetoric and arguments that may have seemed persuasive in the thirties and forties. Understandably, this trend has been accompanied by a more enlightened approach on the part of management, which has learned the art of keeping the workplace union-free by giving the workers the same type of forum for their grievances that they would get with unions and also by paying higher wages, giving good fringe benefit packages, and offering improved working conditions.

In spite of declining union membership and more and more decertifications of unions, the union remains a formidable force with which the security director must deal, especially in certain types of industries. This holds true for workers in heavy industry such as autoworkers, steelworkers, miners, and longshoremen. The most notable successes of antiunionism have been in lighter industry with smaller companies. In the smaller companies management is able to gain the confidence of the work force more easily.

Assuming that the security director is faced with dealing with an employee union, there are a number of things with which he must become familiar. It goes without saying that the security chief should master the intricacies of the collective bargaining contract with his company. He also must realize that a number of factors covered under labor law are not necessarily part of a collective bargaining agreement. The first of these is changes in working conditions. No longer is an employer able to change unilaterally the working conditions of the plant even though a particular change may not be covered by a labor contract. It is well established in labor law that any changes in working conditions are subject to collective bargaining. This does not mean that the union must agree to such changes, but that any such change must first be a matter for discussion with the union.

Likewise, the security director must understand a concept known as past practices. Even though a situation is not covered in a labor agreement, if the past operating practice of the company or a particular plant location is a certain standard, then this practice is held to be the same as if it were in the written agreement. Any attempt to make a change in working conditions that have been established, or can be established, as a past practice will result in failure by the employer.

Another area in which the security director must become proficient is documenting disciplinary actions against union members and applying the concept of progressive discipline. There are only a limited number of offenses for which discharge from employment can be imposed in most labor situations. The whole concept of discharge is considered to be capital punishment within the employment setting, and therefore enlightened companies and security directors must be prepared for the imposition of progressive discipline, which over a period of time, leads to discharge. For example, theft, insubordination, fighting, sabotage, and drugs in the workplace generally are considered to be capital offenses in the employment setting. Gambling, on the other hand, is not necessarily a capital offense and must be dealt with through the use of progressive discipline.

Progressive discipline could easily be a written warning on the first offense, a three-day suspension for a second and repeat offense and discharge for a third repetition of the same offense. Of course, to make progressive discipline hold up, the administrator of the contract, whether he be the personnel director or security director, must be able to document prior offenses and disciplinary actions. This must be done in writing and be kept in the employee's personnel file.

One other fact that seems worthy of mention under the heading of present-day realities is that the Taft-Hartley Act (passed in 1947 and amended in 1959) ruled that guard forces cannot belong to the same union as organized the plant in question. There were exceptions made in this ruling for those guard forces that were already members of the same plant union as the employees, but from that time forward, the same union could not attempt organization of a guard force. In many corporate security setups today, we find that the uniformed guard force is unionized—whether it be a contract guard force or an in-house guard force. Seldom, however, have there been any documented instances of the remainder of the security department being unionized. With a guard force organized by a labor union, however, the security director may very well become the first-line administrator of a collective bargaining agreement in his day-to-day supervision and management of that guard force. For further information on day-to-day dealings with unions, refer to an excellent article titled "An Organized Response to Union Activity."[1]

THE UNION AS A POLITICAL ENTITY

If a security chief can come to accept the fact that unions are political in nature and that virtually everything they do can find some connection in the political approach to problem solving, then the director is at least halfway on the road to understanding and dealing fully with labor unions.

The entire union hierarchy is built on the elective process. On the lowest level of the plant itself, the union representative is the shop steward. The shop steward may be a representative of the workers in a particular department or, in a small plant, the workers plantwide. Alternatively, he may be a chief steward for a larger plant, with ordinary shop stewards administering problems on the departmental level.

The security director usually encounters most of his problems with the shop steward. Some shop stewards are entirely unreasonable and are considered thorns in the side of management. The job does not transform people into malcontents or troublemakers upon taking office, but rather this comes about because of the general apathy of the work force, which generally allows a misfit or troublemaker to run for office and to become the shop steward. Most employees are inclined not to attend union meetings or even to vote in the electoral process beyond the election of a shop steward. This allows antagonistic personalities to rise to these posts and is probably the reason for many of the problems that exist between management and labor.

Above the shop steward is the business agent of the local, and this too is an elected position. Here again, most workers seldom vote in these elections and as a result the business agents often are elected by the small militant element of the work force. These jobs are almost always paid positions, and the business agent may very well service a multitude of company contracts under his jurisdiction. Often, however, one will

---

[1]Daniel R. Miller, "An Organized Response to Union Activity," *Security Management*, April 1984, p. 30.

find that the president of a particular local, who also is elected, is in fact an employee of the company, and this then is not a paid union position.

It is in the imposition of security controls that the security director often runs headlong into opposition generated by the shop steward. Many shop stewards have become adept at minimizing their productivity on behalf of the company by enlarging the apparent scope of their union-related activities. Where this situation exists, management is in a constant squabble with shop stewards over grievances or other complaints that may arise.

In the imposition of security controls, many shop stewards feel that they must automatically oppose such controls on behalf of their constituency, even though labor law clearly states that these controls generally are under the purview of management and management alone. Unfortunately, most shop stewards are unschooled in the art of labor contract administration on a day-to-day basis, and thus arise many of the problems in labor-management relations. Oftentimes, some of this opposition can be erased through the intervention of the business agent, but here again, one must remember that he too has a constituency he does not wish to alienate.

Under the heading of investigations, where the possibility of job loss or paying the supreme penalty is a distinct possibility, the security director can expect the stiffest of opposition. Unless investigations are carefully planned, with an element of surprise, they can degenerate into a disaster for the company. Shop stewards and even business agents have been known to step into the center of an internal investigation and advise employees of their so-called rights. These generally include admonitions such as "Don't admit anything and don't sign anything" and "Don't take a polygraph test and refuse to consent to a search of your home." Once this happens, the investigation is at an end for all intents and purposes. No longer can employees be interrogated with the expectation of obtaining an admission of wrongdoing.

Being the political entity that a union is, it is not uncommon for the union to take extra legal measures to thwart or retaliate against management. Unions have been known to call for illegal strikes in violation of a labor contract as a result of internal corporate investigations. Advice to the workers such as "Hit the bricks" is, of course, illegal, and the illegality will be upheld by the courts. The unions know this but realize that it may take the company two or three days to obtain a court order forcing them back to work, and in the meantime they have made their point by punishing the company. Many labor directors of corporations have attempted to get around this possibility by insisting on tough no-strike clauses in labor agreements that provide for quick arbitration and monetary damages for the company in the event of such a strike.

Last, but not least, the security director must become familiar with and skilled in the process of labor arbitrations. A labor arbitration is very similar to a bench trial in front of a judge. It is inclined to be somewhat more informal, however, and the role of the arbitrator generally is designed to get at the truth of the matter. As a result, many labor arbitrators, even though they may be attorneys or retired judges, will allow evidence to be presented that would otherwise be excluded in a courtroom.

One thing about labor arbitrations is that they are always final in nature. Unless the company can show that the labor arbitrator exceeded his authority under the contract, there is absolutely no appeal from a labor arbitration into the courts. For this reason, the security director must become skilled so that he can win security cases that ultimately go to labor arbitration.

Generally, confessions will be attacked by the union attorney, who acts as a defense lawyer in such a proceeding, and he also will try to suppress other forms of evidence. The process of examination, cross-examination, and rebuttal is much the same as in a bench trial. The company's side of the case is very often presented by a labor lawyer who specializes in corporate labor matters, and if it is a security discharge case, then his role becomes very similar to that of a prosecuting attorney. His skill in handling the company's side of the case may well determine the outcome of the arbitration.

Many arbitrations are lost by companies through faulty preparation and presentation at the arbitration itself. Students also should realize the method of selecting arbitrators, which usually is spelled out in the labor contract. The least desirable method is to have the contract call for the appointment of an arbitrator from a panel selected by a state mediation and conciliation service. Most of the arbitrators on these state panels are labor-oriented, and the company would be well advised to steer clear of this type of agreement. The ideal agreement would be to have the contract call for the submission of a list of names by the American Arbitration Association, and then each side—management and union—will alternately strike names that are not acceptable to them until one name remains. This person would then become the arbitrator.

A situation that most security directors face sooner or later is a strike or the threat of a strike. Not to be prepared for such an eventuality is to demonstrate gross neglect in essential planning. Every security director should have a strike readiness plan or at least a commercially prepared document such as the *Strike Preparation Manual.*[2] One major company's guidelines are reproduced in Appendix 7.

---

[2]The *Strike Preparation Manual* is produced by the American Society for Personnel Administration, 30 Park Drive, Berea, OH 44017.

Labor relations is a very complex procedure that cannot be dealt with adequately within the confines of this text. For this reason the security chief is urged to become better educated with a broader understanding of the modern-day labor union through other educational sources. Doing so will ensure a minimum of problems in the administration of his department.

Chapter 13

Control of Contract Security Services

Over the years, many companies phased out in-house guard forces in favor of contract security officers. This has resulted in a prolific growth of the security guard industry. Although the operation of the guard force may now be delegated to an outside company, many of the headaches still remain for the local security chief. No longer is he faced with the mundane problems of recruitment, retention, equipment, training, and scheduling. Now he is faced with periodic monitoring of the outside agency forces to ensure that they comply with standards that have been previously set up for the guard operation.

DEALING WITH OUTSIDE VENDORS

When outside vendors are brought into a corporation, wages and insurance coverage probably are the first considerations. Control of the vendors necessitates steps such as indemnity and hold harmless agreements, polygraph testing of guards, audit rights clauses in guard contracts, and specific training of security guard personnel. In an attempt to ensure that agency guards perform up to corporate desires, many companies have set down standards that they make known to security agencies before the bidding on a particular job commences. Adjustment of compensation allows the client to reduce payment to the agency should it not meet these standards.

Wage Rates versus Agency Rates

The old adage "you get what you pay for" has never held more true than with security agencies. If a security chief wishes to employ a higher caliber of security officer, he must be willing to pay what could be described as premium rates to the agency rather than the prevailing rates that apply for the community. Following through with this concept, the security chief must ensure that this premium rate is shared with the security guards in the form of a higher wage rate. Also, the security chief must provide for periodic wage increases, in advance, if higher caliber personnel are to be retained. This area must be monitored constantly by the security chief, as it has been found that some unscrupulous agencies will withhold scheduled wage increases to the men while at the same time increasing their rate to the client.

Insurance Coverage

Before entering into any agreement with an outside security agency, the security official would be wise to consult the risk or insurance manager of the corporation to determine what types of insurance coverage should be required of the security agency. Many security agencies are underfinanced and carry little or no insurance, which could easily be to the detriment of the corporate client. To give the reader an idea of what may be required from the insurance department, we are reproducing the insurance requirements of a major corporation in dealing with outside security agencies.

> Contractor shall purchase and maintain such insurance as will protect it from claims under Workers' Compensation Acts and other employee benefit Acts, from claims for damages because of bodily injury including death and from claims for damages to property which may arise out of or result from Contractor's operations under this contract whether such operations be by Contractor or anyone directly or indirectly employed by Contractor. This insurance shall be written for not less than any limits of liability specified as part of this contract or required by law, whichever is the greater. Certificates of such insurance shall be filed with the Client and shall bear an endorsement naming the Client as an additional insured.
>
> Contractor shall maintain comprehensive general public liability insurance covering the legal liability of Client and Contractor against claims for personal injury, death or property damage occurring on, in or about the premises and property specified in this contract in the minimum amounts of $250,000 for each claim with respect to any one person, $1,500,000 with respect to any one occurrence and $250,000 for all claims for property damage with respect to any one occurrence. Such coverage shall include but not be limited to false arrest, detention or imprisonment, libel, slander, defamation of character or violation of right of privacy. Certificates of such insurance shall be filed with the Client and shall bear an endorsement naming the Client as an additional insured.
>
> Contractor shall maintain employee dishonesty insurance in a minimum amount of $100,000. A certificate of such insurance shall be filed with the Client and shall bear an endorsement naming the Client as an additional insured.

Contractor shall maintain comprehensive automobile liability insurance affording coverage for vehicle owned and/or leased by Contractor with the following limits:

Bodily injury—$250,000 per person and $500,000 per occurrence;
Property damage—$250,000 per occurrence.

Certificates of such insurance shall be filed with the Client and shall bear an endorsement naming the Client as an additional insured.

In addition to the foregoing insurance coverage, Contractor will carry $5,000,000 excess combined single limit insurance and will file with Client a Certificate of Insurance carrying an endorsement naming Client as an additional insured.

Indemnity and Hold Harmless

The corporate client must endeavor to protect itself from the wrongful acts of an employee of the security agency. This need has given rise to the indemnity and hold harmless agreement. Again, we reproduce such an agreement in use by a major corporation. We particularly call the reader's attention to the wording of the second paragraph, which attempts to give some protection to the corporate client against lawsuits brought by employees of the security agency:

> The Contractor shall indemnify and save harmless Client from and against any and all losses or damages which Client may sustain by reason of damage to property or injury to or death of any person or for losses or damages suffered or sustained by Client for false arrest, false imprisonment, malicious prosecution, libel or slander, by the willfull act, commission or omission of the Contractor or any of its employees other than resulting from negligence on the part of Client or any of its employees or agents.
>
> Contractor agrees that it and its agents or employees will cooperate with Client in any and all investigations and/or other matters involving or affecting the security of the premises named herein and agrees to indemnify and hold Client harmless for any and all claims arising out of such investigation provided such claims are solely attributable to the acts, commissions or omissions of Contractor's agents or employees and including but not limited to such claims as may be brought by Contractor's agents or employees against Client.
>
> Client agrees to give timely notice to the Contractor of any and all claims made upon Client in connection with any of the aforesaid stating the nature of the claims, the amount claimed, the name of the party making the claim and such other information as shall be relevant to the evaluation of the validity of any such claim and further agrees to permit the Contractor, if it so desires, to participate in the negotiation of any settlement thereof or in the defense of any legal or administrative action brought in connection therewith. The Contractor shall not indemnify Client against

losses or damage resulting from the settlement of any claims without prior written consent of the Contractor.

Contractor agrees to indemnify and hold Client harmless from and against all losses to Client's property or claims for personal injury or wrongful death to Client's employees or third parties arising out of the illegal act(s) of Contractor's agents or employees, whether such agents or employees are acting alone or in concert with others.

Polygraphing of Guards

Many corporations today spend tens of thousands of dollars each year in an effort to screen applicants for security-sensitive and executive jobs. This effort may take the form of security interviews, polygraph examinations, written honesty tests, background investigations, and reference checking. Without question, such companies are concerned about the protection of their assets, both human and material. Because of this great effort, we often find the paradox that at five o'clock, when the plant closes and everyone goes home, the security and well-being of the company's assets are turned over to a security guard who is only vaguely known to management and whose background may not even begin to approach even the most rudimentary security standards the company has set down for its own employees.

Security history is replete with instances of dishonesty on the part of the guard force—sometimes in collusion with the plant's own employees but more often with no involvement in theft other than by the guards themselves.

The authors feel very strongly that any guard assigned to a client's premises should have the most thorough screening possible. It goes without saying that the strongest approach in this direction would be through a polygraph examination. Even in some of the states where restrictive laws apply to polygraphing, these can be legally and successfully circumvented, as the guards generally are not employees of the company and are only being assigned to the client's premises by the agency. In other words, the client should take the position that if a guard wishes to work at his place of business and receive the benefits of premium pay and superior working conditions, then he must be willing to undergo a polygraph examination. For the benefit of the reader, the following language is suggested as a part of any proposed guard contract:

Polygraphing of Guards: The Contractor agrees to polygraph all personnel assigned to Client and furnish a written copy of such polygraph examination to Client's security department. If, in the judgment of the Client, the quality of the pre-employment polygraph examination of prospective guards who will be assigned to Client's property is not adequate, the Client reserves the right to administer such pre-employment tests utilizing his own polygraph personnel.

For Restricted States (another option): The Contractor agrees to screen by polygraph examination all personnel assigned to Client. A copy of written report of such examination to be furnished to Client. In the event any personnel declines to take such polygraph examination, that person will be administered a Reid Report by the Client. Results of such report will then become the determining factor for security clearance to Client's premises. If, in the judgment of the Client, the quality of the pre-employment polygraph examination of prospective guards who will be assigned to the Client's property is not adequate, the Client reserves the right to administer such pre-employment tests, utilizing his own polygraph personnel.

Audit Rights

Corporate security departments should insist on an audit rights clause in any guard contract entered into by operating personnel at a particular location. The reasons for this are obvious when one realizes that unscrupulous agencies have been known to withhold pay raises from guard personnel while passing an increased rate along to the client, and also that a local dishonest executive of the client might enter into a collusive scheme with the agency to arrange for a personal kickback on guard charges. Again, some suggested language is presented for the reader's benefit:

> The payment by Client of invoices submitted by Contractor shall be without prejudice to the Client's right to an examination of Contractor's books and records of services performed under this contract in order to verify charges made by Contractor to the Client. At its option, Client may at any reasonable time upon three days prior notice to Contractor during the term of this contract or within one year after the termination of this contract cause a complete audit to be made of Contractor's records relating to services provided to Client under this contract. Such an audit shall be at the sole expense of Client.

Guard Standards and Training

Security chiefs also should ensure that standards set forth for bidding purposes include minimum requirements for the guards themselves. These would take in items such as literacy, ability to write reports, lack of a criminal record, acceptable credit history, physical and mental condition with no serious impairments, and successful screening by either polygraph or written honesty test.

Security agencies should be put on notice beforehand that training will be required of all security guard personnel in fire prevention and reporting. This would mean the recognition and reporting of obvious fire and safety hazards. Security officers also should be trained in fighting fires, at least in their incipient stages. They should know and understand the workings of sprinkler systems and how to control these systems in the event of failure of a sprinkler head. They should be schooled in the apprehension and detention of personnel. If firearms are required for a particular security officer job, then the security chief must ensure that adequate training on a regularly scheduled basis be given to the guards. This insistence can be made upon the agency, but in the case of in-house guards, it becomes incumbent upon the corporate security staff to arrange for and provide such training.

Along with the above mentioned detention, guards should be well schooled in search-and-seizure procedures. On many occasions, the guard is faced with an act of theft on the part of an employee after hours when no members of management are around. He must be able to respond in a predetermined manner to preserve, at least, the corpus delecti so that security officials can take further action the next day. In this regard, the following material has been extracted, with permission, from a corporate guard manual on what to do if the guard encounters an attempted theft during his tour of duty.

DISCOVERY OF CACHES OF CONTRABAND:

In the course of routine duties, it is possible that the security guard may discover caches of contraband such as drugs, alcohol, gambling paraphernalia, stolen merchandise, weapons, etc. In such cases, where no employee is directly involved with the contraband, *NO SEIZURE* is to be made by the security guard. Instead, a full written report is to be made of the location and the contents. The guard should make every effort to not alert any suspects that such a discovery has been made. Use an Incident Report Form.

THEFT & THEFT PREVENTION:

A. Employees Discovered Stealing:
   1. If you should see an employee leaving the building with unauthorized company property:
      a) If possible, prevent the goods from leaving the property, by making a seizure, but do not restrain the employee. Ask the employee to remain on a voluntary basis.
      b) Notify your supervisor immediately.
      c) Place the stolen goods in front of you and secure as much of the following information as possible (to be written up on an Incident Report Form):

1. Time
2. Date
3. Location
4. Offender's Name
5. Department
6. Supervisor
7. Clock No.
8. Shift
9. Date of Birth

Secure the offender's home phone number, present address and a physical description giving height, weight, color of eyes, hair, etc., if possible.

d) When the security supervisor arrives, the information on your report is to be handed over to him.
NOTICE: The guard shall not interrogate nor take statements from the offender. No threats or promises are to be made. The employee shall not be questioned extensively by the guard regarding the theft, as that may hinder further investigation by Corporate Security.

B. Employees Suspected of Dishonesty.
1. If you should *suspect* that an employee has committed a dishonest act, or evidence has shown that a dishonest act has occurred:
   a) Be very careful not to alert the employee to your suspicion.
   b) Consult with your supervisor.
   c) Record the incident on an Incident Report Form.
   d) Never speak of security instances openly, inform your supervisor and the security person relieving you only.

Last, but not least, training requirements should include schooling on personal appearance, conduct, and general deportment. Even if all the above are in place, if a security officer's attitude toward employees and members of management is surly and undiplomatic, this becomes a reflection on the whole security organization, even up to the level of corporate security.

Adjustment of Compensation

As an administrative tool, the adjustment of compensation section of a guard contract allows the client to reduce amounts of payment to the agency for its failure to meet certain obligations that have been spelled out previously. The section should set out acts or omissions that would cause this clause to be activated and also should state a maximum sum that the agency may be penalized whether it be by the day or by the incident. As an example, the reader is referred to the sample contract in Appendix 8 and, in particular, to that section titled "Adjustment of

Compensation." A review of the provisions of this section will quickly show that this is where the "teeth" are in the contract and in its enforcement by the client.

INVESTIGATIVE COMPANIES

One of the most common things a security administrator may encounter in working with an investigative company is the need for a letter of authorization. Oftentimes, this will be requested by an outside agency that is about to undertake an investigation on behalf of the corporation. This letter is necessary so that an outside agency may gain access to certain information that is not in the possession of the corporation. It more or less opens the door for the agency in dealing with third parties and other companies and goes a long way toward giving the agency the same mantle of authority that might be possessed by an employee investigator working directly for the corporate security office.

In writing such a letter, the director of security must be sure to include the general scope of the investigation and a realistic time limit for the authorization. Not to do these things and, in effect, give carte blanche to an outside agency could turn into a disaster for the company.

Other Safeguards

As with security guard companies, a prudent security director will insist on similar insurance coverage from the agency, along with an indemnity and hold harmless agreement. Although polygraphing is not necessarily practical for each and every operative of the agency who may be assigned to do a limited amount of work on a particular investigation, polygraphing is an absolute must for any undercover agents who may be assigned to the client's place of business. As with security guards, not to polygraph or otherwise screen (by a written honesty test) undercover agents is to invite an unpleasant security incident.

Directing the Investigation

As with the letter of authorization, the security director should exercise some control over the investigation itself. Not to do so simply means that the investigative company may step into areas that could prove uncomfortable or even embarrassing to the corporation. Regardless of the skill and talents of the agency's director of investigations, there is no way that that person can know the personality of the corporation, which investigative steps will be readily accepted, and which steps will not. This is the function of the security director who, hopefully, will have investigative talent of his own and can direct the agency personnel to his satisfaction. Many agencies advertise investigative services, but in reality do so only as a client convenience. They are experts in the security guard business but have limited or no talent in the investigative business. For this reason, the security director of the corporation must be able to choose the right agency to do an investigative assignment for him.

POLYGRAPH EXAMINERS

Recognizing the controversial nature of a pre-employment polygraph program, the authors feel that it is necessary to comment on such programs and, in so doing, perhaps strip away some of the mystique of such a venture.

Potential Problems

Many companies have attempted broad pre-employment polygraph programs. Some of these programs have met with failure and have been abandoned, while others have met with outstanding success. One large multibillion dollar corporation has had a successful nationwide polygraph screening program in effect since 1954. This is an example of what can be done if the problem is approached correctly.

In examining the failures of such polygraph programs, it becomes evident that some of the reasons can be enumerated as follows:

1. Examiner, acting on his own, asks improper and non-job-related questions.
2. Client pressures examiner to ask improper and non-job-related questions.
3. Examiner is undiplomatic and handles client's personnel poorly.
4. Examiner and/or client have set unrealistic minimum standards of behavior for acceptance of applicants.
5. Misuse of polygraph information by client results after receiving same from examiner.
6. Poor or nonexistent quality control exists over examiner's work. (A few examiners are able to operate successfully without the need for quality control. The majority, as in any profession, need a more experienced hand overseeing the results of their work.) In a few agencies, this quality control is present, and in some cases qualified

examiners on the client's own staff may provide quality control over the work of outside examiners. Whatever the case, quality control is essential to a sound, long-term polygraph program.

7. Disputes often can occur between the polygraph examiner and the personnel department of the company, which occasionally feels that polygraph is an intrusion into their sphere of responsibility. When such ill feelings persist on the part of an internal department of a corporation, they become an irritant that sooner or later will force the abolishment of such a program.

Validity of Specific and Pre-employment Tests

Much has been written about the validity of Specific polygraph examinations. Detractors of the polygraph technique grudgingly admit that in some cases the polygraph is approximately 75 percent accurate. They temper this statement with the caution that in order for the polygraph to produce, there must be a fear of detection on the part of the subject. Although the authors recognize that the fear of detection is important to polygraph technique, they maintain that this is not necessary to achieve a 75 percent validity rating. Beginning polygraph students practicing on volunteers and using hypothetical situations regularly can achieve a validity of 75 percent. With the fear of detection thrown in and also the fact that the situation at hand is not hypothetical but a real-life situation, there is no reason why an experienced polygraphist cannot achieve a success rate of 90 to 95 percent.

There have been many scientific studies concerning the validity and reliability of polygraph examinations, but unfortunately, these have all been directed toward Specific testing. The Specific test, under structured conditions, can be verified and thus a statistic established. With pre-employment testing, however, this is much more difficult, and few validity studies have ever been accomplished. The body of knowledge that does exist in this area is empirical at best, and even within the polygraph industry itself, there is a wide divergence of opinion about the scientific validity of a pre-employment test.

Pre-employment testing involves a wide multiplicity of issues and because of this, the usual control or "known-lie" questions that one sees on a Specific test, have a questionable usefulness in this situation. The senior author, with solid professional polygraphic credentials, is more inclined to think of pre-employment tests as a probing interview aided by the polygraph technique. The purpose of the interview is to search for sensitive areas that must then be explored through normal interviewing techniques. Because of lack of control questions on the typical pre-employment test, the examiner normally cannot conclude that deception is present.

He can, however, conclude that unresolved areas of concern exist, which must be explained by the examinee. Such explanations can then be verified by a polygraphic technique known as a clearing test. If no explanations are forthcoming, the unresolved response is left hanging, and no verification is ever possible. This is why validity studies are virtually impossible for pre-employment testing.

In actual commercial practice, however, the polygraphist is, in reality, a personnel specialist who utilizes a scientific instrument to aid him in his interviewing techniques. Experience has shown that most such specialists have a "batting average" showing that of the total number of applicant rejections, four out of five are rejected because of their own admissions. Only one out of five will be found to be rejected solely by unresolved responses.

From a statistical standpoint, the one person out of five who is rejected by polygraph screening cannot be confirmed as deceptive or proven to be the victim of a mistake on the part of the examiner. Companies must then decide for themselves whether this one rejection by instrument, as opposed to admissions, is an acceptable level for job denial. In the meantime, polygraphists continue to serve industry in an ever-increasing volume. They perform a service that has proven its ability to upgrade the workforce and substantially reduce internal theft.

Chapter 14

Security and Outside Relations

Corporate security departments have a variety of relationships with sources outside the company. We have discussed some of these in previous chapters and present a few more here.

OUTSIDE SERVICES TO OTHER CORPORATIONS

In recent years, it has not been unusual to find one corporate security department rendering aid to another. Usually requests for assistance or aid have come about because of close friendships developed between security directors who may, at one time, have worked for the same company or perhaps have developed a close relationship through professional societies such as the ASIS. Aid of this type usually is requested and rendered with the understanding that it will be reciprocated, when appropriate, in the future.

Requests for mutual assistance usually come as a result of a job that must be completed in a remote location that is not convenient for the security department of the requesting corporation to access. It may very well be convenient for the security department of another corporation to handle the job because of its close proximity to the location. This could take the form of background investigations, interviewing, or surveillance. In the area of surveillance or interviewing and interrogating employees, the corporation doing the work should routinely ask for an indemnity and hold harmless agreement from the corporate security department that has requested the assistance. This is especially important where no profit is involved and it is only a question of rendering assistance on a convenience basis with time and expenses to be reimbursed.

PROPRIETARY VENTURES

A newer development, which may be a logical outgrowth of mutual aid endeavors, is that of the corporate security department offering commercial security services to other corporations. At least one major airline and a large apparel manufacturing company have embarked on this route. An expansion of this type of service would depend, in large part, on the extent of the commitment of the parent corporation to get involved in the private security field. Another restrictive factor could be the difficulty in obtaining licenses in each state in which the security department wished to offer commercial services.

The one danger is the possibility that such a venture would take up more attention than was warranted, with the result that in-house corporate problems might be neglected in favor of assigning security personnel to commercial endeavors that were producing profit. The operative philosophy obviously must be that the parent corporation's security work comes first and that any other effort in the commercial vein is secondary.

It becomes clear, however, that even a moderate effort in this direction could produce sufficient profits to defray the cost of internal security operations. To expand such an operation, advertising and promotional effort obviously is required. The reader also should be cautioned that this type of activity might very well require additional insurance coverage that the corporation may not normally possess. In particular, an errors and omissions coverage would seem to be mandatory if the corporate security department intended to offer its services on a commercial basis. Not to have adequate insurance coverages would mean that the entire parent corporation could be placed in jeopardy in the event of a massive lawsuit along these lines.

An example of a proprietary system offering its capabilities to nearby businesses is a situation in which the proprietary alarm monitoring station of twenty branch banks offered alarm monitoring to nearby businesses that could link up to the banks' system.[1] Doing this helped make the most use of the proprietary monitoring station and helped to defray the costs of the station, thus adding to the bottom line. Another example of creating a profit was where a security department sold shredded paper pulp to a recycler. This paid for the shredding equipment in the first year and generated profits in later years.

Another example of a proprietary security function that provided protection to outside clients was one that started with a residential

---

[1]Kerrigan Lydon, "Editorial," *Security World*, April 1985, p. 9.

community patrol.[2] It should be noted that the guards who were hired to accomplish the residential community patrol were mentally and physically fit; had a high school education, an unblemished police record, and a good driving record; and were licensed by the state. They were given new uniforms, and an in-depth background investigation was conducted on each. They also took a pre-employment polygraph test, received four weeks of an in-house training program before they were sent out on the job, and were under supervised probation for ninety days. This proprietary security function eventually formed a separate company to offer security services to the community. This provided a reduction in cost and an income, and in four years, the commercial end of this operation was supporting about 75 percent of the proprietary security function's operating costs.

Many proprietary corporate security functions have extensive experience and expertise in certain areas. Some of these areas include investigations, polygraph testing, training, alarm monitoring, and surveys. An innovative and imaginative corporate security director can capitalize on this expertise and market it to outside clients. For instance, a security and safety department made a film regarding fire safety training, which was earmarked for twenty-five thousand tenants in the high-rise development of this particular corporation.[3] The cost of producing this film was $56,000. After gaining national attention, copies of the film were sold to other organizations, and the film has been previewed by a national film company for possible distribution.

Turning a profit or helping to defray costs of the security department is a serious consideration. One contract fire department monitored an alarm board twenty-four hours a day. Since the personnel were there anyway, they sold their monitoring services to outside clients and began monitoring all types of alarms, not just fire alarms.[4] The system was designed and customized based on the customer's needs to report specific conditions, which included tracking an intruder through a building. The selling of this monitoring service has helped to reduce overhead and is an asset because the personnel were on twenty-four-hour-a-day duty already.

One corporation involved in the protection of executives in their homes decided to utilize the existing corporate headquarters security system as the central monitoring point rather than using an outside

---

[2] "Propietary Security with Contract Clients: Can It Work?" *Security Management,* April 1985, p. 31.

[3] " 'Firesafe' Gains National Attention," *Security World,* February 1984, p. 11.

[4] "An Alarming Idea," *Security World,* April 1984, p. 12.

central station.[5] In this instance, the corporation utilized existing company personnel at no additional staffing cost. It gave the corporation more control over its protection program, and a study projected a 20 percent cost savings over a fifteen-year period.

There are many things to consider before offering your corporate security expertise to outside clients. In the alarm monitoring situation, some of the factors to consider are:

Communication expenses
Equipment expense
Installation expense
Depreciation
Operating expenses
Staffing
Maintenance
Power supply redundancy
Warranties
Insurance and liability
False alarm fines
Taxes
Underwriters' Laboratories approval
Response posture and attitude.[6]

There are many sources to which you can market your security expertise. Law enforcement executives listed the following as some potential activities for contracting out private security services:

Public parking security
Parking enforcement
Parking lot patrol
School crossing guards
Public parks control
Animal control
Traffic control

---

[5]Alan B. Abramson, P.E., "Executive Security Goes to Work," *Security World,* May 1984, p. 49.

[6]Cherlyn Kirk, "Alarm Monitoring: Propietary versus Contract," *Security World,* June 1985, p. 32.

Noninjury accident investigations
Special events security
City/county code violations
Funeral escorts
Court security
Prisoner transport
Housing project patrol.[7]

One should also remain aware of the efforts at the privatization of government. The federal government, in an effort to cut costs, is reviewing all federal government jobs every five years and encouraging federal agencies to transfer jobs done by civil service employees to the private sector. The question the government asks is whether a particular job can be done for less by a private contractor.

CUSTOMER RELATIONS

The corporate security department can enhance its relationship with its various subsidiaries, franchisees, and customers. If, for example, the parent corporation services a large number of retail outlets, the security department can give these customers something extra. In a retail situation, the corporate security department can assist these retail stores in areas such as antirobbery tactics, employee robbery training, shoplifting, bad checks, and employee theft. It also can give loss prevention seminars and other advice about things such as reducing window signage to provide a clearer view, lowering shelves and displays to a height of 5 feet, and raising sales counter floors 6 inches.

The corporate security department can assist its customers with advice in areas such as personnel interviewing and screening. Should the retailer have any specific security problems, the corporate security office is in a position to give advice. For example, a retail customer may wish to give polygraph tests, where legal. The corporate security director can help the retail customer select a competent, qualified, and professional polygraph examiner for that particular situation.

Making an income or profit for the corporate security department cannot be accomplished by caretaker management. An aggressive, energetic, imaginative, and innovative posture on the part of the corporate

---

[7]William C. Cunningham and Todd H. Taylor, *The Hallcrest Report: Private Security and Police in America* (Portland, OR: Chancellor Press, 1985), p. 185 (hereafter cited as *The Hallcrest Report*).

security director is required. Although all security goals remain the same, each corporate situation may be different depending on the makeup of the community and the corporation's peculiar problems, areas of expertise, and geographic location. Just because security historically has been known as a non-income-producing entity does not mean that it must necessarily, in all instances, remain so today. Capitalizing on income-producing opportunities is the corporate security manager's challenge of the future. And selling security to senior management will be easier if there is income in that future.

Chapter 15

Security in the Future

What lies ahead for private security? While it is often difficult to predict the future, detailed studies and research show trends of growth in many directions. A recent new direction transforming the lives of Americans is the shift from relying on the traditional institutional (government, corporations, and the like) help to the concept of self-help.[1] The growth of crime, the rebellion against higher taxes, and the reduction in police manpower, equipment, and response, have caused, among other things, ". . . an enormous increase in private security police."[2]

THE GROWTH OF PRIVATE SECURITY COMPANIES

In 1982 eleven of the United States' fastest growing private companies in the top 500, and in 1983 nine of the fastest growing companies in the same category, were private security entities.[3] One of these companies grew because it supplied radio telemetry equipment as an alternate to dedicated lines. Another grew because of its ability to supply affordable equipment to the needs of the changing security market. A third fast-growing company supplied wireless communication equipment. Its "public safety officers" (not guards) received 110 hours of prejob training.

As for the growth of the guard service industry, one study shows that in 1963, 23 percent of the protective workers were from contract companies. The study predicted that in 1990, roughly 60 percent of the protective workers would be employed by contract companies.[4] Another study showed that protective services growth in 1979 continued at the rate of 15 percent per year and was predicted to slow down to 10 percent

---

[1]John Naisbitt, *Megatrends*, p. 154.

[2]Ibid.

[3]"The Big Business of Security," *Security World*, January 1984, p. 13.

[4]Robert G. Kingwell, "What Lies Ahead?" *Security Management*, September 1981, p. 19.

per year. In connection with this, guard and investigative service revenues for 1985 were projected at $5.7 billion, an increase of 113 percent over 1978, and were estimated to be $11.6 billion in the 1990s.[5]

The guard service industry will change because of the impact of new technologies and will come to be known as a protective service. More reliance will be placed on computers in the operational and administrative areas, which will aid in planning schedules, guard rosters, costs, payroll, and lists of accounts. This industry will receive more training and higher pay, including fringe benefits and cash incentives, and will see more psychological testing in the selection process. Management will need to be more competent, knowledgeable, and aggressive to survive in this competitive business.

The protective service industry of the future will add to the range of services it now offers and will upgrade its capacity to respond. This protective service aspect will be involved in more services that traditionally have been supplied by the police or fire departments. These include traffic control, accident investigation, funeral escorts, alarm response, and fire-fighting services. The industry will get more business from the U.S. government due to government requirements to contract out its work if certain percentages of money can be saved. The industry will become more decentralized (in keeping with Naisbitt's *Megatrends* predictions), and more control will go to the local management of the protective service industry. The industry will increase its involvement in designing total security plans for specific situations, and there will be an increase in local and state legislation that will affect the security field.

ELECTRONIC CONTROLS

The protective service industry of the future will become equipment-intensive.[6] The biggest problems for security managers, which are common to all, remain employee theft and unauthorized access. Forty percent of the readers surveyed in this study plan to integrate their security functions—such as access control, closed-circuit television (CCTV), and intrusion detection—in the next three years into a single computer-controlled unit. The computer-controlled unit can be integrated into building management functions such as fire detection and energy management, and unit operators also will be able to prioritize alarm signals.

---

[5]Mary Alice Kmet, "Guard Industry Check-Up: Staying Fit in the 1990's," *Security Management*, September 1981, p. 10.

[6]Kerrigan Lydon, "Reader Survey: Trends in Equipment Applications," *Security World*, January 1985, p. 29.

Security professionals want more wireless alarm equipment and sensors.[7] They also want more reliable equipment, more reliable service, and more equipment that has state-of-the-art capability. They would like adaptable and flexible systems so that they can continually upgrade and integrate these systems on a cost-effective basis with other systems already in house. They foresee a trend toward more use of proprietary stations as opposed to central stations or alarm company stations. The sales of security-oriented equipment will see enormous growth.[8] According to Predicasts, Inc., sales of security equipment in 1983 were $2.6 billion. They are anticipated to be $4.4 billion in 1988 and will almost double to $8 billion in 1995.

Because of rapid breakthroughs in the electronics field, more security equipment will be more affordable for those choosing to buy it. In connection with the above study, for an eleven-year period from 1972 to 1983, there was a 52 percent increase in the sales of security equipment in the access control market, a 22 percent increase in sales in the electronic alarm market, and a 23 percent increase in sales in the CCTV market. They predict that while access control equipment was 82 percent of the market in 1972, it will be only 54 percent of the market in 1995. Also, while detection equipment was 17 percent of the market in 1972, it will be 45 percent of the market in 1995, with CCTV dominating the field. As we enter an information society, it is anticipated that there will be a 22 percent increase in sales of data encryption equipment through 1995.

Commercial and financial institutions, which are 40 percent of the market, will continue to be the main purchasers of security equipment. Other large purchasers are the transportation and manufacturing industries. The growth rate of equipment purchases for all four industries will be approximately 10 percent annually through 1995.

Robots

Exciting new technology and the upgrading of in situ equipment will assist the private security industry in accomplishing its task. Today, there are approximately 8,000 robots in industrial use in the United States, and it is predicted that there will be from 80,000 to 100,000 in use by 1990.[9] In that year, our country will produce some 17,000 robots per year. Second-generation robots are now programmed to perform a

---

[7]"Security Equipment: What the Pro's Want," *Security World*, September 1984, p. 40.

[8]"Researchers Predict Market Growth," *Security World*, September 1984, p. 3.

[9]Gordon Williams, "What Will 'Smart' Robots Mean to You?," *Family Week*, 6 January 1985, p. 7.

variety of tasks and to do the dull and hazardous work humans would rather avoid.

Robots are about one-third the price of humans and, in their security application, will be equipped with sensors, which, in effect, makes them nonstationary, or mobile, detectors.[10] Robots will be able to patrol large areas in the dark and report conditions affected by light, sound, motion, or smoke. An advantage of utilizing robots in the security industry is that many of them can be monitored and instructed by one human being manning a central station. As more sophisticated software packages are developed, third-generation robots will become more intelligent and of greater use to the industry.

Identification through Physiology

Biometrics, a fairly recent development in the field of access control, is a statistical study of biological data and uses unique individual physiological characteristics to positively identify people.[11] This is done by recording, recognizing, and comparing the stored patterns of retinal configurations of the eye, fingerprints, and the geometry of one's palm or hand. Research in this area continues to perfect identification by signature manner or dynamics' analysis, voice, facial identification, brain waves, and typing rhythms (which may have special application to computer security). At present, biometrics access controls are expensive and, while they currently supplement other access controls systems, interest in their use will increase as the cost comes down. It is predicted that in two years, the cost of this type of control will be one-half of what it is today.

Verifiable identification is becoming more of a necessity in our world, and hundreds of different applications of this type of access control will evolve as its technology is developed and its cost reduced. Some uses of biometric access control include identification by users of cafeteria systems, automated teller machines, safety deposit box entry, check cashing, and entry to programming rooms in the computer field.

Better Armor

Various materials used in the private security field will become lighter, stronger, easier to apply, more comfortable to use, and less expensive.

---

[10]William Cole Cathey, "The Robots Are Coming!" *Security Management*, September 1983, p. 112.

[11]Michael Thompson, "The Newest Wave: Biometric Security," *Security World*, February 1985, p. 40.

Bullet-resistant materials, for example, can be categorized into three areas: body, vehicle, and window armor.[12] Soft-body armor, which is made of fibers and fabrics, is becoming lighter, stronger, and more comfortable to wear. Because of increasing kidnappings and terrorism, the need for vehicle armor has become more compelling. It, too, has become lighter and stronger through the use of new alloys, plastics, and laminates. Window armor, or antiballistic laminates, is becoming more bullet and bludgeon resistant and can be had in plastic, glass, or acrylic; in some instances, it can be glazed on existing windows. It should be noted that for window armor, there are Underwriters' Laboratories standards.

CCTV Improvements

In the field of CCTV, there will be new features, increased reliability, additional options, less maintenance, and reduced cost.[13] The vacuum tube in the camera is being replaced by more dependable solid-state technology. There will be an increasing use of microwave transmission for video signals. Flat monitoring screens will hang on the walls, and color imagery will be improved. There will be a greater use of CCTV for residential security, such as identifying visitors or watching children play outside. Greater use will be made of tape recording and log capabilities in this field. At present, CCTV is a tool to assess conditions. In the future, however, it will become a part of the intrusion-detection system. Video motion detection will have a vision system that will allow the "smart" CCTV to become a discriminating sensor, which will alert the console operator via annunciator to a change in normal conditions. This will ensure a more reliable and continuous detection capability by decreasing the human error quotient.

More Sophisticated Alarms

The future will see alarms becoming more common, more sensitive, and more sophisticated. State and local governments will revise and expand fire codes, which will be more in keeping with the National Fire Protection Association codes.[14] More cities and towns will pass false alarm ordinances, resulting in administrative fines, and this will help force alarm companies to design better products and users to be more careful.

---

[12] Kerrigan Lydon, "The Bullet-Proof Business," *Security World*, February 1984, p. 55.

[13] "The Growth of New Technologies: CCTV," *Security Management*, January 1982, p. 10.

[14] Larry C. Brown, "What's on the Security Horizon?" *Security Management*, January 1984, p. 49.

There will be a growth in outdoor perimeter protection, which will include fence sensors and seismic detectors. More end users will monitor their own alarms instead of utilizing the services of a central station or alarm company. Proprietary monitoring will grow, as the alarm system will be integrated into a building's system.

Alarm sales in Europe will grow 46.2 percent in the next ten years.[15] The anticipated growth in European alarm sales will be from $437 million in 1982 to $1.09 billion in 1992, due to a rise in crime and insurance contracts that demand security systems. The largest markets for alarm sales will be Germany, Britain, France, Italy, and Spain. In the United States, alarm response will be handled more by private enterprise, due to the increase in false alarm ordinances and the decrease in law enforcement manpower and resources.[16] This confirms a part of the Hallcrest Report,[17] which indicated that law enforcement is receptive to relinquishing its responsibility in certain areas to the private sector.

The future of intrusion detection will depend on the standards set forth by the Department of Defense and the Department of Energy. Protecting nuclear weapons requires extensive use of exterior intrusion-detection devices such as buried cable and triggered fencing systems.[18] Technological advances will increase the reliability of intrusion-detection devices, and there will be an increase in the use of passive infrared detectors, which sense a change in temperature. Passive infrared detectors are easily installed, have a relatively trouble-free performance, and are comparatively cheap. Sales for passive infrared units have doubled since 1982, and these units appear to be replacing ultrasonic and microwave devices. Ultrasonic and microwave detectors, whose beams can penetrate walls, are susceptible to a higher false alarm rate, and sales of these units will decline. There will be limited use of sonic, seismic, and shock sensors used in open areas, on walls, and on roofs.

Computers

The security manager of the future will make more use of microcomputers as managing security functions becomes more and more com-

---

[15]"Security Market Expected to Expand Abroad," *Security World*, May 1983, p. 3.

[16]"Private Patrols Roll into Alarm Service," *Security World*, August 1983, p. 15.

[17]William C. Cunningham and Todd H. Taylor, *The Hallcrest Report*.

[18]"Intrusion Detection: The Future Unfolds," *Security Management*, September 1984, p. 93.

plex.[19] The use of microcomputers will be necessary to achieve greater cost-effectiveness and return on investment because there will be a demand for greater productivity and accountability and because of increasing automation and the spreading out of business. The security department of any given company can make use of specialized applications of the microcomputer to help manage, develop, monitor, and update things such as lists, schedules, manpower allocations, resources, information summaries, activity reports from outlying areas, and inventory controls. The computer also can be used to track alarms, the response time to each alarm, and the cost breakdown of nuisance alarms.

Information is a key resource for any security department, and fast accessibility to information is sometimes of utmost importance. One private investigating firm[20] has massive amounts of information in more than five hundred computer data bases. These records consist of court indices, real estate records, other public records, technical fields, business histories, expert witnesses, and lawsuits. The utilization of a computer in obtaining information of this sort saves time and money.

PRIVATE SECURITY IN POLICE AND CORRECTIONAL FUNCTIONS

The Hallcrest Report has provided interesting information about the future of law enforcement and security.[21] At the present time, private security resources employ approximately 1.1 million people and have an annual budget of roughly $22 billion. Of these people, 449,000 are employed in the proprietary area and 641,000 in the contract realm. Law enforcement's annual budget is approximately $14 billion, which includes local, state, and federal officers, and it employs approximately 580,000 persons.

Increased Role

In 1981, 44 percent of the law enforcement agencies advised that they had the same number or fewer personnel in that year than five years before. Due to budgetary restrictions law enforcement has been forced into narrowing its focus of police service by having to reduce its service

[19]William J. Sako, "Computers and Security: A New Management Language," *Security Management*, September 1984, p. 20.

[20]Thomas J. Serb, "Computerized Investigations," *Security World*, April 1984, p. 42.

[21]William C. Cunningham and Todd Taylor, "A Preview of the Hallcrest Report: Security/Police Relationships," *Security Management*, June 1983, p. 27.

calls, by screening cases, and by spending less money for vehicle replacement, training, overtime, and capital investments. This means that private security will bear more of the crime prevention burden and will accept more responsibility in areas such as burglary alarm response, preliminary investigations, and misdemeanor incidents. Private security also will be more responsible for incidents on privately protected property. As new property areas are developed, the purchaser may have an opportunity to "broker" the purchaser's desired mix of protective services.

Private security officers will receive special police officer status and respond to and resolve more minor criminal incidents. These officers will receive more training and be certified, with private business bearing the expense. Research will be conducted into the different types of non-crime-related workloads of police departments to see which activities can be performed by the private sector. Some potential activities for private security in the future include school crossing guards, animal control, public building security, parking enforcement, parking lot patrol, noninjury accident investigation, traffic control, special events security, court security, prisoner transportation, and funeral escorts.

Incarceration is a growth industry in the United States. The privatization of the correction function will continue and increase as private enterprise takes over more of the financing, building, and operating of prisons. Private enterprise can do it on a more cost-effective basis. Private enterprise now owns or operates twenty-four major correctional facilities, and this growth is expected to continue.[22]

Impact of Illegal Drugs and Terrorism

The drug trade in the United States is an $80 billion a year business, and the use of drugs by employees is affecting the United States' ability to compete in the marketplace. An incredibly high percentage of white- and blue-collar workers admit to using drugs while on the job. The global drug trade continues and will increase due to the lure of the fabulous wealth involved, which has its concomitant corruption. Drug export crops are measured in tons, and this activity threatens the security of some countries. In 1984 seven of thirteen major drug-producing nations boosted their output of marijuana, coca, and poppy crops.

A problem of the future is "designer drugs,"[23] which are cheap,

---

[22]Martin Tolchin, "As Privately Owned Prisons Increase, So Do Their Critics," *New York Times*, 11 February 1985, p. A-1.

[23]Arthur Brown, "Synthetic Heroin, Real Threat," (New York) *Daily News*, 17 March 1985, p. 4.

easy to produce, easy to market, hard to detect, and three thousand times more powerful than heroin. Synthetic or designer drugs are produced in laboratories and are legal because they are not on the list of controlled items as promulgated by the Drug Enforcement Agency. Simply by making some small change in the molecular structure of a drug, criminal chemists avoid running afoul of current scheduled drug laws.

There will be an increase in drug screening for prospective employees. IBM Corporation, for example, screens prospective employees to make sure there is a safe and productive working environment. The Federal Aviation Administration has recommended that regular drug screening be given for air traffic controllers and others in safety-related jobs. Private industry has gone a long way toward implementing employee assistance programs for problems such as alcoholism. The private sector will need to learn more about drug abuse and develop programs for dealing with this insidious modern problem.

The corporate security manager will need to guard against terrorism, both domestic and foreign, as this form of political expression is expected to continue and worsen.[24] Risks International estimates that in the next ten years, one-third of all terrorist operations will affect business and that the trend of targeting U.S. firms will continue.[25]

Government Boost

Private security will get more business from the U.S. government, which wishes to transfer many programs to private enterprise.[26] The government has identified some eleven thousand commercial activities, including fire and protective services, that can be performed by private contractors. In 1985 some ten thousand security guards were under contract with the government's General Services Administration (GSA). These guards were supplied by 235 guard contractors on a nationwide basis. The GSA soon will require that these guards pass a certification test developed by the Government Federal Protective Service, which is the law enforcement arm of the GSA.[27]

The future of private security is exciting. As overburdened taxpayers pressure state and local governments to cut costs, private se-

---

[24]Alvin H. Buckelew, "The Reality of Terrorism in the U.S.," *Security Management*, February 1984, p. 42.

[25]Wayne Siatt and Sally Matteson, *Trends in Security*, p. 34.

[26]Martin Tolchin, "U.S. Pressing Plan to Contract Work," *New York Times*, 11 February 1985, p. 1.

[27]"Certification Set for GSA Guards," *Security World*, February 1985, p. 14.

curity will encroach even further on what historically has been government's exclusive domain. The increased scope of the types of tasks to be performed, the availability and affordability of sophisticated equipment, and challenges not yet known today will cause this industry to explode in size. The security practitioner will have to become more professional as the demands of his chosen career dictate more education and constant monitoring of the latest changes and trends. Private security is only now growing out of its infancy. The next few decades will see it mature into an exacting, diverse, necessary, and highly profitable industry.

FINANCING OF EDUCATION

Numerous colleges, universities, professional associations, and businesses offer various forms of continuing security education through seminars, lectures, conferences, and workshops. These cover virtually all aspects relating to the private security industry and range in time from several hours to a week. Some are very expensive and are located out of town, but if you keep your ear tuned to local events, you will find that more and more lectures and seminars are being conducted locally and for a reasonable fee.

In attempting to finance the receipt of some of these educational opportunities, you should not forget that there are numerous co-op programs available in which industry finances a student's education and the student is able to have a work experience for that instruction. Hundreds of colleges and universities participate in co-op programs. For instance, Northern Arizona University and the Honeywell Process Management Systems Division have a co-op program that takes students off the campus and puts them to work at Honeywell's plant in Phoenix.[28] The students receive five months of in-depth, hands-on security experience while earning a salary and college credit.

Another method of financing your education is by receiving tuition refunds from either the corporation or government body employing you. A third method is scholarships. The number of scholarships that pertain to private security has increased in the past few years. The ASIS Foundation awards annual scholarships to college or university students and also to graduate students. More and more during the past few years, local ASIS chapters have awarded thousands of dollars in scholarships to worthy or needy students.

---

[28]"Training Ground For Security Directors," *Security Management*, May 1982, p. 58.

BROADENING THE HORIZONS

Any professional worth his salt must stay up to date in the changes and trends in the dynamic private security industry. The authors strongly suggest that some or all of the following be accomplished:

1. Join and become active in a professional association such as the ASIS. You will learn a lot and develop valuable contacts.
2. Subscribe to various professional magazines and journals, such as the following:

   Security Management
   1655 North Fort Myer Drive
   Suite 1200
   Arlington, VA 22209

   Security World
   1350 East Touhy Avenue
   Des Plaines, IL 60018

   Journal of Security Administration
   London House Press
   1550 Northwest Highway
   Park Ridge, IL 60068

   The Protection of Assets Manual
   The Merritt Company
   1661 Ninth Street
   Santa Monica, CA 90406

3. Answer some security advertisements and request information. This will put you on mailing lists, and in a short time, you will be inundated with mail pertaining to all sorts of security products. This will give you the opportunity to keep abreast of current trends and state-of-the-art products.
4. It is recommended that those security professionals who have not completed their college education return to college and earn their degree.[29]
5. Read, read, read, and read more! There are plenty of books on the market that discuss in detail whatever your individual security problems are. While they may not solve a particular problem in all cases, they will give you a sense of direction and will be a guide to acceptable industry standards.

---

[29]Charles A. Sennewald, *Effective Security Management,* p. 257.

Before enrolling in any seminar or college or university course, obtain information about the course. Determine not only the expense and course duration but, more importantly, the identity and reputation of the instructors, the text and/or other materials used, a syllabus of the course content, what handouts will be issued, and what type of credit you will receive (continuing education units or college credits). It has been the unfortunate experience of the authors that some seminars are either a complete squandering of valuable time, redundant in nature, or able to be mastered on your own without wasting your time and the corporation's money.

It is believed that the most effective approach to a college or university education in the loss prevention area would be a multidisciplinary or scholarly approach, which should be the core concept for the development of degree programs in this area.[30] In 1976, the Task Force on Private Security noted that there was no curriculum model available for baccalaureate and graduate degree programs, and they suggested the following:

A. *Model for Baccalaureate*
   Ten per cent of courses in sociology and psychology.
   Ten per cent of courses in law enforcement/criminal justice.
   Twenty per cent of courses in security administration.
   Twenty per cent of courses in business administration.
   Forty per cent of courses in general education.

B. *Model for Masters*
   Twenty per cent of courses in sociology and psychology.
   Forty per cent of courses in security administration.
   Forty per cent of courses in business administration.[31]

For the convenience of the reader, three different curricula appear in Appendixes 9–11, which will assist you in measuring and comparing different curricula and course contents, not only in the event that you wish to take courses, but also as a gauge for detailed comparison if the security director is sending his or her employee to school. It also will be helpful to review the content of the appendixes when reviewing the educational backgrounds of new or potential employees. Note that the programs may differ so as to meet local needs.

With the rapid changes taking place in the security profession, academic training in the future will be more widely available, and

---

[30]Michael J. Palmiotto, "Who Teaches Private Security: Staffing for a New Discipline," *Journal of Security Administration*, June 1981, p. 61.

[31]*Private Security: Report of the Task Force on Private Security* (Washington, DC: National Advisory Committee on Criminal Justice Standards and Goals, 1976), p. 274.

security will become a more popular course of study.[32] Further information about what colleges and universities are offering in academic programs may be obtained from the American Society for Industrial Security, 1655 North Fort Meyer Drive, Suite 1200, Arlington, VA 22209. Ask for the booklet titled *Career Opportunities in Security and Loss Prevention.*

---

[32]David L. Berger, *Industrial Security* (Los Angeles, CA: Security World Publishing Co., 1979), p. 334.

Appendix 1

Job Descriptions

STAFF INVESTIGATOR

(Entry-Level Position)

1. Must be able to work undercover in the company's various locations. This work might consist of almost any job in the building, for instance, janitor, shelver, order filler, receiving clerk, shipping clerk, or sales clerk. If not already an actor, a staff investigator must learn to be one so as to portray a thief, in order to gain the confidence of other thieves. Investigator must be able to mix freely with other employees and on their own level. Where drinking groups are found to exist during lunch, or after working hours, investigator is expected to participate. Where gambling is found to exist, investigator is expected to participate and gather physical evidence of such whenever possible.
2. Investigator should have the basic ability to operate openly as an investigator and conduct necessary inquiries such as background investigations. Investigator also must be willing to undertake surveillances and tail jobs whenever assigned, both by foot and automobile. A working knowledge of photography is helpful.
3. Investigator must be able to render concise, detailed daily reports on any type of investigation to which he is assigned.
4. Investigator must be free to relocate to another city approximately once every six months. There is also some short-term travel involved on occasion. All of this is at the company expense.
5. Investigator occasionally will assist company security officers in the conclusion of major investigations. This would include making searches and seizures, transporting suspects, processing and inventorying recovered physical evidence, and occasional taking of statements and interrogation. Frequently, the task involves long hours without rest. This type of activity would be rather infrequent, how-

---

Courtesy McKesson Corporation.

ever. Also, investigator is expected to work harmoniously with, and lend assistance to, any police officer who may also be investigating a company case.

6. Investigator also must be able to organize evidence and be able to testify in a dignified and courteous manner in court or quasi-legal proceedings. Investigator's conduct must be such at all times that it will not cast unfavorable reflections on the company's security department.
7. Excellent advancement opportunities exist in both the security department and management for all investigators who are willing to work and further their careers. The opportunity for transfer to another department is open at all stages of a security career.
8. Starting salary is negotiable.

STAFF INVESTIGATOR

Primary Accountabilities

A staff investigator's primary responsibility is effectively to work alone on undercover investigations but also be capable of conducting other types of investigations. A staff investigator must be knowledgeable in all areas of law enforcement and possess the ability to utilize investigative equipment.

A staff investigator works in a strictly staff capacity, contributing information and perhaps advising his superiors as to various follow-up actions. The job requires exercising considerable initiative and judgment, since decisions often must be made without recourse to advice or counseling.

Scope

A staff investigator's job has a considerable impact in that his goal of a successful investigation results in increased profits and higher employee morale. Within the corporate structure a staff investigator must be considered as a rather unique specialist.

Organizational Relationships

A staff investigator reports directly to the chief investigator and indirectly to the director of security.

CHIEF INVESTIGATOR

Primary Accountabilities

The primary responsibilities of the chief investigator are recruiting, hiring, training, and supervising staff investigators and assisting the director of security in coordinating the conclusion of major investigations. The chief investigator also conducts special investigations at the direction of the director of security.

The chief investigator occasionally must fill in for the regional security managers, so he has the responsibility of conducting annual security inspections, employment audits, special security surveys, and interrogations. Principally, the chief investigator serves in a staff capacity, although he also is delegated line responsibilities for some investigations.

Scope

In that the job definitely affects profits, it has a great impact on the total company, although these results often are difficult to measure accurately.

Organizational Relationships

The chief investigator reports directly to the director of security. The staff investigators report directly to the chief investigator.

REGIONAL SECURITY MANAGER

Primary Accountabilities

The primary responsibilities of the regional security manager involve security inspections and surveys; review of systems and procedures to insure compliance with minimum corporate standards; monitoring of guard and watchman functions; property and personal protection; talks to management groups; and talks to employees.

The regional security manager also conducts special investigations singularly or in conjunction with other security personnel.

If qualified, the regional security manager may utilize the polygraph in granting security clearance to new employees or job applicants for sensitive positions. This function requires mature, realistic judgment in making independent decisions on selection, retention, or discharge of personnel.

Scope

The regional security manager handles all security problems and programs in his geographical area, which covers most company locations. This job has a definite impact on the profits of the company by minimizing losses.

Organizational Relationships

The regional security manager reports directly to the head of the security department.

Appendix 2

Cluett-Foremost Staff Investigator Undercover Training Outline 1981

Arrival Night: WELCOME and Introductions.

Required Reading: "UNDERCOVER INVESTIGATION" Chpts. 1, 2, 3 (pgs. 18–23) chpt. 4 pg. 40 (credit rating) and pages 42, 43.

"12 WAYS TO GO BROKE" booklet.

Movie: "UNDERCOVER TRAINING" (part I).

1st Day: *Part I—General:*

A. History and Orientation of Company.
B. History of Undercover Investigation and Operation.
C. History of Department and its Organization.
D. Difference between Police and Corporations.

Part II—Administration:

A. Company Forms (distribution).
B. Expense Reports (sample sheet; sample hotel bills).
C. Handling of Money.
D. Overtime (sample request format).
E. Re-polygraph.
F. Establishing Credit.
G. Medical Claims.
H. Financial Advances.
I. Moving Expenses.
J. Memory Test; Fingerprints; I.D. Card.

Required Reading: "UNDERCOVER INVESTIGATION" Chpts. 5, 8. Two General Investigation Cases.

Critique and discussion with trainer after each case.

2nd Day: *Objectives of U/C Investigation:*

Report Writing:

A. *Three types of investigations*
   1. General—Undercover.
   2. Special—Short-term special work.
   3. Major—"Bust."

B. *Frequency and Format*
   1. Answer Interrogatives
      a) Who
      b) What
      c) When
      d) Where
      e) How
   2. Write reports in 3rd person.
   3. Frequency of reports.
   4. Accuracy of reports
      a) Facts vs. Hearsay
      b) Facts vs. Opinions
      c) Facts vs. Conclusions
      d) Completeness
      e) Brevity
      f) Impartiality
   5. Heading of reports
   6. Format for surveillance reports (distribution)

C. *Practical Exercise.*

Required Reading: "UNDERCOVER INVESTIGATION" Chpts. 3 (pgs. 23–35), 6, 7. Booklet—"U.S. vs. MADDOX", Gambling & Entrapment sections. Two General Investigation Cases.

Critique and Discussion with trainer after each case.

3rd Day: *Training:*

A. Drugs
B. Drinking and Gambling
C. Gathering and Marking of Evidence
   1) Envelope Sample—date, time, initials, place
   2) Ultra violet crayon and Black Light Demo
D. Body Language (The Sixth Sense)

Roping and Entrapment:

A. Discussion of "Maddox vs. U.S." and Entrapment sections

B. Roping
   1) It takes a thief to catch a thief
      a) Visual Aids (Roping movie)
   2) Accountability of merchandise

C. Co. Guest lecture (lectures)

D. What to Expect—Morale and Patience

E. Undercover Training movie (part II)

Required Reading: "UNDERCOVER INVESTIGATION" Chpts. 4, 9. One General Investigation and Arbitration.

Critique and discussion with trainer.

4th Day: *Cover Story:*

A. Three main ingredients of a cover story
   1) Keep it simple
   2) Make it believable
   3) Keep it as close to the truth as possible

B. Practice on Application Form (in detail & in pencil)

C. Review with trainer

D. In case of burn
   1) React
   2) Make counter accusation
   3) Step up roping activities

Collateral Investigations:

A. Crimes committed outside Company—must coordinate
   ex. in U/C INV.
   pages 64–66
   Peoria, IL.

B. The Test

Miscellaneous Investigations (Orientation only)

A. Surveillances—Special Investigations

B. Shopping

C. Busts

Required Reading: One General Investigation Case and "THE BIG DECISION" Chpts. 1, 2, 3, 4 (pgs. 34–40), Chpts. 7 (pgs. 68–75), 9, 10 (pgs. 89, 90, 103 & 104), Chpts. 13 (pgs. 130–133), 14 (pgs. 139–142), 15.

Critique and discussion with trainer

6:00 PM—Group dinner, and informal discussion.

5th Day: Critique and Group Discussion on "THE BIG DECISION" and any remaining General Investigation cases.

Final Examination

Individual Briefings and Conferences

Miscellaneous and Farewell.

Appendix 3

Loss Prevention Report

Distribution:
ORIG. - Plant Manager
DUP. -
CC: - Corporate Security
- Regional Security
- Mgr. Internal Audit
- D.H. & S.

Name & Address of Location: ____________

Date of original inspection ____________
Date of last inspection ____________
Date of this inspection ____________

Officials interviewed during survey:

____________ (Name) ____________ (Title)

Instructions: All "NO" answers to be explained on separate page. Also, all descriptions called for and any questions where improved control is needed.

Petty Cash Count:

Cash authorized ____________
Cash on hand ____________
Receipts & Vouchers ____________
Over/Short ____________

Volume in last fiscal year ____________

$ Overage or (Loss) in last fiscal year:
- Raw Materials ____________
- In Process ____________
- Finished Stock ____________

Total Number of Personnel (everyone headquartered in building)

Warehouse	Factory	Drivers	Off.	Salrd Supvrs. & Exec.

Type of Building (describe fully)

PERSONNEL	Y	N
1. Is the application form completed properly and signed?		
2. Where a security screening program is in effect, have polygraph tests or Reid Reports been administered to all applicants for sensitive positions?		
3. Are references of applicants for sensitive positions checked by either letter or telephone and placed in file?		
7. Are company rules adequate, in writing, and posted?		
10. Are disciplinary actions reduced to writing and placed in personnel files?		
11. Are regular safety-security meetings held? a) Did you review the minutes of the last three meetings? b) Date you last participated in supervisors' meetings at this location.		
12. Is the Incident Report Form regularly in use?		
13. Is the Monthly Loss Prevention Report in use? Date of last report: ____________		
14. Has responsibility for overall security been delegated to one employee? Name: ____________		
GUARDS & WATCHMEN		
21. Are guards or watchmen utilized at this location? Attach post No's and hours of coverage if any change since last report.		
22. Is coverage adequate for this location?		
24. Describe current rate of pay for guards and watchmen. ____________		
25. If agency guards, what do we pay agency? ____________ What do men receive? ____________		
27. Is the guard manual up to Corporate standards? (Attach any changes in guard manual since last report).		
30. Is a guard's log maintained giving full particulars of all persons entering and leaving the building, except at starting and quitting time? a) Is a permanent access or pass system in effect for off-hours? Covers: (List by name and title) ____________		

	Y	N
31. Is the Guard's Daily Report in use? Who receives the report, and takes follow-up action? ____________ Did you review the past six months of reports?		
33. List type of firearms (and serial # if Company owned), and other equipment owned by Co., Guard Agency, or personal property of guards. ____________ Did you inspect any firearms?		
36. Is instruction and training given to guards and watchmen in the use of firearms and fire protection equipment? By whom? ____________		
37. Did you make a clock round with the guard? Is the number of stations adequate? Describe frequency of rounds, type system used.		
38. How often are watch clock tapes or discs examined? ____________ By whom? ____________ Are tapes or discs retained until they are examined by insurance inspectors and corporate security officers?		
KEYS, ALARM & WATCHCLOCK SYSTEMS		
41. List key holders by name, position, locks or doors, type of key. Number of master keys? ____________ Where and how are spares secured? ____________ Normal opening and closing times of office door if not on alarm.		
42. Are keys withheld from alarm Co.?		
43. Are locks changed when a key is lost?		
44. Are locks changed when a key holder leaves the company? Date locks were last changed: ____________ (Change every two years).		
45. Are guard's building keys and gate keys maintained in secure place when not actually in use?		
46. Are the buildings equipped with burglar or other type alarms? If so, describe type of alarms - i.e. central station and name of company, local alarm to police, F.D., outside bell, internal day alarms, etc.		

(Rev. 8/82)

LOSS PREVENTION REPORT

Cluett, Peabody & Co., Inc.

	Y	N
47. List burglar alarm circuit No. area covered, title of card holders and normal opening and closing times by days.		
48. Was a review of alarm company or time recorder lock reports of unusual openings and closings since last inspection found to be negative?		
49. Are all alarm systems tested regularly? Did you personally make a test of all perimeter alarms? Types of system tested? ____________		
50. Describe any changes since last report in floor-plan showing the following: a) Entrances and exits (including overhead doors). b) Exits connected with alarms and/or padlocked. c) Watchman's clock stations, numbered in sequence. d) Guard stations. e) Fire stations.		
TRANSPORTATION SECURITY		
54. Are adequate security procedures taken when merchandise is left in trailers or box cars?		
55. Is responsible person present on docks at all times when receiving and shipping doors are open? Title:		
56. Are shipping and receiving rooms properly separated?		
57. At warehouse locations, are shipping activities, which are performed during other than normal working hours, subject to extra security measure? Explain:		
58. Are truck driver movements restricted from the stock areas? (Describe amount of access).		
59. Is a well defined and carefully executed plan in effect for the use of security seals on Company or leased trucks which are used to transfer products or finished goods between inter-companies, plants and warehouses? Describe plan, name person in charge of supervision of plan and method used for custody of seals.		
60. If seals are not used, have paper controls been set up? (If so, describe fully).		
INTERNAL CONTROLS		
61. Describe how visitors, repairmen, and other non-employees are controlled in the plant.		
62. Is employee identification adequate?		
63. Is procedure for handling returns and/or seconds adequate for security purposes?		
64. Does procedure for disposal of waste cartons, trash, etc. minimize opportunity for theft? Did you inspect the trash? (Describe controls setup).		
65. If there are restricted areas, buildings, or offices on the premises, are these areas protected? (Describe)		
66. Are janitors, maintenance men, and clean up crews properly supervised for control of theft activity? (Describe)		
67. Are employees required to enter and leave the building only via the ____________ door?		
68. Are employees prohibited from taking lunch boxes, packages, purses or handbags, etc., into stock and working areas?		
69. Are employees' packages which are brought into the building, stored in their lockers or other place approved by management?		

	Y	N
70. Are the locker space and restrooms outside stock and working areas?		
71. Describe security and control of unusual piece rate tickets. a) Describe procedure for manually changing rates and dozens on the tickets. b) Did you make a spot check audit of processed piece rate tickets?		
72. Is there local physical inspection of handbags, packages, lunch boxes, etc., made as employees leave the building? Is the inspection complete as opposed to a spot check? Did you personally observe or make an inspection? Who makes the inspection? ____________ Where is the inspection performed? ____________ How often is the inspection performed? ____________		
73. Does the package pass system meet corporate standards? List names and titles of authorized package pass signers.		
74. Are employees prohibited from remaining in stock and working areas during lunch periods?		
75. Is a supervisor on duty during lunch periods?		
76. Is procedure for pick-up of employee purchases in conformity with good security? (Describe fully)		
78. Are employees' cars parked only in areas a secure distance from shipping and receiving doors?		
80. Did you make an inspection of lockers, work stations, sensitive areas, etc? List names of questionable products, location and name of employee.		
81. Are lavatories and refuse containers free of improper items?		
82. Are all cases in the full case area full and unopened?		
PERIMETER SECURITY		
106. Did the perimeter security check reveal that proper security measures are in use? (Outside of buildings, ground floor, basement windows, flood-lights, skylights, doors, approach to roof, etc.)		
107. Did you walk the fence line? Is the present condition of fence perimeter adequate? List any holes, breaks, etc. Describe height, type and material of fence. ____________		
108. When fence gates are not in use, are they kept closed?		
109. When gates are not guarded, are they securely locked?		
MISCELLANEOUS		
115. List any security deficiencies remaining since last inspection.		
116. List any personal observations during this Security Inspection that indicate laxness in administration of security, gambling, drinking, leaving work place, sleeping on job, etc.		
117. Describe any unusual political, labor practices or crime activity that could have some bearing on security.		
118. On Security Department copies only, show date of your last personal contact with local police sources.		
Submitted by: ____________		

Appendix 4

Loss Prevention Survey Worksheet

LOCATION:
DATE(S) OF SURVEY:
COMPLETED BY:
PERSON(S) INTERVIEWED DURING SURVEY PERIOD:
NUMBER OF EMPLOYEES (BY CATEGORY):
WAREHOUSE DRIVERS OFFICE SALES EXECUTIVES
NUMBER OF SHIFTS:

Company(ies) Involved		YES	NO	COMMENTS
	A. PHYSICAL:			
All	1. External Conditions:			
All	Perimeter fence (describe)	___	___	___
All	Illumination (describe)	___	___	___
All	Lighting depend on human effort	___	___	___
All	Signs of vandalism	___	___	___
All	High crime area	___	___	___
All	Police protection by			___
All	History of civil or labor disturbance	___	___	___
All	Visibility around area obscured	___	___	___
All	Materials stored against building, fence	___	___	___
All	2. Building Construction and Condition: (Describe the building, # floors, floor construction, roof construction, square footage)			___
All	Physical location			___
All	Area (Industrial, residential, etc.)			___
All	Weakness in structure	___	___	___
All	Doors well made and properly framed	___	___	___

Company(ies) Involved		YES	NO	COMMENT
All	Interior doors properly placed	___	___	___
All	Common walls	___	___	___
All	Interior walls extend to roof	___	___	___
All	Roof easily accessible	___	___	___
All	Windows have security devices (describe)	___	___	___
	Other comments: ___			
All	3. Locks and Door Functions:			
All	Locks of sufficient quality	___	___	___
All	Location involved in lock changing program (Best)	___	___	Date last change: ___
All	Thumb turns used in critical areas	___	___	___
All	Chutes properly secured	___	___	___
All	Warehouse doors controlled against unauthorized access during the day (How?)	___	___	___
Drug	Punch button locks installed (Where?)	___	___	___
Drug	Punch button combinations changed every 30 days	___	___	___
Drug	Access list posted on employee door to warehouse	___	___	___
Drug	Employee door to warehouse self-closing and self-locking	___	___	___
All	Overhead doors reinforced with locks	___	___	___
All	Elevator locked in place at night	___	___	___
	Other comments: ___			
Drug	4. Vaults, Safes and Drug Abuse Cage(s):			___
	a. Vault: (Describe make, construction, location and doors)			___
Drug	Vault contain items other than controlled substances	___	___	___

Company(ies) Involved		YES	NO	COMMENT
Drug	If other items in vault, has DEA approved	___	___	___
Drug	Construction satisfy governing regulations	___	___	___
Drug	Any opening at top or bottom of day gate	___	___	___
Drug	Day gate self-closing and self-locking	___	___	___
Drug	Day gate blocked open to facilitate movement in and out of vault	___	___	___
Drug	Exposed day gate hinges sealed, welded or constructed to inhibit removal of pins	___	___	___
Drug	Combination changed annually or when knowledgeable person leaves	___	___	___
Drug	Location create unnecessary traffic	___	___	___
Drug	Access list posted on the vault door	___	___	___
Drug	Access personnel security cleared	___	___	___
	Other comments: ___			
All	b. Safe(s): (Describe make, construction, location and ratings)			___
Drug	Safe contain items other than controlled substances	___	___	___
Drug	If other items in safe, has DEA approved	___	___	___
Drug	Safe meet DEA specifications against attack	___	___	___
Drug	Combination changed annually or when knowledgeable person leaves	___	___	___
Drug	Contents of safe			___
Drug	If contains controlled substances, has DEA approved	___	___	___
Drug	If less than 750 lbs, has safe been anchored	___	___	___

Company(ies) Involved		YES	NO	COMMENT
Drug	If contains controlled substances, is access list posted on safe	___	___	___
Drug	Access personnel security cleared	___	___	___
Drug	Location create unnecessary traffic	___	___	___
	Other comments: ___			
Drug	c. Main Drug Abuse Cage: (Describe construction, location and number of doors)			___
Drug	Cage walls constructed of 10 gauge steel screening, with openings not more than 2½″ across the square	___	___	___
Drug	Cage walls attached to steel posts at least 1″ in diameter	___	___	___
Drug	Supporting posts set in concrete, or attached to floor with steel bolts and nuts peened or spot welded	___	___	___
Drug	Supporting posts not more than 10′ apart, with horizontal 1½″ reinforcements every 60″	___	___	___
Drug	If cage walls less than 14′ in height, is cage ceiling also 10 gauge steel screening; or top is attached to structural ceiling of building	___	___	___
Drug	Nuts on bolts attaching steel screen panels have been peened or spot welded	___	___	___
Drug	Any space at bottom of cage walls or doors has been closed	___	___	___
Drug	Cage door(s) are both self-closing and self-locking	___	___	___
Drug	Door(s) to cage are 10 gauge steel screening, attached to metal door frames, and in a metal door flange	___	___	___

Company(ies) Involved		YES	NO	COMMENT
Drug	Exposed door hinges are sealed, welded or constructed to inhibit removal of pins	___	___	___
Drug	Doors being blocked in open position to facilitate movement in and out of cage	___	___	___
Drug	Access list posted on cage door	___	___	___
Drug	Access personnel are security cleared	___	___	___
Drug	Cage is DEA approved	___	___	Date of approval: ___
	Other comments: ___			
Drug	d. Auxiliary Drug Abuse Cage: (Describe construction, location and number of doors)			___
Drug	Construction of walls, top and door(s) equals or exceeds that of main cage	___	___	___
Drug	Top covered if less than 14′; or attached to structural ceiling of building	___	___	___
Drug	Nuts on all bolts attaching support posts to floor and steel screen panels to frames have been peened or spot welded	___	___	___
Drug	Door(s) are both self-closing and self-locking	___	___	___
Drug	Door(s) being blocked in open position to facilitate movement in and out of cage	___	___	___
Drug	Location create unnecessary traffic	___	___	___
Drug	Access list posted	___	___	___
Drug	Access personnel are security cleared	___	___	___
Drug	DEA approved	___	___	Date of approval: ___
	B. <u>ALARMS</u>:			
All	1. Contract Data, Reports and Certification: (Describe areas protected, type of equipment, etc.)			___

Company(ies) Involved		YES	NO	COMMENT
All	Contractor			______
All	Central station, police connected or local			______
All	Direct wire connected	___	___	______
All	Date and term of contract, including changes by riders			______
All	Contract available and reviewed (attach copy)	___	___	______
All	Other contractor should be considered at renewal time	___	___	______
All	Opening reports received from contractor on time	___	___	______
All	Opening reports reviewed (By whom)	___	___	______
All	Schedule of protection complete (attach copy)	___	___	______
All	Any maintenance problem with contractor	___	___	______
	Other comments: ______			
All	2. Alarm Characteristics:			
All	Coverage sufficient	___	___	______
All	Can circuits be reduced	___	___	______
All	Control instruments inside protected areas	___	___	______
All	Conventional line security provided	___	___	______
All	Any obvious gaps in coverage	___	___	______
All	Wiring clean and unbroken	___	___	______
All	Standby power source for motion units	___	___	______
Drug	Vault and drug abuse cage on one separate circuit	___	___	______
Drug	Vault and cage circuit(s) have defeat resistant (random coded sequence) line security	___	___	______
Drug	Vault and cage circuit(s) have *complete* UL Grade AA certification, and certificates on file	___	___	______
Drug	Vault, cage and safe circuits tested annually by contractor, and tests are recorded	___	___	______

Company(ies) Involved		YES	NO	COMMENT
Drug	Vault, cage and safe circuits tested weekly by management and tests are recorded	___	___	___
Drug	Test records reflect date contractor advised of any defects in alarm, and date corrected	___	___	___
Drug	Records on alarm tests retained for 24 months	___	___	___
All	System detect unusual openings without prior notice when merely turned off	___	___	___
	Other comments: ___			
	3. Alarm Operation:			
All	Modifications in alarm coverage coordinated with RSM	___	___	___
All	System operates properly	___	___	___
All	Management walk-tests motion units and records tests	___	___	___
All	Frequency of false alarms		___	
All	False alarms explained	___	___	___
All	Penalty assessed by local government or contractor for false alarm registrations	___	___	___
All	Alarm registrations responded to by whom	___	___	___
All	Contractor has premise keys	___	___	___
All	Frequency of special openings			___
Drug	Contractor and/or police advised in writing of normal opening and closing schedule	___	___	___
Drug	Telephone procedure has been established for any special openings—not to include the vault and cage	___	___	___
Drug	Written advance notice is given the contractor and/or police before any special opening of the vault or cage	___	___	___

Company(ies) Involved		YES	NO	COMMENT
Drug	Contractor and/or police advised of high risk classification of drugs and requested to afford priority response to alarms	___	___	___
Drug	Contractor and/or police provided with *current* list of supervisors and home telephone numbers who will respond to alarms and other emergencies	___	___	___
All	Business hours generally coincide with opening and closing hours	___	___	___
All	Code cards issued by the contractor	___	___	___
All	Code card numbers listed and available in the files	___	___	___
All	Unnecessary code cards issued	___	___	___
All	Holdup devices properly placed (Where?)	___	___	___
All	Employees know how to use holdup devices	___	___	___
Drug	Holdup devices are tested quarterly and tests recorded	___	___	___
Drug	Motion detection on cage(s) extend the protection outside the cage(s)	___	___	___
All	Alarm circuits identified at the telephone terminals	___	___	___
	Other comments: ___			
All	4. Fire Alarm and Fire Protection:			
All	Premises sprinklered	___	___	___
All	18″ clearance below sprinkler heads	___	___	___
All	Sprinkler supervised	___	___	___
All	Manual fire alarm	___	___	___
All	Automatic fire alarm	___	___	___
All	Number, type and location of fire extinguishers and hoses in the area			___

Company(ies) Involved		YES	NO	COMMENT
All	Type of extinguishers on trucks			____
All	Extinguishers appropriate in areas where located	____	____	____
All	Extinguishers inspected at appropriate intervals	____	____	____
All	Smoking permitted in the warehouse	____	____	____
All	Fire exits posted and clear of obstructions	____	____	____
Drug	Doors intended as fire exits have annunciators	____	____	____
All	Fire exits secured or locked from the outside	____	____	____
All	Fire doors function as intended	____	____	____
All	Evacuation plan made and posted	____	____	____
All	Drills conducted to test evacuation plan; or plan reviewed at employee safety meetings	____	____	____
	Other comments: ____			

C. OPERATIONS:

1. Key Control:

Company(ies) Involved		YES	NO	COMMENT
All	Keys issued against receipt	____	____	____
All	All keys accounted for	____	____	____
All	Any keys issued unnecessarily	____	____	____
Drug	Record maintained on number of keys issued for vault and cage(s); persons to whom issued; and method of control	____	____	____
Drug	Where are keys for the vault and cage(s) used during operations kept after closing	____	____	____
Drug	Where are spare keys for vault and cage(s) secured in DC			____
All	Truck keys safeguarded	____	____	____
All	Keys found "stashed" in warehouse or office	____	____	____

Company(ies) Involved		YES	NO	COMMENT
All	Unnecessary persons have access to the building or parts of the building	___	___	___
All	Cleaning personnel allowed to enter after hours	___	___	___

All

KEY HOLDER	POSITION	KEYS & LOCKS	TYPE KEY

Other comments: ___

2. Pedestrian Traffic Control:

Company(ies) Involved		YES	NO	COMMENT
Drug	Visitors identified and logged	___	___	___
Drug	Badges issued and controlled	___	___	___
All	Maintenance personnel show bonafide identification before entering the warehouse	___	___	___
Drug	Badges sequentially numbered and accounted for each day	___	___	___
Drug	Lost or not returned badges permanently cancelled and so noted in front of the registration book	___	___	___
All	Can a casual visitor penetrate any opening to the warehouse	___	___	___
All	Employees Distinguishable	___	___	___
All	Visitors supervised while in the warehouse	___	___	___
All	Opening time present ambush potential	___	___	___
All	Closing time present ambush potential	___	___	___
Drug	Warehouse and other critical areas empty at break and meal times	___	___	___

Company(ies) Involved		YES	NO	COMMENT
Drug	Picker aprons and uniforms inspected before laundry pickup	___	___	___
All	Any unlocked entrance present clear danger of undetected intrusion	___	___	___
All	Office to warehouse entrance monitored	___	___	___
All	Presence of night shift create potential for ambush attack	___	___	___
All	Exterior doors remain open to facilitate entry/exit if 2d/3rd shifts	___	___	___
All	Only designated persons given access to and enter secured areas	___	___	___
All	Employees take unnecessary items into the warehouse	___	___	___
All	Package control system in effect	___	___	___
All	Employees pass management check upon exiting after work	___	___	___
All	Door checks made on a random basis	___	___	___
All	Employees provided with lockers and means of securing lockers	___	___	___
All	Management has duplicate keys to the lockers	___	___	___
All	Lockers inspected on a random basis	___	___	___
All	Employees fill their own orders	___	___	___
	Other comments: ___			
	3. Receiving:			
All	Receiver receives from a correct document (What?)	___	___	___
All	Receiver checked by anyone	___	___	___
Drug	*Space designated in receiving for specific controlled substance receiving	___	___	___

Company(ies) Involved		YES	NO	COMMENT
Drug	*Only authorized individuals allowed in designated controlled substance receiving area	___	___	___
Drug	Valuable or sensitive items kept on dock for prolonged periods	___	___	___
Drug	Controlled substances move directly to secured areas	___	___	___
All	Receiving area physically separated from shipping area	___	___	___
All	Receiver has access to shipping area	___	___	___
All	Drivers allowed in the receiving area	___	___	___
All	Operations personnel supervise receiving	___	___	___
All	How are rail cars secured overnight	___	___	___
All	Receiver leave the area unattended	___	___	___
	Other comments: ___			
	4. Order Control:			
All	Orders controlled (How?)	___	___	___
All	Customers can be verified (How?)	___	___	___
Drug	Special purchase orders originating at DC signed by DCM and IM	___	___	___
Drug	Registered mail accepted anywhere except office	___	___	___
Drug	Registered mail received at DC only by exempt employee	___	___	___
Drug	Registered mail picked up at Post Office by non-exempt employee is delivered directly to exempt employee at the DC	___	___	___
Drug	Except emergency, is sale of controlled substances prohibited on waiting or will call orders	___	___	___

Company(ies) Involved		YES	NO	COMMENT
Drug	On normal waiting or will call orders, is name of person to pick up order requested	___	___	___
Drug	Authenticity of any questionable order verified by call back to customer	___	___	___
Drug	Identification and signature required before delivering a waiting or will call order	___	___	___
Drug	Will Call Record (Log) being maintained	___	___	___
Drug	Schedule II orders filled in vault, checked and sealed by supervisor	___	___	___
Drug	Schedule III, IV and V orders filled in the cage, checked and sealed by a supervisor	___	___	___
Drug	Controlled items sent through the picking lines	___	___	___
Drug	Controlled items shipped in sealed packages	___	___	___
All	Orders shipped only to address of actual purchaser	___	___	___
Drug	Narcotic blank forgeries	___	___	___
Drug	Unusual or suspicious purchases of controlled substances reported to DEA	___	___	___
Drug	Telephonic reports to DEA followed by letter sent certified mail	___	___	___
Drug	Record maintained on reports of any suspicious purchases made to DEA	___	___	___
All	Merchandise is properly closed out	___	___	___
All	Breakage being controlled	___	___	___
	Other comments: ___			
	5. Shipping:			
All	Shipping area is physically separated from the receiving	___	___	___

Company(ies) Involved		YES	NO	COMMENT
All	Shipper checked by anyone	___	___	___
All	Valuable or sensitive items kept on dock for prolonged periods pending shipment	___	___	___
Drug	Defined area in shipping for controlled substance orders	___	___	___
All	Shipper has access to receiving area	___	___	___
Drug	Drivers receipt for controlled substance orders before loading	___	___	___
All	Drivers have access to merchandise not intended for their particular truck	___	___	___
All	Operations personnel supervise the shipping	___	___	___
Drug	Controlled drug orders sent via the U.S. Postal Service	___	___	___
Drug	Orders sent via postal service registered mail—return receipt	___	___	___
Drug	Packaging of orders sent through postal service indicate contents	___	___	___
Drug	Postal orders are delivered to the registry window and receipt is obtained	___	___	___
Drug	Large shipments of controlled drug orders sent via the mails are escorted to Post Office	___	___	___
All	Shipper leave the area open and unattended	___	___	___
	Other comments: ___			
	6. Customer Delivery Operations:			
All	Drivers acknowledge responsibility in writing to lock their truck when the truck is not attended, to allow no unauthorized			

Company(ies) Involved		YES	NO	COMMENT
	riders and to not use company trucks for personal reasons	___	___	___
Drug	Controlled drugs are secured in the locked rear of the truck when transported (not in cab)	___	___	___
Drug (All)	Drivers require customer signature for Schedule II–V orders	___	___	___
All	Drivers pick up returns	___	___	___
All	Returns checked for verification	___	___	___
Drug	Controlled items remain outside designated secured areas when returned	___	___	___
All	Drivers pick up COD's	___	___	___
All	COD's turned in promptly and against receipt	___	___	___
All	COD's secured against loss (How?)	___	___	___
All	Security of COD's of drivers returning after hours	___	___	___
All	History of a COD loss	___	___	___
All	Drivers return after normal business hours	___	___	___
All	Drivers vulnerable to ambush	___	___	___
All	Trucks suggest the product being carried	___	___	___
All	Trucks equipped with alarms	___	___	___
All	Alarms operate properly	___	___	___
All	Records kept on shorts by drivers	___	___	___
All	Excessive breakage reported by any driver	___	___	___
All	Loaded trucks stored outside protection before being sent on delivery	___	___	___
	Other comments: ___			
	7. Night Operations:			
All	Presence of 2nd, 3rd shifts negate value of alarm	___	___	___

Company(ies) Involved		YES	NO	COMMENT
All	Presence of night shift necessitate exterior doors be unlocked	___	___	___
All	Night employees isolated from areas not required for proper operation	___	___	___
All	Night employees exit building for meal breaks	___	___	___
	Other comments: ___			
	8. Computer Operations:			
All	Room inside warehouse	___	___	___
All	Night operation	___	___	___
All	Night operator safe	___	___	___
All	Management restrict access to those having business in the room	___	___	___
Drug	Access list is posted	___	___	___
All	Door kept locked when room not in use	___	___	___
All	Any door between room and warehouse (How secured?)	___	___	___
All	Room sprinklered	___	___	___
All	Burglar alarm protect room	___	___	___
All	Holdup device in room	___	___	___
	Other comments: ___			
	9. Armed Robbery Procedures:			
Drug	Employees indoctrinated on robbery attack procedures	___	___	___
Drug	Front door being kept locked at all times	___	___	___
Drug	Electric strikeplate installed on office entrance door	___	___	___
Drug	Office entrance door is both self-closing and self-locking	___	___	___
Drug	Required sign is posted on entrance door	___	___	___
Drug	Persons not recognized present bonafide identification before permitted entrance	___	___	___

Company(ies) Involved		YES	NO	COMMENT
Drug	Shipping and Receiving doors are closed and latched when not in use	___	___	___
Drug	Employee door to warehouse is both self-closing and self-locking	___	___	___
Drug	Employee door to warehouse posted "No Admittance—Authorized Employees Only"	___	___	___
Drug	Outside pedestrian doors equipped with annunciators	___	___	___
Drug	Annunciators sound alarm in immediate area of door opened	___	___	___
Drug	Exit doors with annunciators are posted to announce that alarm will sound if the door is opened	___	___	___
Drug	Management tests annunciators and records tests	___	___	___
Drug	Mirrors/viewers installed outside solid entrance or overhead doors	___	___	___
Drug	If holdup devices installed, has DCM developed predetermined plan of action with responding police	___	___	___
Drug	If holdup devices installed, are the employees familiar with location and operation of the devices	___	___	___
Drug	*Batteries in portable holdup devices replaced every six months and date recorded in log or on battery	___	___	___
Drug	Vault door equipped with escape mechanism for emergency exit	___	___	___
Drug	If vault is not equipped with emergency escape mechanism, is holdup device installed in vault	___	___	___
Drug	Employees working after hours can be protected by perimeter alarm	___	___	___

Company(ies) Involved		YES	NO	COMMENT
Drug	Emergency numbers posted on each telephone instrument	___	___	___
Drug	Names and telephone numbers of management posted on the outside of the building	___	___	___
Drug	Management verifies authenticity of after hours calls concerning emergency or alarm at DC before reacting	___	___	___
Drug	As many employees as possible present when employee door is opened	___	___	___
Drug	Authorization to open any exit from building is denied until full complement of employees are present	___	___	___
Drug	Vault and/or cage remains locked until substantial employees are on the premises	___	___	___
Drug	Supervisor is present at opening of vault and cage	___	___	___
Drug	All exits closed during open period of vault and cage	___	___	___
Drug	Vault and cage are scheduled to be closed, locked and alarmed following business day or last DEA order	___	___	___
Drug	Supervisors remain on premises in any failure of vault or cage alarm at closing until repairs are made, and all exits are kept closed and locked	___	___	___
Drug	Visual check of premises made at closing to insure doors and windows are closed, and no "lock ins" are in building	___	___	___
Drug	Pre-arranged signal established with alarm contractor and police to investigate any delay in closing when such delay was not previously made known	___	___	___

Company(ies) Involved		YES	NO	COMMENT
Drug	Procedure to reduce vulnerability of robbery of employees making bank deposits or other transport involving risk	___	___	___
	Other comments: ___			
	10. Miscellaneous:			
All	Security clearance procedures being followed	___	___	___
All	Polygraph waiver completed by all applicants regardless of job considered	___	___	___
All	Prescribed procedures for use of outside examiner being followed	___	___	___
All	Any "Not Recommended" on the payroll	___	___	___
All	Previous employers being checked	___	___	___
All	Work rules established, clearly presented and posted	___	___	___
All	Housekeeping a problem	___	___	___
All	System for issuing samples	___	___	___
Drug	Procedure for the disposal of controlled substances	___	___	___
All	Serial numbers of office machines recorded	___	___	___
All	Procedure for the disposal of waste cartons and trash	___	___	___
All	Inspection of lockers, work stations, sensitive areas and desk drawers by RSM	___	___	___
All	Gasoline issuance and storage	___	___	___
All	Control of vehicle fuel credit cards and purchases	___	___	___
All	Method of making bank deposit	___	___	___
All	Receivable and bank deposit functions properly separated	___	___	___

Company(ies) Involved		YES	NO	COMMENT
All	Any unexplained change in gross profits	___	___	___
All	Any noticeable change in the personal behavior of any employee	___	___	___
Chemical	Deposit containers storage and inventory	___	___	___
W&S	Gallonage reports received by RSM on time	___	___	___

Other comments: ___

___

___

D. RECOMMENDATIONS:

1. ___
2. ___

___ Enclosures

DISTRIBUTION:

Appendix 5

Computer Loss Prevention Survey

Distribution:
Orig ____________________
Dup ____________________
Trip ____________________
Quad ____________________

Location: ____________________

____

Date: ________________ By: ________

Officials interviewed: ____________________

____

____

____

Instructions: *All "No" answers to be explained on separate pages;*
All "Yes" answers expanded as necessary.

General:	Y	No
1. Describe physical construction and lay-out of facility.		
2. List equipment and describe functions, i.e. information storage vs. input only.		
3. Number of personnel and shifts. Are all personnel properly supervised to include night shift?		
4. Is this facility on line with another? If yes, describe.		

	Y	No
5. Value of hardware, software, supplies		
6. Have there been any changes since last inspection? Has the Insurance Mgr. been advised of changes that increase or decrease value of facility?		
7. Are all areas of computer room and key punch in full view of the supervisors at all times?		
Fire and Physical Exposure 16. a) Is there an approved emergency plan which includes procedures and priorities in the event of fire, flood, or other disaster, and is it posted and understood? b) Has delayed evacuation been analyzed for hazards?		
17. a) Are all areas of facilities accessible to fire department regardless of time of emergency? b) Have officers of Fire Dept., actually been familiarized with facility and its emergency procedures?		
18. How do E.D.P. personnel distinguish between fire drills and actual emergency situations?		

	Y	No
19. Describe fire fighting equipment available—both installation equipment (sprinklers) and accessory equipment (fire extinguishers). State which specific areas are covered, and if equipped with sprinklers, what kind: dry, wet, on/off, etc.		
20. Is all fire fighting equipment checked periodically and inspected thoroughly, at least annually?		
21. Are all personnel trained in the use of fire fighting equipment?		
22. a) If the facility is equipped with automatic flooding fire suppressing device such as CO^2 or Halon, is there a preactivation warning alarm in the event of actuation? b) Can actuation be aborted?		
23. Is fire detection or smoke detection equipment tested periodically, at least annually?		
24. Are "No Smoking" restrictions strictly enforced in the E.D.P. facility?		
25. Are waste paper and other fire hazards not allowed to accumulate in the computer room?		

	Y	No
26. Is there a power cut-off switch located inside the computer room and outside?		
27. Are all fixtures and furniture within the computer room non-combustible?		
28. a) If there is a raised floor, is the area beneath the floor kept clean? b) Are floor panel lifters readily available?		
29. Are computer service contractors on call to clean and dry components after fire or sprinkler discharge?		
Special Loss Prevention: 40. Is there adequate emergency lighting for coverage of the computer room library and means of ingress and egress?		
41. How is facility monitored for low or high heat, intrusion, loss of power, water flow, etc.? Describe in full.		
42. Has there been any new construction or renovations within the computer facility? If so, describe in full.		
43. Has all work been done according to local building codes and National Life Safety Code?		

	Y	No
50. If facility includes information storage—what is format? i.e.: cards, discs, tape? Describe physical security.		
51. Describe the work fields for which information is stored, i.e. payrolls, inventory, accounts payable, etc.		
52. How is access to equipment controlled physically (card key, etc.)?		
53. How is access to computer function controlled, i.e. password to go on line, password to access a given computer program?		
54. Are terminals themselves limited in their ability to access programs and work fields?		
55. What records are kept of terminal use/time. Are operator logs kept?		
56. What records are kept of programs "brought up" and work fields accessed?		
57. What programming is done at site? Is programmer familiar with passwords and programs of central facility (Troy, Royersford, etc.)? Does programmer operate computer?		

	Y	No
58. Are critical jobs rotated periodically?		
59. a) Is our computer's use restricted at all times to our own company? b) If "No", is there a written agreement for use by others? c) Are our programs and all files fully secured? d) Do our personnel always operate the computer?		
71. a) Have all personnel been cleared through the security program? b) What positions have been designated as sensitive positions? c) Have polygraphs or Reid Reports been administered to all sensitive positions?		
72. a) Is a log maintained of all computer processing? Is the log compared to standard run times and all exceptions investigated? b) Are spot checks made of operator activity?		
73. Are tapes and discs kept in secured areas during non-working hours?		

	Y	No
74. Is there a written record of tapes issued and returned?		
75. Is there a current list of personnel authorized to sign out confidential material?		
76. Is there a secure on-site storage facility for maintaining back-up copies of vital data programs?		
77. Is there numerical control and accountability for checks and other pre-numbered forms?		
78. Is there a procedure established that prevents programs from being changed without the knowledge and consent of the user's department?		

Appendix 6

Safety Inspection Report: Cluett, Peabody & Co., Inc.

Page 1

Distribution:
Orig. - Plant Manager
Dup. -
Trip. - Corporate Safety
Quad. - Regional Security

Date: ____________

Name & Address of Location: ____________

Official interviewed during survey:

____________ ____________
(Name) (Title)

Instructions: All negative (N) answers to be explained on separate page; Positive (Y) answers should be expanded as necessary.

		Y	N
	FIRE PROTECTION:		
1	Is the facility free of evidence indicating smoking violations?		
2	Is housekeeping good in all areas including: a) kitchen and cafeteria areas b) floors, aisles, passageways c) loading docks and adjacent areas d) storerooms e) under cutting tables		
3a	Is a minimum clearance of 18" maintained under sprinkler heads?		
b	Is a minimum of 36" clearance maintained where combustibles are stored on pallets or on racks to a height of more than 12' or in closely packed piles to a height above 15'?		
4a	Are all fire extinguishers inspected at least monthly and do they have properly completed record tags?		
b	Are all extinguishers free of signs of actuation, tampering, physical damage, corrosion, or other visible impairments?		
c	Are all in place at their marked locations?		
d	Are they all readily accessible?		
e	Do all ABC extinguishers more than 5 years old bear a record or tag of metal or equally durable material, showing the date of test, within the last 12 years, test pressure, name or initials of persons or agency making the test?		
f	Is the maximum walking distance to a fire extinguisher from any point 75 feet?		
5a	Are all fire hoses properly installed on their reels or racks so that they may be removed very quickly (check for intertwining with the reel spokes and tie downs)?		
b	Are all lined hoses tested once per year at two hundred psi for at least 15 seconds, by insurance Co., or fire department?		
c	Are all defective obsolete linen hoses replaced with lined?		
6a	Are highly flammable materials, oil paints, lacquers, solvents, stored in UL-approved containers?		
b	Are accumulations of oily rags stored in approved cans from which they are removed daily?		

		Y	N
6c	Are flammable solvents restricted and used only with great caution and under strict supervision?		
d	Does management control presence of chemicals from approved list?		
7	Is there a complete absence of anything that would prevent fire doors from closing?		
8	Is there an effective , scheduled program to prevent build up of lint or dust? Is management aware of the (explosive) fire propagation characteristics of dust?		
9a	Is the installation equipped with employee alarms audible above the background noise? Have they been tested as part of the regular fire drill?		
b	Do the fire alarm systems work perfectly? When were they tested? If there has been no recent test, they should be tested.		
c	Have mandatory two fire drills been held? a) Date of last drill: w/warning ______ Time ______ w/o warning ______ Time ______		
10	Has an effective Plant Emergency Organization been organized and trained? Are they instructed to deal only with incipient fires? (Attach a copy of PEO list).		
11	Is the emergency plan adequate? Has a hazard analysis been performed? Does the Plan address all hazards? Are salvage operations included?		
13	Has the local fire department been invited to cooperate where possible?		
14	Are any installations of kitchen stoves protected by chemical packs or other authorized fire suppressant systems?		
15	Within the last six (6) months have the premises been inspected by any outside organization? (Attach copies) a) Have all major safety recommendations made in the last six months by Corporate Safety or other loss prevention engineers been carried out? If not, please specify. What was date of last reminder?		
17a	Is a proper fire watch maintained with protective curtains, fire extinguishers, etc. during times of cutting and welding?		

Cluett, Peabody & Co., Inc.
SAFETY INSPECTION REPORT

Page 2

	Y	N
17b Is ventilation where welding, cutting and brazing performed adequate?		
18a Are LPG or gas-powered vehicles always fueled in a designated, well ventilated, safe location? If possible, is this outside? b If gasoline, is any spillage properly dealt with? c Are there any signs of leaking hydraulic fluids on lift trucks?		
19 Are Oxygen and acetylene cylinders: a) Kept away from radiators and sources of heat and live electrical conductors? b) fastened in an upright position during use and storage so that they cannot fall over? c) Valves closed during moving, when not in use and when empty? d) Stored at least 20' apart or separated from each other or highly combustible material by a 5' non-combustible barrier with 1/2 hr. fire rating? e) Kept capped when not in use? f) Including valves, couplings, regulators, hose and apparatus kept away from oil and grease in any form?		
20 If facility has hose houses, are they properly maintained?		
21 Sprinkler System a) Are riser valves open? b) Are post indicator valves open and equipped with unbroken wire seals, frangible locks or tamper switches? c) Are they checked at least weekly? How was this determined? d) Are records acceptable to the F+EC carrier maintained, and readily accessible?		
22 Are all sprinkler branch lines and mains free of anything draped over, suspended from or fastened to them?		
23 a) Is the temperature in hose/pump houses maintained safely above freezing? b) Are areas with wet (water filled sprinkler) systems maintained at a temperature safely above freezing?		
24 Where wet automatic sprinkler systems of not more than 20 heads are installed in small unheated areas they require special treatment. a) Have they been shut off and drained? b) Or have they been drained and filled with an anti-freeze solution? c) Is the protected system free of the usual automobile type anti-freeze solutions which are contrary to health regulations? How was this determined?		
25 Are all sprinkler heads free of paint or other coverings?		
26a Are chute and conveyor openings through floors properly fire proofed? b Are all floor or wall openings closed by approved methods? c Are openings protected and fire doors kept closed when not in use, such as at the end of the work day?		

	Y	N
PERSONAL SAFETY 30a Are all needle guards properly positioned and effective? Have there been any needle punctures reported? b Do supervisors stress safe procedures such as removing foot from treadle during threading?		
31 Are all fans that can be brought within 7' of the floor equipped with guards having maximum openings of 1/2" and taut that they cannot be pushed into the fan blades?		
32a Are work rests of abrasive wheel machinery (bench grinders) kept adjusted closely to the wheel with a maximum opening of 1/8"? b Are all parts of a grinding wheel enclosing guard in proper position? c Does the grinder operate without vibration? d If the abrasive wheels are so designed, are blotters (compressible washers) used between flanges and the surface of the wheel? e Is the abrasive wheel free of chips, uneven wear, cracks, etc.? f Are goggles always worn when operating the bench and other grinders? g Is the machine equipped with an eye shield? Is the shield clean, free of cracks, and in place?		
33a Are all tools, personally or company owned, in safe usable condition? b If an employee carries tools in a tool-carrying belt, does he carry them safely at the side? c Are employees prohibited from carrying screw-drivers or other pointed tools unguarded in their pockets?		
34a Are movable parts of the fire escapes in working order? When were they last checked? ________ b Are aisles leading to their access windows and doors maintained free of obstruction? c Do all access windows or doors operate freely? d Are fire escapes kept free of ice? e Are the areas, including steps, outside of emergency exit doors, kept free of snow and ice and parked cars and trucks? How?		
35 Are eye wash stations available wherever needed e.g. boiler rooms where boiler water is treated?		
36a Are trucks, vehicles, containers, shelving, tables, etc. free of splinters, projecting nails, broken welds, sharp or jagged edges? b Are wheels on all work trucks free to roll?		
37 Are all work bundles tied in quantities that are within reasonable weight limits for work force?		
38a Are wood ladders free of cracks, breaks, protruding nails, screws, or paint? b Are they maintained in a snug condition so that they cannot wobble? c Are straight ladders equipped with anti-slip shoes?		
39a Are floors maintained in a non-slippery condition? b Are floors free of holes, protruding nails, warped boards?		

Cluett, Peabody & Co., Inc.
SAFETY INSPECTION REPORT

Page 3

	Y	N
40a Are vehicles, e.g. tractors, forklift trucks, etc. operated at safe speeds? b Do forklift trucks travel with their forks in lowered position? c Is unsafe riding of powered trucks prohibited? d Is the operation of a powered truck restricted to experienced operators? e Are all walls, storage bins, doorways, etc. free of any signs of damage indicating improper or careless use of powered industrial trucks? f Do all industrial truck operators have a record of their training in their personnel file?		
41a Are first-aid kits maintained according to company standards? b Is the bed linen in the first aid room clean? c Is there always at least one person fully trained in first-aid available? Have they been certified within the last three (3) years? (list names in report) d List those persons who have received first aid training and are designated for OSHA purposes.		
42a Are truck and/or trailer wheels chocked when they are being boarded by powered industrial trucks or on inclines? b Are fixed jacks used when necessary to support a semi-trailer and prevent up-ending during loading or unloading when the trailer is not coupled to a tractor? c Are all bridge plates adequate as to load, and secure when in place? d Is the edge of a dock or platform guarded when a removable section of guardrail has been temporarily removed? Is this removable section replaced just as soon as the need for a gap in the rail is satisfied? e Are the interiors of trucks and trailers adequately lighted?		
43a Is there an emergency lighting system? b Is it properly maintained?		
45 Are all employees in the vicinity of equipment being cleaned with compressed air required to wear: a) goggles? b) dust masks as necessary? c) Are the masks NIOSH approved for type of exposure in question?		
MISCELLANEOUS		
46 Have all cracks and/or broken glass been safely repaired or replaced?		
47a Are there two boiler low-water cut offs for any boiler not constantly attended? b Are the low-water cut offs dismantled and cleaned by contract personnel, or other authorized persons under the supervision of insurance company engineers? c Is this done at least once a year? d Is there a boiler shutdown inspection of water-side surfaces once per year conducted jointly with the water treatment contractor and the insurance carrier's engineers?		

	Y	N
48 Is the food being handled in accordance with accepted sanitary procedures?		
49 Are toilet rooms kept: a) clean? b) well lighted? c) supplied with tissues and towels? d) are refuse containers emptied before they become full? e) Is plumbing in working order?		
50 Are all drinking fountains working properly?		
51 Is the lighting of all means of egress, interior, and exterior, being properly maintained so that there are no portions in darkness?		
52 Are all means of egress being kept clear of obstructions?		
53 Is there an established preventive maintenance program? Is it in writing?		
55 Does all equipment acquired since the last inspection conform to the OSHA Act regulations on guarding, grounding, sharp edges, anchoring, etc.?		
58 Is material stored with or without pallets, on high racks by fork lift trucks safely balanced and supported by the rack?		
60 Are exits being maintained free of locks and fastenings that would prevent free escape from the inside of the building?		
61 Are all electrical appliances such as light bulbs, hot plates, coffee makers, irons, etc. being operated a safe distance from combustibles?		
ELECTRICAL		
70a Are the doors and covers of all electrical boxes kept closed? b Are all lighting and power panel components, fuses, circuit-breakers and switches, normally cool? If not, has cause been determined? c If any plug (screw) fuses that were found warm or hot were screwed tight, did they subsequently cool off? d Are all cartridge fuse clips their normal copper color? If they run hot, they should be replaced.		
71 When work is being performed on electrical equipment, is its power source de-energized and tagged?		
72 Is the working space around electrical equipment kept clear and free of storage? (at least 30")		
74 Are overhead electrical distribution ducts in straight, level lines, free from sag that could indicate loss of support?		

Cluett, Peabody & Co., Inc.
SAFETY INSPECTION REPORT

Page 4

	Y	N
75 Extension cords are intended for temporary use with portable equipment. a) Are all appliances, tools and similar equipment which are normally used at one specific location connected directly and without an extension cord to a receptacle located near the equipment? b) Are extension cords on temporary duty placed where they could not be damaged against hot surfaces, in aisles, where trucks could damage them, etc.?		
76 Is the location free of the use of flexible cord: a) as a substitute for the fixed wiring of the structure? b) where run through holes in walls, ceilings, or floors, or under carpets. c) where run through doorways, windows, or similar openings? d) where attached to building surfaces?		
77 Are all flexible cords used without splices or taps?		
78 Are all junction box covers in place and all knock-out holes plugged?		
79 Are all electrical controls labeled where their purpose is not obvious?		
81 Are all water coolers grounded through a 3-conductor cord with a 3-prong plug inserted in a grounded tested outlet without a pigtail adapter?		
83 Are all portable electrical tools either insulated or equipped with a 3-conductor cord terminating in a 3-prong grounding plug?		
OSHA		
91a Is the OSHA Job Safety & Health poster prominently displayed? b Are OSHA Forms 100, 101 (or its equivalent) and 102 being maintained at the location?		
92 Is the building free of obvious fire and safety hazards?		
WORKERS' COMPENSATION		
94 Is a specific person assigned to handle Workers' Comp. paperwork? Who? By name: ______________________		
95 Is there someone principally responsible for safety? Who? By name: ______________________		
96 Does the Personnel Officer or Plant Mgr. personally follow Workers' Comp. cases on a daily basis?		
97 Are Workers' Comp. claimants informed immediately of the statutory nature of their benefits? i.e.: that benefits are set by law; that there is a waiting period; and that there are both medical and indemnity benefits.		
98 In those states where appropriate, has a poster been displayed naming the panel of Workers' Compensation physicians? Have these physicians become acquainted with job descriptions?		
GENERAL		
101 Have any losses occurred since the last Corporate inspection which are related to outstanding recommendations?		
102 Are preventive maintenance principles being followed per current Corporate bulletins?		
103 Are there any occupational or cumulative trauma cases reported since last Corporate inspection?		
104 Is the Cluett Hearing Conservation program functioning according to Corporate guidelines?		
105 Are there both a safety education program and a safety incentive plan in effect?		
106 Are losses discussed by safety committees and is there a narrative summary of the matters posted on a safety bulletin board?		
107 Where there are knitting operations, are workers observing basics of cotton dust program? i.e.: are masks used for "blow down"? Are personnel restricted during "blow down" to only necessary manpower?		
110 General summation - overall impression:		
111 Goals/objectives to be achieved by next inspection:		

Submitted by: ______________________

Appendix 7

Strike Readiness Plan

In the beginning it should be remembered that organized labor has three fundamental and basic rights:

1. the right to engage in peaceful picketing
2. the right to strike
3. the right of assembly.

These rights are guaranteed by the Constitution of the United States and the States. There are numerous labor laws which act as a guide and provide the foundation of rules, regulations, and decisions. The Federal laws of importance are attached as Enclosure I.

There should be at least three separate categories for consideration:

1. pre-strike plans
2. strike operations
3. post-strike operations.

They require different resources and involve different time frames. The first category to be considered will be pre-strike plans.

PRE-STRIKE PLANS

The Security Department must determine from management if the facility involved is to continue operation or to close down. If the decision is to continue operation, will you encourage employees to cross the picket line? Will you attempt to hire *replacement* or interim production employees? Will you use salaried and/or sales employees to operate the plant? Will you attempt to use a combination of the above? If the decision is to continue operation, the following should be adhered to:

1. Determine the property line for the facility in question. Have available a sketch of the facility, indicating all entrances and exits, fence

lines, window locations and building locations with dimensions drawn to scale.

2. Obtain a copy of the law relating to assault and simple assault.
3. Notify/visit local police of the strike situation. Maintain a list of the officials in the community and country, particularly the Chief of Police, Sheriff's Office, City Attorney, etc. In the event of a strike, these individuals must be contacted and made aware of the situation and, when appropriate, the company's position.
4. Notify the alarm company central station of the strike situation.
5. Notify/visit the local fire department of the strike situation.
6. If guards are to be used, instructions should be in writing and discussed with the guards prior to being placed on a duty status (no show of force unless absolutely necessary).
7. Trucks or vehicles which will not be needed during the strike should be moved to a safe location.
8. Will management/supervisors live in or report for work daily? If the decision is to live in, consideration must be given to renting/purchasing cots, linens, and a supply of canned food on the premises.
9. All fire extinguishers and fire fighting equipment should be checked and inspected no matter what the decision (business as usual or closing). All windows and doors should be measured so that if the need arises, plywood or sheet metal for glass doors may be readily ordered.
10. Access to the roof must be provided for as well as a hose which can be attached to a convenient faucet in the building to reach all parts of the roof.
11. If the facility has drapes or blinds, they should be closed during operating hours.
12. Establish a management team of observers to man each entrance to the plant where picket lines may be established. Observers should be instructed to record all incidents, listing date, time, names, etc. Provide tape recorders.
13. In the case of a location stocking controlled substances, move the items to a safer location prior to the strike.
14. Perimeter lighting must be checked and replacement bulbs available within the branch, as well as portable emergency lighting.
15. Safeguarding cash and/or valuable documents must be provided for as well as protection for the Computer Room.
16. The decision should be made as to who is in charge of the operation during the strike, and who is second in charge. Know how to correctly replace or terminate strikers under state and federal law. Know what the reinstatement rights and requirements are of replaced strikers. Over-extend yourself to insure all individuals receive fair and equal treatment. Be alert for and knowledgeable of

actions by strikers which may constitute unprotected union activities. Be keenly aware of conditions or actions by the company which could lead to unfair labor practice charges against the company and possibly convert the strike from an economic strike to an unfair labor practice strike. Know the "rights" of strikers.

17. A system of communications must be set up so that those persons working during the strike will be kept informed of any changes which take place during non-operating hours.
18. Hire a photographer to record incidents or have a security officer take motion pictures of any incidents.
19. Check the housekeeping. Remove all trash and/or flammables from the area.
20. Secure or lock power source meters as well as water supply and telephone box.
21. Determine if security department will keep low profile or visible profile.
22. Company will prosecute strikers. Can always back off.
23. Legal counsel should be contacted as well as Corporate Industrial Relations staff. Plan to provide adequate protection for property, facilities, equipment, vendors, company shipments and all non-striking personnel. Develop strike surveillance activities and locations for placement of photographers for best surveillance coverage to document all "incidents." Obtain telephone message equipment to record pertinent strike information. Update list of "authorized" personnel in the event of strike. Update gate procedures and consider installing gate and fence telephones where needed. Prepare parking arrangements inside fenced areas. Review and/or provide for medical and first aid facilities. Review entrances and exits to plant facilities. Review night lighting, possible effects of glass or window breakage and location of fire fighting equipment. Prepare for providing 24-hour guard/security service of the plant and grounds.
24. Suppliers should be contacted and announcement made to customers.
25. Consideration should also be given to I.D.s.
26. Temporary barriers?
27. Telephone systems?
28. Wild cats?
29. Protection for working moving goods?
30. People working in or having any business with the company have a right to pass freely in and out of the plant. Pickets must not block a door, passageway, driveway, crosswalk or other entrance or exit to a struck plant. Profanity on streets and sidewalks is a violation

of the law. Company officials, with the assistance of local law enforcement agents, should make every effort to permit individuals and vehicles to move in and out of the plant in a normal manner. Union officials or pickets have a right to talk to people going in or out of a struck plant. Intimidation, threats, and coercion are not permitted, either by verbal remarks or physical action. Sound truck should not be permitted to be unduly noisy—it should have a permit and must be kept moving. If acts of violence or trespassing occur on company premises, plant officials should file complaints or seek injunctions. In cases of violence on one's person, the aggrieved person should sign a warrant for the arrest of the person or persons causing such violence. Fighting, assault, battery, violence, threats, or intimidation are not permissible under the law, nor is the carrying of knives, firearms, clubs, or other dangerous weapons.

31. Do not offer extra rewards to non-strikers and make statements that returning strikers will not have the same reward, or attempt to withhold the "extras" from strikers once the strike has ended and some or all strikers are reinstated. Do not threaten employees or strikers. Do not promise benefits to individuals or groups of strikers in an attempt to end the strike or undermine the union. Do not threaten employees with discharge for taking part in a lawful strike. Do not discharge non-strikers who refuse to take over a striker's job.

STRIKE OPERATIONS

During the strike it is recommended that the following procedures be strictly adhered to:

1. Communication with the strikers should be through designated individuals.
2. If operations are to continue on a "normal" basis, a central location must be designated for communications. Matters concerning internal operations and strike strategy and other questions dealing with the prevalence of violence and assurance of physical protection must be coordinated through the designated chief.
3. Communications between the strikers (Union) must continue.
4. Ingress and egress should be kept to a minimum such as leaving for lunch. The decision should be made if food will be brought in on a daily basis or if a designated member will go out and return with lunches or dinners.

5. During a strike, "baiting" by the strikers will be prevalent. Supervisory personnel must be briefed to ignore completely comments made by the pickets.
6. A strike log must be maintained and kept up to date.

POST-STRIKE OPERATIONS

1. Establish a system to notify employees of termination of the strike.
2. Establish a system to notify customers of the termination of the strike.
3. Gather any necessary records and documentation before and after photographs of damage for insurance and tax purposes.

Another company published the following amendment to its corporate strike plan:

Supplemental to the Strike Plan
If the Decision Is Made to Do Business as Usual

A. Guard Service
   1. Meet at least 10 days prior to a strike.
      a. To insure experience in this area.
      b. Outline general duties—in writing.
      c. Specify areas of special concern, i.e., electrical power, terminals, telephone lines, truck parking area and other areas of concern.
      d. Specify dress. If riding our trucks through secondary boycott picket lines, no uniforms or other identification allowed.
      e. Insure the guards carry no guns, clubs, knives or anything else that implies a weapon.
      f. Make sure guards do have communications, i.e., walkie-talkies and that one radio on premise has capabilities of reaching law enforcement agencies.
      g. Make sure each guard has a camera and he knows how to use it.
      h. Instruct guards to take picture of any questionable action or account and write a detailed report regarding that action or occurrence.
   2. Meet with supervisors to review the above procedures at the 11th hour.

B. Meet with all visiting personnel and instruct them on how to cross a picket line.
   1. Minimize crossings at the change of shift if the location is working on a three shift basis. Have a van or utilize one of our rigs to take everyone across at the same time.
   2. If possible have meals catered.
   3. Arrange with the vending company to service the machines daily. It may call for a supervisor of that vending machine to do so.

C. Have the Corporate Labor Relations Department assign a local attorney to represent us in this matter.
   1. Meet and brief the attorney 10 days or so prior to the strike.
   2. Inform the attorney as to the feelings of the pending pickets, etc.
   3. Inform the attorney of our plans.
   4. Obtain special instructions regarding secondary boycott.

D. Meet with management and decide on a freight depot that will allow us to pick up freight.
   1. Decide if that freight is to be reconsigned to another depot and if so, this has to be done at least 10 days in advance.
   2. Instruct the depot as to the reconsignments.
   3. If we are to pick up our own freight then rent three or four 18 ft. straight trucks which is the equivalent of one 45 footer to allow flexibility.
   4. Make certain we have drivers capable of driving those 18 ft. straights and are licensed appropriately.

E. Trust your good judgment and common sense and if that doesn't work, pray.

Appendix 8

General Conditions of Guard Service

CONTRACT ______________
(Page 1 of 9 Pages)

ADJUSTMENT OF COMPENSATION—Upon the occurrence of any of the acts or omissions listed below, there shall be an equitable downward adjustment of your charges to reflect the reduced value of your services fairly. This adjustment shall be determined by mutual agreement between and you. Pending agreement on the amount of downward adjustment, may deduct from your billing the sum of one hundred dollars ($100) for each occurrence per day per incident. If and you fail to agree within two (2) months after each deduction, the amount actually deducted by shall be deemed acceptable. shall provide you with written notice of its intention to make a deduction. Acts of omissions to which this clause applies are:

1. Failure to provide a guard required for a post or a shift as specified in the "Statement of Work".
2. Failure to train in advance before assignment to premises, a substitute guard force numbering at least one half of the total guards required by this agreement without cost to .
3. Failure to assign a trained substitute guard as a replacement.
4. Allowing a guard to work in excess of twelve (12) hours per twenty-four (24) hour period or in excess of sixty (60) hours per week without written waiver from 's Representative or Delegate.
5. Failure to provide a guard with a minimum twenty-four (24) consecutive hours off in a week.
6. Failure to maintain complete records of all hours each guard assigned to 's premises is engaged in work for which payment is computed on the basis of actual hours worked.
7. Not paying a guard the minimum amount specified in this agreement.
8. Failure to produce documentation required by the clause "Standards" for a guard prior to assignment.

CONTRACT ______________
(Page 2 of 9 Pages)

9. Failure to assign a correctly dressed guard.
10. Failure of a non-resident agency supervisor to appear for unannounced daily inspections during each shift and at each shift change.
11. Failure to replace any guard within eight (8) hours upon the request of 's Representative or Delegate.
12. Failure to provide the training specified under the clause "Training" to a guard before assignment to premises.
13. Failure to furnish all equipment and material necessary for the performance of the Work.
14. Allowing a resident guard supervisor to perform relief duties for more than a total of two (2) hours in any one day in the aggregate.

Nothing in this section shall be deemed to limit rights or remedies in the event actual damage exceeds the amount withheld from the billing. failure at any time to require performance of the provisions of this section shall in no way affect right to enforce it for subsequent occurrences.

ARRESTS AND COMPLAINTS—Guards shall make no arrests or detentions without the express consent or written instruction of 's Representative or Delegate unless otherwise specified in written instructions furnished to you by . Guards shall not sign a complaint on behalf of and any request by governmental (local, state or federal) authorities to sign a complaint shall be referred to 's Representative or Delegate.

AUDIT—You shall maintain complete records of all hours of direct labor employees engaged in Work for which payment under this agreement is to be computed on the basis of actual hours worked, at a fixed rate per hour and all other costs, if any, payable by under this agreement. Such records shall be maintained in accordance with recognized commercial accounting practices so they may be readily audited. You shall permit to examine and audit these records and all supporting records at all reasonable times. All payments, if any, made under this agreement by shall be subject to final adjustments as determined by such audit(s). You shall retain all such records for a period not less than one (1) calendar year after the completion date of this agreement.

CONTINUITY OF SERVICES—You recognize that it is the responsibility of the guard personnel to guard and protect 's plants, premises, material, facilities and property. In the event your personnel are

CONTRACT ______________
(Page 3 of 9 Pages)

faced with a strike, threatened strike, stoppage of work or other interferences, guard personnel will continue to report for duty, remain at their posts, discharge their duties in the regular manner and discharge such other plant protection duties as are determined to be necessary and proper under the circumstances by 's Representative or Delegate. Should they not do so, or should any other circumstances prevent their performance as specified under this agreement, may arrange for guard service to be performed by other guards, in which event, you shall be responsible to for all expenses incurred in such performance in excess of the price specified in this agreement.

EQUIPMENT AND UNIFORMS—You shall furnish all equipment and material necessary for the performance of the Work, including uniforms and firearms, except for fire-fighting equipment. At no time shall firearms be stored on 's premises when the premises are unattended by your employees. If weapons storage is necessary during attended hours, will furnish a suitable cabinet having a combination lock. will furnish you, without charge, the office equipment and space, including the maintenance and utilities, 's Representative or Delegate deems necessary. All such facilities shall remain property and shall not be used for any purposes other than those which are required in the performance of guard duties.

GENERAL—Guards shall be responsible for all phases of building protection, including, but not limited to: guarding the premises against fire, theft, pilferage, malicious injury, damage and destruction; permitting only authorized persons to enter the premises; reporting violations of fire and safety regulations; making tours of the premises; and, when so instructed, controlling traffic in parking lots.

Written instructions (including a guard manual) specifying days and hours of the week when guards are to be provided, number of guards required, duties to be performed by each, and the location of guard rooms and guard logs will be prepared by 's Representative or Delegate and furnished to you. All guard manuals furnished to you must be returned to 's Representative or Delegate upon the termination of this agreement or upon request. 's Representative or Delegate may make changes in any of these instructions at any time, except that twenty-four (24) hours notice shall be provided to you regarding changes in days and hours of the week when guards are to be provided and the number of guards required. You may charge the overtime rate

CONTRACT ______________
(Page 4 of 9 Pages)

indicated in this agreement for any overtime hours worked by the guards as a result of a failure by 's Representative or Delegate to provide such notice. A substitute guard force numbering at least one half the total guards required by this agreement shall be trained in advance at no expense to , and assigned when replacements are required. Resident supervisory guard personnel shall not perform relief duties for more than a total of two (2) hours in any one day in the aggregate.

All persons performing Work shall at all times be recognized as your employees and under your control and supervision. However, you, your agents, and employees shall, in the performance of the Work, comply with the written or verbal instructions received from 's Representative or Delegate.

All guards shall sign in and sign out in the guard log which will be furnished by and located as specified in written instructions issued pursuant to the second paragraph of this clause "General".

At the conclusion of each tour of duty, each guard shall submit a written report to 's Representative or Delegate covering all unusual or hazardous conditions encountered during the tour. No information contained in a report or obtained by a guard relating to or its employees shall be disclosed by you or your employees without the written consent of

It is understood by the parties that personnel performing guard duties must be alert at all times. You, therefore, shall not assign any person to perform guard services under this agreement who will have worked in any capacity in excess of twelve (12) hours per twenty-four (24) hour period or in excess of sixty (60) hours per week. Each guard will have a minimum of twenty-four (24) consecutive hours off each week. Under extraordinary circumstances, these conditions may be waived in writing by 's Representative or Delegate.

For purposes of this agreement, the work week shall commence with shifts beginning on or after midnight on Sunday and end the next Sunday at midnight.

In the event United States Government Security Clearances are required after the inception of this agreement, agrees to renegotiate the compensation aspects of this agreement regarding those personnel involved, if not otherwise covered in this agreement.

HIRING AND REPLACING PERSONNEL—No guard shall be hired by to work at a former duty location within one (1) year following termination of that guard's employment with you.

You shall promptly replace any guard performing services under this agreement who, in the sole judgement of 's Representative or Delegate, may be undesirable. Any guard replaced shall not be reassigned to any location.

IDENTIFICATION CREDENTIALS— may, at its discretion, require your employees to exhibit identification credentials, which may issue, in order to gain access to 's premises for the performance of Work. If, for any reason, any of your employees are no longer performing Work, you shall immediately inform 's Representative in the speediest manner possible. Notification shall be followed by the prompt delivery to 's Representative of the identification credentials involved or a written statement of the reasons why the identification credentials cannot be returned.

LABOR RELATIONS—You shall be responsible for your own labor relations with any labor organization either representing or seeking to represent your employees and shall negotiate and seek to adjust all disputes between you and your employees or any union representing such employees. Except as otherwise provided in this section, and subject to the terms of this agreement, you may freely enter into any contract with any union representing employees employed by you to perform the duties on 's premises that are contemplated by the requirements of this agreement. You shall enter into no contract that purports to obligate to the union, either as a successor or assignee of yours, or in any other way, on the termination of this agreement, or at any other time. You warrant that you are not a party to any existing union contract purporting to so obligate . In the event you have knowledge that an actual or potential labor dispute prevents or threatens to prevent timely performance under this agreement you shall immediately give notice thereof to 's Representative or Delegate. The notice shall include all relevant information concerning the dispute.

LIMIT OF EXPENDITURE—Notwithstanding any other provisions in this agreement, the total amount payable by for the Work shall be

Appendix 9

Model Curriculum: Center for the Study of Crime, Delinquency, and Corrections at Southern Illinois University

MODEL CURRICULUM (Shaped by Security Directors)

The following model curriculum, leading to a baccalaureate degree in security management, was prepared for the Center for the Study of Crime, Delinquency, and Corrections at Southern Illinois University, Carbondale, Illinois.

This curriculum was shaped to a large extent by the directors of corporate security for many of the largest and most prestigious corporations in the United States. Letters requesting their views were sent to fifty security executives, all of whom are members of the American Society for Industrial Security (ASIS). An attempt was made to include a cross section of industries and sizes of corporations, although security executives working for corporations based in Illinois were given first preference (thirty-three of those who responded fit this category).

No attempt was made to randomize the selection procedure. Instead of being interested in polling a sampling of ASIS members, ideas were solicited from security directors in corporations likely to hire program graduates, or offer internship positions.

The letters simply asked the executives about the type of curriculum they felt would best prepare students for careers in corporate security. Although the responses did reflect some diversity of opinion, the following curriculum generally includes suggestions provided by all.

This appendix is reprinted from Howard W. Timm, "Create a Curriculum," *Security Management,* June 1982, pp. 62–63. Reprinted with permission.

Required Classes

(Substitutions are permitted with written approval of the student's academic advisor.)

Accounting

221-3 ACCOUNTING I. Basic concepts, principles, and techniques used in the generation of accounting data for financial statement preparation and interpretation. Asset liability and owners equity valuation and their relationship to income determination.

222-3 ACCOUNTING II. A continuation of Accounting I with emphasis on the analysis and interpretation of accounting reports, including ratios and funds flow analysis. The use of accounting information for managerial planning, control, and decision making through budgeting, cost and variance analyses, and responsibility accounting.

Administration of Justice

200-3 INTRODUCTION TO CRIMINAL BEHAVIOR. Multidisciplinary study of the etiology and patterning of offender behavior.

201-3 INTRODUCTION TO CRIMINAL JUSTICE SYSTEM. Survey of the agencies and processes involved in the administration of criminal justice: the history of English law; the criminal justice process and system, including underlying ideologies, procedures, and fundamental legal concepts; and the roles and functions of police, courts and correctional services.

303-3 BEHAVIORAL ASPECTS OF INVESTIGATION. Principles of behavioral science are applied to the recurrent patterns of criminal investigation as a social and fact-finding process; a survey of criminalists.

305-3 CRIMINAL LAW—INTRODUCTION TO PROCEDURAL ASPECTS AND POLICE POWERS. An introduction to the procedural aspects of criminal law pertaining to police powers in connection with the laws of arrest, search and seizure, the exclusionary rule, civil liberties, eavesdropping, confessions, and related decision-making factors.

395-6-12 SUPERVISED FIELD EXPERIENCES IN THE ADMINISTRATION OF JUSTICE. Familiarization and direct experience in applied settings. Under supervision of faculty and adjunct staff, the student assumes a student-participant role in a security position.

403-3 ENFORCEMENT OPERATIONS IN ADVANCED INVESTIGATION. This course offering provides a broad coverage of law enforcement activities from detailed investigative work through required specialized management techniques.

490-3 INDEPENDENT STUDY IN THE ADMINISTRATION OF JUSTICE. Supervised readings or independent investigative projects in various aspects of security administration.

Administrative Sciences

302-3 ADMINISTRATIVE COMMUNICATIONS. Creating and managing interpersonal administrative communications including the analysis, planning, and practice of composing different types of internal and external communications in various administrative and business contexts.

304-3 ORGANIZATION ADMINISTRATION. Basic concepts of the administrative process are considered with emphasis on executive action to develop policy, direction, and control based on traditional and behavioral science approaches to decision making.

385-3 PERSONNEL MANAGEMENT. An introduction to the development, application, and evaluation of policies, procedures, and programs for the recruitment, selection, development, and utilization of human resources in an organization.

Computer Science

212-3 INTRODUCTION TO BUSINESS COMPUTING. An introduction to concepts and features of computing systems with reference to business information processing. Includes a basic treatment of standard programming language.

Health Education

334-3 STANDARD FIRST AID. Provides students with first aid knowledge and skill competencies necessary to care for injuries and meet emergencies. The course leads to instructor authorization in the American National Red Cross Program and includes ANRC procedure.

Industrial Technology

341-3 MAINTENANCE. Principles and practices of maintenance department organization, preventative procedures, and typical equipment problems. Also, includes related topics such as plant protection, custodial services, and maintenance of power plants.

465-3 INDUSTRIAL SAFETY. Principles of industrial accident prevention; accident statistics and costs; appraising safety performance; recognizing industrial hazards and recommending safeguards. Includes a study of the Occupational Safety and Health Act and the Coal Mine Health and Safety Act.

Political Science

436-3 ADMINISTRATIVE LAW. The procedural law of public agencies, particularly the regulatory commissions but also executive branch agencies exercising regulatory functions. The exercise of discretion and its control through internal mechanisms and judicial review.

Psychology

320-3 INDUSTRIAL PSYCHOLOGY. A study of the use of psychological methods in the analysis of human factors problems in business and industry.

323-3 PSYCHOLOGY OF EMPLOYEE RELATIONS. Job satisfaction and morale, psychological aspects of labor relations, interviewing methods, and human relations training.

SUGGESTED GENERAL STUDIES COURSES

Southern Illinois University requires students to take forty-five semester hours from the General Studies Program for a baccalaureate degree.

101-3 ENGLISH COMPOSITION. Basic principles of sentence structure, paragraphing, and organization.

104-3 MORAL DECISIONS. Introduction to contemporary and perennial problems of personal and social morality, and to methods proposed for their resolution by great thinkers of the past and present.

106-2 MARTIAL ARTS. (a) Self Defense, (b) Judo, or (c) Karate.

107-4 INTERMEDIATE ALGEBRA. Properties and operations of the number system. Elementary operations with polynomials and factoring. Elementary operations with algebraic fractions. Exponents, roots, and radicals. First and second degree equations and inequalities. Functions and graphing. Systems of equations and inequalities. Exponential and logarithmic functions.

112-2 BASIC CONCEPTS OF STATISTICS. Illustrates basic concepts of statistical theory. Emphasis on concepts rather than computational techniques. Main topics include data reduction, probability sampling, statistical estimation, and decision procedures.

118-2 TECHNICAL REPORT WRITING. An introductory course in technical report presentations both written and oral, in library research methods, and in elementary business correspondence.

153-3 PUBLIC SPEAKING. Principles of communication as applied to settings (speaker/audience). Developing research and speaking skills in the preparation and presentation of various types of messages.

201-2 HEALTHFUL LIVING. Personal and community health. Designed to meet general health education needs and to develop wholesome health attitudes and practices in college students.

202-3 INTRODUCTION TO PSYCHOLOGY. An examination of the variables related to the origins and modifications of human behavior using the viewpoints and techniques of contemporary psychology.

203-4 THE SOCIOLOGICAL PERSPECTIVE. A survey of topics that investigates the range of social relationships among people; basic sociological concepts and theories, social groups, social institutions, social and cultural change, and social deviance.

204-3 ECOLOGY. Fundamental biological and ecological processes important in the individual and community life of organisms (including humans) are discussed in the context of ecological systems.

221-3 SURVIVAL OF MAN. Topics discussed include the interrelated ethnological, technological, sociological, moral, and ethical aspects of the environmental problems concerned with technology, air pollution, urbanization, natural resource utilization, agriculture, and aesthetics. Emphasis is placed on understanding the total context in which environmental problems must be considered.

302-3 PSYCHOBIOLOGY. A survey of the role of biological processes in the behavior of humans and other species. Topics covered include structure and function of the nervous system, behavioral endocrinology, psychopharmacology, sensorimotor functions, sleep and waking, motivation, emotions, reinforcement, psychopathology, learning, and memory.

363-3 PHILOSOPHY OF SCIENCE. Introductory survey of the nature and significance of scientific method and its applications. Topics include: the role of value judgments in scientific research, the rationality of scientific method, and the relation of science to common sense, religious institutions, and technology.

325-3 RACE AND MINORITY RELATIONS. To acquaint students with race and minority group relations as a social problem: forms, extent, distribution, trends, causes, effects, and evaluations of proposals for reduction of prejudice and discrimination. The problems of Blacks, Mexican-Americans, Indians, Japanese-Americans, and others in South Africa, India, and other countries are included.

390-3 CONTEMPORARY AMERICAN THOUGHT. Introductory survey of the main currents of contemporary philosophy in America and their relevance for legal, political, and educational developments.

Plus ONE course to be selected from the following courses:

111-3 ECONOMIC DEVELOPMENT OF WESTERN CIVILIZATION. Emphasizes the underlying trends and forces that have led to the present economic structure of the developed world. The commercial and industrial revolution as well as the rise of the market system and capitalism are treated in their historical context.

106-3 CHEMISTRY FOR NON-SCIENCE MAJORS. Selected discussions of inorganic, organic, and biological chemistry and their relationship to our standard of living and quality of our health and environment. Three lectures with one voluntary help session per week.

299e-3 VALUES, SYSTEMS, AND SOCIETY. Values and ethics in evolutionary systems and cultural perspectives will be critically analyzed. A review of the basic problems of survival and further evolution of civilization.

Appendix 10

Model Curriculum: ASIS Suggestions

The American Society for Industrial Security, in a 1978 booklet titled *Establishing Baccalaureate Programs in Security and Loss Prevention,* presented the following suggested model curricula for a baccalaureate degree and for security as a specialization within another major, together with course descriptions.

SUGGESTED MODEL CURRICULA

I. INDEPENDENT MAJOR
   (120 Semester Hours Required)
   A. General Education Courses
      (30 Semester Hours)
      1. English (Composition and/or Literature) (6 Hours)
      2. Natural Science (6 Hours)
      3. Social Science (9 Hours)
      4. Humanities (9 Hours)
   B. Major Courses
      (30 Semester Hours)
      1. Required
         a. Introduction to Security
         b. Security Administration
         c. Security Law
         d. Technological Aspects of Security
         e. Special Problems
         f. Field Practicum

This appendix is reprinted from "Establishing Baccalaureate Programs for Security and Loss Prevention," The American Society for Industrial Security (Arlington, VA: 1978), pp. 47–54. Reprinted with permission.

2. Electives
    a. Criminal and Civil Law**
    b. Commercial and Retail Security
    c. Fire Prevention and Occupational Safety
    d. Industrial Fire Protection Technology and Systems
    e. Environmental Security
    f. Computerized Systems Security
    g. Document and Personnel Security

C. Cognate*
(30 Semester Hours)
1. Accounting
2. Business Law
3. Business Administration
4. Public Administration
5. Introduction to Criminal Justice**
6. Organizational Psychology
7. Economics
8. Ethics
9. Research Methodology
10. Criminal Investigation**

D. Free Electives***
(30 Semester Hours)
1. International Politics
2. Political Psychology
3. Personnel Administration
4. Sociology of Organization
5. Social and Political Philosophy
6. Finance and Budgeting

II. SECURITY AS A SPECIALIZATION WITHIN ANOTHER MAJOR
(120 Semester Hours Required)

A. General Education Courses
(30 Semester Hours)
1. English (Composition and/or Literature) (6 Hours)
2. Natural Science (6 Hours)
3. Social Science (9 Hours)
4. Humanities (9 Hours)

---

*Substitutions of similar courses may be made.

**Criminal justice courses in curricula that seem warranted by private security responsibilities.

***The student should be encouraged to pursue his/her individual interests, whatever they may be. The courses are merely suggestions of those which might be especially relevant to the general area of security.

B. Major Courses
   (30 Semester Hours)
   1. Required
      Courses depend upon major field (Criminal Justice, Business Administration, etc.)
   2. Electives****
      a. Introduction to Security
      b. Security Administration
      c. Security Law
      d. Technological Aspects of Security
      e. Special Problems
      f. Field Practicum

C. Cognate
   (30 Semester Hours)
   If security specialization is part of major department, cognate courses would be similar to independent major curriculum. If security specialization is outside the major field, Cognate course work should include security electives noted above.

D. Free Electives
   (30 Semester Hours)
   Same as independent major.

COURSE DESCRIPTIONS

1. Introduction to Security (3 Credits)

   The historical, philosophical, and legal basis of security. The role of security and the security practitioner in modern society; the concept of professionalism; a survey of the administrative, personnel, and physical aspects of the security field. The relationship of security to the criminal justice process.

2. Security Administration (3 Credits)

   Organization, administration and management of security and plant protection units. Policy and decision making, personnel, and budgeting. Programs in business, industry and government, including retailing, transportation, public and private institutions. Private guard and alarm services.

3. Security Law

   The legal process as it relates to the security field.

****Assuming security specialization is part of major department.

4. Technological Aspects of Security

   The impact of technology on the security field. The peculiar security problems posed by sophisticated data storage system, the potential for terrorist exploitation, and the implication of technology as a monitor and controller of behavior patterns.

5. Special Security Problems (3 Credits)

   A study of the security requirements in specific fields and types of organizations. Topical subjects would be in bank, campus, computer, hospital and transportation security programs, executive protection/terrorism, etc. The emphasis placed on each subject would relate to the specific needs associated with the community and the area the degree program would service:

   Special Security Problems—Projected Emphasis:

   Bank Security
   A study of the principles and practices of security measures for banks and other financial institutions, and the preparation of rules establishing minimum standards under current federal and state legislation.

   Campus Security
   A study of the security requirements at all levels of educational institutions. Security's role in problems involving student discipline, vandalism, use of drugs, theft and theft control through educational programs, demonstrations, riots, occupation of buildings, maintaining the freedom of movement and control of personal liberties, liaison with civil authorities, traffic control, intelligence gathering, the training of campus police to deal with students, first-aid and emergency services, and physical security controls using alarm devices, video, surveillance, etc.

   Computer Security
   Basic security concepts of providing protection for the computer facility. Includes techniques for access control, storage and handling of data and emergency procedures. Covers physical protection of the area and data, usage of alarms and surveillance systems, as well as implementation of security procedures. Protection of information in cold storage from unauthorized access is also developed.

   Hospital Security
   The function of protection in the health industry. Medical security administration including study of health care providers; trends in hospital law; security from injury, fire and loss in the medical

world. Security methodology for safeguarding specialty areas; the security role in mass casualty management and emergency preparedness; the concept of professionalism; community liaison; and patient attitudes toward security.

Transportation Security
A study of security for the various types of transportation such as by truck, railroad, air, and ship. Methods of protection against theft, pilferage and hijacking; the preparation of shipping orders and manifests and the concealment of the identity of valuable cargo as effective security measures; the economics of transportation security and the fine balance between investment for security and potential loss.

6. Field Practicum (3 Credits)

   Practicum designed to broaden the educational experience of students through appropriate observational and work assignments with governmental agencies and private firms. Correlation of theoretical knowledge with practice in participating organizations.

7. Criminal and Civil Law I (3 Credits)

   Exploration of the major problems of criminal law as a device for controlling socially undesirable behavior. It is intended to give students a working knowledge of the basic questions of public policy involved in the administration of criminal justice, and of the legal principles of determining criminal and civil liability in light of the theories advanced to justify punishment and other methods of correction. The course includes a consideration of vital constitutional issues including self-incrimination, search and seizure, wiretapping, coerced confessions, right to counsel and conduct of trial.

8. Commercial/Retail Security (3 Credits)

   The operation of security departments including the functions of mercantile establishments; dishonest employees, shoplifters; management and public relations; receiving, shipping, and warehousing; special laws and procedures.

9. Industrial Fire Protection Technology and Systems (3 Credits)

   Implementation of a fire loss prevention program within the structure of an industrial organization; techniques of hazard analysis; risk management; administrative procedures; economics of fire protection; training and motivation; emergency planning; survey of fire protection equipment and application to industrial hazards; use of fire codes and standards.

10. Document and Personnel Security (3 Credits)

    A detailed study of procedures for handling and control of classified and other sensitive information; a survey of control systems from manual to semi-automated systems using data processing equipment. The fundamentals relating to personnel security, specifically: governmental and proprietary concepts, background investigations, loyalty and suitability criteria.

    A study of the Department of Defense Industrial Security Program; and relationship between private enterprise engaged in the program and monitoring government agencies; applicable federal statutes and executive orders; the role of the Cognizant Security Office (DCASR—Defense Contract Administration Services Region); the facility clearance, personnel security problems and the rights of appeal, security requirements and procedures for handling government classified information; physical security controls; visitor control; security education program; security problems regarding subcontractors and vendors; security classification management; the interaction of protective measures for proprietary information and classified information.

11. Security Aspects of Environmental/Occupational Safety and Health (3 Credits)

    The impact of the Industrial Age upon man and his physical environment; topics to be covered will include familiarization with the various local, state and federal regulatory agencies monitoring air/water pollution, waste disposal, toxic substances, radiation and occupational safety and health. Specific emphasis will be given to the interrelationship of security with the internal monitoring and loss control functions of an industrial organization or public utility.

12. Computerized System Security

    The unique security problem posed by sophisticated computer systems especially data storage and retrieval. Analysis of automated security systems and their vulnerability.

Appendix 11

Model Curriculum: University of New Haven

The Security Management concentration at the University of New Haven in West Haven, Connecticut, requires forty-five graduate credits in the following topics for a Master's degree:

Required Courses: (27 Hours)		Credit Hours	
SH602	Safety Organization and Management	3	
CJ601	Seminar in Interpersonal Relations	3	
CJ605	Social Deviance	3	
CJ612	Criminal Justice Management	3	
CJ614	Survey of Forensic Science	3	
CJ669	Dynamics, Evaluation & Prevention of Structural Fires	3	
CJ675	Private Security Law	3	
CJ676	Security Management Seminar	3	
CJ677	Private Security in Modern Society	3	
		27	
and two from among: (6 Hours)			
EC625	Industrial Relations	3	
EC687	Collective Bargaining	3	
PA625	Administrative Behavior	3	
CJ637	Contemporary Issues in Criminal Justice	3	
		33	33
Elective Courses: (12 Hours)			
EC625	Industrial Relations	3	
EC687	Collective Bargaining	3	
PA601	Principles of Public Administration	3	
PA625	Administrative Behavior	3	
A621	Managerial Accounting	3	
MG637	Management	3	
MG645	Management of Human Resources	3	
SH605	Industrial Safety Engineering	3	

SH611	Occupational Safety and Health Seminar	1	
SH620	Occupational Safety and Health Law	2	
CJ637	Contemporary Issues in Criminal Justice	3	
CJ649	Fire Scene Investigation and Arson Analysis	3	
CJ667	Fire and Building Codes, Standards, Practices	3	
CJ668	Fire and Casualty Insurances Practices	3	
CJ690	Independent Study (Private Security)	3	
CJ697	Thesis I (Private Security)	3	
CJ698	Thesis II (Private Security)	3	
			45

The Professional Certificate Program, an adjunct program to New Haven's master's degree, consists of eighteen graduate credits and is limited to those already holding baccalaureate degrees. Credits earned in this program may be transferred to the master's degree program. The required courses for a professional certificate are:

SH602	Safety Organization and Management	3	
CJ612	Criminal Justice Management	3	
CJ669	Dynamics, Evaluation and Prevention of Structural Fires	3	
CJ675	Private Security Law	3	
CJ676	Security Management Seminar	3	
CJ677	Private Security in Modern Society	3	
			18

Index